# Guided
# Writing
# and
# Free Writing

# Guided Writing and Free Writing

## A Text in Composition for English as a Second Language

### SECOND EDITION

## Lois Robinson

FORMERLY OF THE CITY COLLEGE
OF THE CITY UNIVERSITY OF NEW YORK

**HARPER & ROW, PUBLISHERS**
NEW YORK  EVANSTON  SAN FRANCISCO  LONDON

Sponsoring Editor: George J. Telecki
Project Editor: David Nickol
Designer: Emily Harste
Production Supervisor: Will C. Jomarrón

**GUIDED WRITING AND FREE WRITING**
A Text in Composition for English as a Second Language
SECOND EDITION

Library of Congress Cataloging in Publication Data

Robinson, Lois.
  Guided writing and free writing.

  1. English language—Composition and exercises.
2. English language—Text-books for foreigners.
I. Title.
PE1408.R634   1975   808′.042   74-15721
ISBN 0-06-045525-X

# Contents in Brief

# Contents in Detail

---

## Section D   130
Adverbials
The Progressive Past Tense

**Section J  240**
Gerunds and Infinitives
Spelling: Rules 7 and 8

# Preface

This book is intended for students of English as a second language who are eager to take at least some work in their field of specialization the following term.

The second edition of *Guided Writing and Free Writing* continues to use the technique of controlling the variety of errors a student can make in any one exercise. However, the text has been broadened by work in eight new areas.

First, there is a great increase in the number of topics suggested for free writing. Second, the students are invited early to add a paragraph of their own to the guided exercise that they have just completed. ("The Moon," page 11, gives the first such invitation.) Explicit work is given in the English-American habit of plunging into one's subject immediately, and in making a coherent outline of one's writing.

The section on the articles, too difficult in the first edition for many students, has been greatly expanded in the number of exercises offered and decidedly simplified in the grammatical explanations.

Letter writing, a feature called "Listen and Write," and the use of paragraphs of dictation for spelling and punctuation are all new.

Finally, a new section, "The First Term Paper," has been added. (A student's future instructors, if they assign term papers, will assume that the student knows how to write them. The student had better practice in the shelter of his composition course.)

Because they are seasoned students, the most determined can go from writing their first composition at the beginning of the term to producing a short term paper by the end of approximately 75 class hours. This means concentrated work on writing, not writing as part of a general course.

The unremitting effort required first to prepare to use a new structure and then to use it freely in writing is demanding for the students, but the effort frees them to do what they have come to do—to work in their special field.

**Lois Robinson**

# Guided Writing and Free Writing

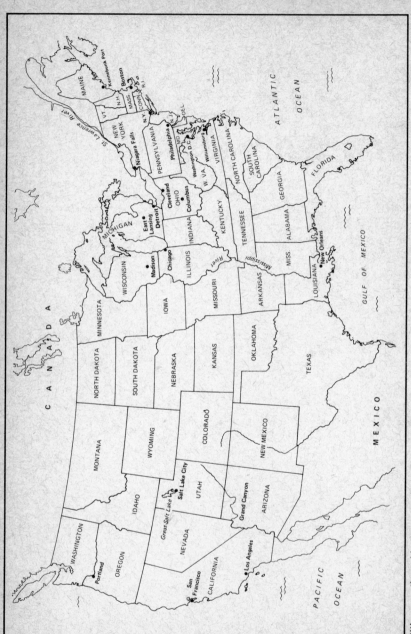

Cities mentioned in the exercises.

# Section A

---

## The Simple Present Tense
## Outlining and Free Writing

**TO THE STUDENT**

*Guided Writing and Free Writing* recognizes the fact that you have already had a course in English grammar, probably more than one. It assumes that you cannot yet write the standard English you need to be able to write. Here is the plan of the book:

*Grammar* Each point of difficulty (structure) is first presented in a brief grammatical statement to be referred to when necessary.

*Oral Practice* Each structure which is going to be practiced in writing is first practiced orally. Why? Writing is partly getting

To the instructor: It will help the class to become acquainted with the book quickly if you yourself read from the beginning to the first assignment, *A 1*, everyone following in his text. Time spent acquainting the class with what the text can do will be time well spent. Encourage discussion, but see that each student has made a successful start on *A 1* before the close of the first full class period.

..n on paper in standard form what you are already saying to yourself silently.

*Guided Writing*    Guided writing helps you practice a difficult structure repeatedly in paragraphs. It helps you feel certain that you are doing the right thing. You follow instructions and change or complete sentences. As you write, you can analyze. "So this is the way it is done," you may say to yourself. "This is how to get beyond writing lists of sentences to writing English prose."

*Free Writing*    As soon as you can do the guided work on a structure, you are given a composition topic which makes it possible to use freely what you have just practiced. When enough good habits are established by this process, you are ready to write with competence in the field of your special interest.

## Steps in Oral Practice

1. The instructor puts the name of the structure to be practiced on the blackboard and adds a few examples in writing.
2. Immediately, or almost immediately, oral practice begins, the students' books closed, the instructor's book open.
3. First the group and then individuals respond strongly.
4. After the oral practice has been completed, the class brings up any points remaining obscure.
5. The connection between the assignment, placed on the blackboard before class, and the oral practice just completed, is pointed out by the instructor.
6. To make doubly sure that the assignment is clear, a paragraph or two of the guided exercises assigned may be read orally by members of the class.

*The Assignment—When?*    Ideally, the work of the whole class hour leads up to the assignment. Actually, an assignment made at the end of the hour is likely to be made under pressure. On the whole, it is probably better to put the assignment on the blackboard before class and have the students copy it as they come in as a part of established class procedure. It will be necessary only occasionally to drop or to modify an item later.

## PREPARING FOR THE FIRST ASSIGNMENT
### Grammar: <u>be</u>[1]

---

These are the forms of *be* in the present tense:

| *Singular* | *Plural* |
|---|---|
| I **am**; he, she, it **is** | We, you, they **are** |

Note the differing position of the verb in questions and in statements.

|  | *Verb* | *Subject* | *Verb* |  |
|---|---|---|---|---|
| Question: | Is | the teacher | ——— | here? |
| Statement: | ——— | The teacher | is | here. |

In a **be** question, some form of **be** comes first in the sentence; in a statement, the subject comes first.

---

### Oral Practice

Directions: When you are given a question, change it into a statement in chorus. (Do not begin with *yes*.)

1. Are the students in this classroom in earnest?
   (The students in this classroom are in earnest.)
2. Is the teacher in this classroom in earnest?
   (The teacher in this classroom is . . .)
3. Are the teacher's directions clear?
4. Are the students' responses prompt?
5. Is the class wide-awake during oral practice?
6. Is the classroom reasonably cheerful?
7. Is the blackboard reasonably clean?
8. Are the lights bright but not too bright?
9. Are the chairs fairly comfortable?
10. Are the halls fairly quiet?

---

[1] Only two types of questions will be used by the students in Section A: *be* questions and *do* questions, also called *yes/no* questions. The instructor will sometimes use *wh*-questions, but questions of this type will not be required of the students until Section B.

## Grammar: omitting <u>do</u>[1] in statements

|  | Subject | Verb |
|---|---|---|
| Question:  Do | I, you, we, they | know  that man? |
| Statement:  ——— | I, you, we, they | know  that man. |

*Do* is used in questions but NOT IN STATEMENTS. In statements, omit *do* and make your word order as it is in the Oral Practice below: subject, verb, rest of the sentence.

### Oral Practice

Directions: In chorus, change the question given into a statement beginning with "I."

1. Do you have a good vocabulary?
   (I have a good vocabulary.)
2. Do you hear new words every day?
   (I hear new words every day.)
3. Do you remember some of them?
   (I remember . . .)
4. Do you forget some of them?
5. Do you own an English dictionary?

Directions: Next, respond with *we*.

6. Do you understand spoken English quite easily?
   (We understand . . .)
7. Do you like English?
   (We . . .)
8. Do you **love** English?
9. Do you need English?
10. Do you intend to learn a lot more about English?

### Sampling Guided Writing

Directions: Read both the Question Paragraph and Your Paragraph in chorus with your instructor.

[1] For *do* in negative statements, see p. 13. For "emphatic *do*," see p. 37.

Question Paragraph

Are foreign students exceedingly busy persons? Do they study at least five and a half days a week? Are weekends a little different? Do even the busiest students try to spend a few hours with their friends Saturday evening or Sunday afternoon? When such friends meet, do they often relax over a quiet meal?

Your Paragraph

Foreign students are exceedingly busy persons. They study at least five and a half days a week. Weekends are a little different. Even the busiest students try to spend a few hours with their friends Saturday evening or Sunday afternoon. When such friends meet, they often relax over a quiet meal.

## Deciding on the Directions for the Term[1]

Since you are going to try guided writing in class in a few minutes, turn now to "Directions for the Term," p. 306. Read this list with your instructor, check the items he wishes you to observe throughout the term, and write in the margins the additions and modifications he desires.

## Practicing Writing A 1

Before you begin to write A 1 on "good paper," practice on a piece of paper already partly used—"scrap paper." Keep your texts open to "Directions for the Term."

You will probably not get everything right the first time. When you discover that you are ignoring a direction, simply cross out what you have written and go on. Your instructor will come around to see how you are doing as promptly as possible, but depend upon yourself. When you can see that you understand the process, ask your instructor to review your work and then, with his permission, begin A 1 on the paper you are going to hand in.

[1] *To the instructor:* Students will absorb "Directions for the Term" rapidly if you put the first paragraph of A 1 on the blackboard precisely as they direct.

**A San Francisco cable car.**
[Phil Palmer, Monkmeyer]

## A 1 / The Cable Cars in San Francisco

Directions: Change the four following paragraphs of questions into four paragraphs of affirmative statements. Do not copy the questions. Do not write *yes*. Do not write *do*. Begin, "The streets are steep in San Francisco. They run . . . "

Are the streets steep in San Francisco? Do they run uphill and downhill at angles astonishing to a newcomer? Do a few of the steepest streets have a unique[1] means of transportation called cable cars?

Is a cable car tall and clumsy compared to a modern bus? Is it pulled up and down hill by a steel cable under the street? Are cable cars a survival from the days before electric power?

Is the front section of the car open to the weather at all times? Do the passengers in this section sit parallel to the sidewalk? Do timid newcomers hold onto a pole to keep from sliding into the street?

[1] *unique:* the only one of its kind.

Do athletic young San Franciscans jump onto the narrow running board without waiting for the cable car to stop? (Is the maximum speed of a cable car nine miles an hour?) At the end of the line, do the passengers get out and help the motorman push the car around on its revolving platform for the return trip?

Are the cable cars more expensive to run than buses? Do they create a deficit[1] for the city every year? Do San Franciscans like them and keep them anyway?

## Grammar: adding s after "the third person singular"

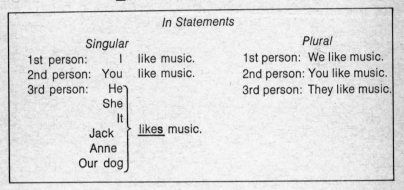

After a third person singular subject, *s* or *es* is added to the simple form of any verb except *be* and *have*. Otherwise, the simple form is used alone in the simple present tense.

### Oral Practice I

Directions: When you are given a question, respond with an affirmative statement, adding a loud, firm *s* to the verb.

1. Does an active boy like sports?
   (An active boy **likes** sports.)
2. Does he like to play outdoors?
   (He **likes** . . .)
3. Does an American boy play baseball?
   (An American boy **plays** . . .)
4. Does he play football, too?

[1] *create a deficit*: the cable cars make less money than it costs to run them.

5. Does he ride a bicycle?
6. Does he dream of owning a motorcycle?
7. Does he read a sports magazine regularly?
8. Does he follow his favorite team on TV?
9. Does he remember the scores of this team all season?
10. Does he hope to be on a college team some day?

**Oral Practice II**

Directions: When you are given a question, again respond with an affirmative statement, adding *s* to the verb.

1. Does a university library contain thousands of books?
   (A university library **contains** thousands of books.)
2. Does it contain hundreds of magazines?
   (It **contains** . . .)
3. Does it take some foreign newspapers?
   (It **takes** . . .)
4. Does it have dictionaries on every floor of the building?
   (It **has**[1] . . .)
5. Does it have the *Encyclopaedia Britannica?*
6. Does it have the *Encyclopedia Americana?*
7. Does it have other kinds of encyclopedias?
8. Does the library open early and close late?
9. Does it provide a convenient place to study?
10. Does it serve the students well?

## Grammar: <u>does</u> in questions

| Statement: | ———— | Lee plays the piano. |
|---|---|---|
| Question: | Does | Lee play the piano? |

When a statement uses the s-form, the question form is *does,* followed by the simple form.

**Oral Practice III**

Directions: In the two practices just finished, the instructor used *does* in a question and you responded with a statement adding *s* to the verb. Now reverse the process:

[1] The form used in *have* statements after a third person singular subject is *has.*

Example:

Instructor:   Lee **plays** the piano.
Class:          **Does** Lee play the piano?

1. Lee **attends** the university in the daytime.
   (**Does** Lee attend the university in the daytime?)
2. He **carries** a briefcase all day.
   (**Does** he . . .)
3. He **takes** the 8:00 o'clock bus every morning.
   (**Does** . . .)
4. He **attends** classes all morning.
5. He **hears** lectures in two of his classes.
6. He **asks** questions in his composition class.
7. He **eats** lunch in the cafeteria every noon.
8. He **goes** to the speech laboratory three afternoons a week.
9. He **reads** the college paper in the library lounge.
10. He **types** his compositions in the library typing room.

## A 2 / The Fog in San Francisco

Directions: Change the following paragraph of questions into a paragraph of affirmative statements. In the statements, s must be added to four of the verbs. Underline the four s's. Begin, "Water surrounds San Francisco on three sides. Fog . . . "

Does water surround San Francisco on three sides? Does fog drift in from the Pacific Ocean late in the afternoon, particularly in July and August? Do the buoys[1] floating in San Francisco Bay begin to ring their bells in warning to approaching ships? Do the ships themselves blow their foghorns? Does the fog close in around hills, tall buildings, and cable cars? Does the sun, scattering the fog the following day, leave the flowers brilliant[2] and the inhabitants comfortably cool?

## Grammar: What is a paragraph?

A paragraph is a group of sentences which belong together because they deal with one topic. The following topics, for ex-

---

[1] *buoys:* objects with a bell, anchored and floating in water to warn of danger. Rising waves make the bells ring.
[2] *brilliant:* pleasingly bright.

ample, are touched on briefly in the five paragraphs of the next exercise, *A 3*, on San Francisco's Chinatown:

Paragraph 1: Chinatown introduced

Paragraph 2: Grant Avenue described

Paragraph 3: Objects for sale mentioned

Paragraph 4: A "tea lunch" described

Paragraph 5: The residents mentioned

The first sentence of each new paragraph begins about an inch to the right of the rest of the sentences in the paragraph. (This starting to the right is called *indenting*.) In English, even the first paragraph is indented.

## A 3 / San Francisco's Chinatown

Directions: Change the five following paragraphs of questions into five paragraphs of affirmative statements. Be sure to indent five times.

Is San Francisco's Chinatown the largest Chinese community in the United States? Do at least 45,000 Chinese live there? Does Chinatown occupy some of the choicest land in downtown San Francisco? Does it have a beautiful view of the Pacific Ocean?

Is Grant Avenue the heart of Chinatown? Do the restaurants lining the avenue have red and gold dragons curling around their doorways? Do ornamental dragons hold up the street lights with their claws? Do red neon signs shine with Chinese letters? Are a few signs regrettably Western in style? Do lines of cars politely take turns in moving at intersections? Does all traffic wait for pedestrians?[1]

Does the tourist find carved chop sticks, jackets of Chinese silk, and blue and white rice bowls in shop after shop? Are sports jackets and television sets also available? Are Chinese comic books for sale in the "Culture Shop"?

Do a few restaurants offer a "tea lunch," mainly for Chinese patrons? Does a "tea lunch" consist of small pastries[2] filled with pork, shrimp, mushrooms, fruit, or[3] vegetables? Does the waiter bring a tray full of these pastries to the table? Does the patron make

[1] *pedestrians:* persons walking.
[2] *pastries:* rich baked crusts.
[3] *or:* a choice is implied between two or more items. (*Section A*, p. 15).

his selection with pleasure? Do the Chinese call this lunch a "Dim Sum"?

Are the residents of Chinatown American-born? Do the young clerks in the shops speak unusually clear and pleasing American English? Do such young men and women represent the possibility of preserving the best of two cultures?

## Grammar: capitals[1]

In English, a capital letter is used only to begin the name of a particular person, place, or institution; a small letter begins a name which applies to all of its kind. Note the capitals in *A 4:* Fifth Avenue, the Museum of Modern Art, Central Park (but an *avenue*, a *museum*, a *park*).

### A 4 / Fifth Avenue, New York

Directions: Change the three following paragraphs of questions into three paragraphs of statements. When you have finished, make sure that your use of capitals and small letters agrees with the printed page.

Is Fifth Avenue the heart of New York City? Do churches, museums, and department stores line this important street? Are Radio City, St. Patrick's Cathedral, and the Museum of Modern Art close neighbors? Are Greenwich Village and Harlem at opposite ends of the avenue?

Is there a small zoo in Central Park near Fifth Avenue? Do children call to the seals sunning themselves by their outdoor pool on summer afternoons? Do children gather to watch the polar bears cooling themselves in their special pool nearby? Do children and adults gather to listen to the roar of the lions near mealtime?

Is the Metropolitan Museum of Art popular with adults? Is it in Central Park, too? Are both institutions crowded on Sunday afternoons? Is the zoo near Fifth Avenue? Is the museum *on* Fifth Avenue?

### A 5 / The Moon

Directions: Change the three following paragraphs of questions into three paragraphs of statements.

[1] For additional notes on the use of capitals, see *For Reference*, p. 311.

Is the moon the earth's nearest neighbor? Is it only about a quarter of a million miles away? Is this a very short distance compared with other distances in space? Is the diameter of the moon just a little more than one-fourth the diameter of the earth?

Does the moon circle the earth every twenty-eight days? Does it also rotate on its own axis? Does it make one complete turn every twenty-eight days? Does it keep the same side to the earth at all times?

Does the moon get its light from the sun? Does the moon shine during the day as well as at night? Is moonlight really only secondary sunlight?

*Free writing:* Add a fourth paragraph, one of your own, giving further information about the moon.

## Grammar: the negative with **be**[1]

*Not* is placed after *be.* In the following examples, the contracted forms (those in parenthesis) are used mainly in conversation.

Directions: When you are given a *be* question, respond in chorus with a negative statement. (*Your* in a question becomes *our* in the statement.)

| *Singular* | *Plural* |
|---|---|
| I **am not** busy. (I'm not busy.) | We **are not** busy. (We're not busy.) |
| You **are not** in the right line. (You're not in the right line.) | You **are not** in the right line. (You're not in the right line.) |
| He, she, it (Bill, Marie, the car) **is not** in the right line. (He, she, it isn't in the right line.) | They **are not** in the right line. (They're not in the right line.) |

## Oral Practice

Directions: When you are given a *be* question, respond in chorus with a negative statement. (*Your* in a question becomes *our* in the statement.)

[1] *To the instructor:* The contracted negative forms, *isn't, aren't, doesn't, don't,* are standard usage in conversation. In writing, one style uses almost no contractions; a second style uses almost as many contractions as speech. What style or modification of a style a class adopts is left to the discretion of the instructor.

Example:

Instructor:   Is this your first day on the campus?
Students:     This is **not our** first day on the campus.

1. Is this your first class in English?
   (This is **not our** first class in English.)
2. Is it your ninth class?
   (It is **not our** . . .)
3. Is it your nineteenth class?
   (It is . . .)
4. Are these questions on page 200?
5. Are these questions long?
6. Are they difficult?
7. Are they in the past tense?
8. Are they in the future tense?
9. Are they in the present perfect tense?
10. Are they in the past perfect tense?

## Grammar: the negative with <u>do</u> and <u>does</u>

Note in the following sentences that *swim* is made negative by inserting *do not* or *does not* between *swim* and the subject.

|  | Singular | Plural |
|---|---|---|
| 1st person: | I do **not** (don't) swim. | We do **not** (don't) swim. |
| 2nd person: | You do **not** (don't) swim. | You do **not** (don't) swim. |
| 3rd person: | He, she, it (Bill, Marie, our cat) **does not** (doesn't) swim. | They do **not** (don't) swim. |

### Oral Practice

Directions: When you are given a *do* question, respond in chorus with a negative statement. (When a question begins with *you,* respond with *I.*)

1. Do you write your exercises at midnight?
   (I do **not** write my exercises at midnight.)
2. Does Marie write her exercises at midnight?
   (She does **not** . . .)
3. Do you get up at 4:00 A.M.?

4. Does your roommate get up at 4:00 A.M.?
5. Do you run five miles before breakfast?
6. Does Jack run five miles before breakfast?
7. Do most business men run five miles before breakfast?
8. Does the university begin classes at 6:00 A.M.?
9. Do you go to classes seven days a week?
10. Do you study forty days each month?


## A 6 / This Is Not Our Class

Directions: Change the two following paragraphs of questions into two paragraphs of negative statements, underlining *not*. (*Your* in the question becomes *our* in the statement.) Begin, "Our class is *not* in an unusual location. It is *not* . . . "

Is your class in an unusual location? Is it in a television studio? Is it in a movie theatre? Is it on a tennis court? Is it in an airport? Is it in a library reading room?

Do unusual conditions distract the class? Does an unhappy lover sing outside your classroom door? Does the ice-cream man ring his little bell under your windows? Do small boys play and fight under these same windows? Do students shout greetings from one end of the hall to the other? Do the radiators[1] thump and hiss in the winter? Does the instructor ignore the bell indicating class is over?


## A 7 / A Few Geographical Negatives

Directions: Change the two following paragraphs of questions into two paragraphs of negative statements, underlining *not*.

Example:

Question:   Is Mexico north of the United States?
Statement:   Mexico is **not** north of the United States.

Is Canada south of the United States? Is the Pacific Ocean east of the United States? Does the Mississippi River run east and west? Are the Rocky Mountains of the West older than the Appalachian Mountains of the East?

Do most farmers in Florida grow wheat? Do most farmers

---

[1] *radiators*: a set of pipes which give off heat. Radiators working imperfectly give out a heavy, dull knock (a thump) or a hiss (s-s-s).

in California grow corn? Are oranges and grapefruit the chief crops in New England?

## Grammar: or

The word *or* implies a choice:

Will you have tea **or** coffee?

Shall we walk **or** take a bus?

Shall we go to the movies **or** to the baseball game?

The choice may be among three or more items as in the following sentence:

Shall we go to the movies, the baseball game, **or** the free concert in the park?

### Oral Practice

Directions: Your instructor will give you a pair of words or phrases. Ask a fellow student which he prefers.

Example:

Instructor:   tea, coffee
Student A:   Which do you prefer, tea or coffee?
Student B:   I prefer tea.

1. ice cream, cake
2. orange juice, milk
3. soccer, football
4. hunting, fishing
5. dancing, singing
6. a noisy dormitory, a quiet dormitory
7. speaking English, writing English
8. snowy weather, rainy weather
9. a lot of money, a little money
10. traveling by bus, traveling by plane

### A 8 / True Statements

Directions: Make true statements in response to the two paragraphs of questions below, using your own knowledge or referring to your *A 7* paper. Begin, "Here are a few facts which no one denies. Canada is north . . . "

Is Canada north or south of the United States? Is the Pacific Ocean east or west of the United States? Does the Mississippi River run east and west or north and south? Are the Rocky Mountains of the West younger or older than the Appalachian Mountains of the East?

Do American farmers grow a wide variety of crops? Do most farmers in Florida grow wheat, or do most farmers in Florida grow oranges? Do most farmers in California grow corn, or do most farmers in California grow oranges, grapes, or lettuce? Are oranges and grapefruit the chief crops in New England, or is maple syrup the distinctive product of New England?

## FREE WRITING[1]

### A 9 / Living in a Hurry

Directions: Begin, "On weekdays, I hurry from morning until night. I get up . . . " Write one paragraph.

### A 10 / On Sundays

Directions: Begin, "On Sundays I relax. I do not get up . . . " Write one paragraph, including things you *do* and *don't do* on Sunday.

### A 11 / A Busy Person

Directions: Think of a busy person. Your mother? Your father? Your former boss? An older brother? Begin, "One of the busiest persons I know is . . . " Give the relationship of the person to you and possibly his name, and continue, giving one activity after another of one of the busiest persons you know. There is no restriction as to the number of paragraphs.

## LISTEN AND WRITE

The student who is trying hard is likely to write out his compositions first in his own language and then translate them into English. Seemingly, this practice gives him a better chance to think: actually, it makes him produce "foreignisms," even a sentence as impossible as this one:

[1] *To the instructor:* The work in free writing begins casually and continues casually until the habit of writing in English has had a chance to become established. For a formal but simple presentation of the topic sentence and the paragraph, see p. 43.

"I know that if I know the basic I often make mistakes on my paper."[1]

Few sentences as impossible as this one appear in compositions. Nevertheless, in the long run there is nothing to do but gradually to give up the treacherous[2] habit of translating.

One way to begin this long-term change is to do exercises at intervals of the type called "Listen and Write." Such exercises are not dictation. You do not even try to write every word. Rather, you write down the ideas presented, *using the words of the author as often as you can.* The object is to get part of the English phrasing on paper before one of your other languages can get in the way.

### Listen and Write I: The Climate of Haiti[3]

Directions (instructor to class): "I am going to read a paragraph twice. After the second reading, swiftly write down the ideas you remember, using the words of the writer as often as you can. If a sentence does not come quickly, write a few words and go on. These papers will not be collected."[4]

"Now write down this sentence, which will be the first sentence I will read: 'I like the climate of my country, Haiti.'[5] Then relax and listen to the reading."

I like the climate of my country, Haiti. It is not too hot. It is not too cold. Nobody wears a coat to school. Most boys take a swim after school. I much prefer the climate of my country to the climate of the United States.

### Listen and Write II: The Climate of the United States

Directions (instructor to class): "Write down this sentence, which will be the first sentence of the paragraph I am going to read: 'The climate of the United States is varied.' Then relax and listen to the reading."

---

[1] This is a complicated thought. One rephrasing might be, "I know that, even though I understand the basic rules, I often make mistakes on my papers."

[2] *treacherous:* not to be trusted, giving a false sense of security.

[3] *Haiti:* an island republic off the southeastern coast of Florida.

[4] In fact, some students may prefer that the instructor not even glance at their first two or three efforts.

[5] A quotation within a quotation uses single quotation marks.

The climate of the United States is varied. In the southern part of the country, you can go swimming in the winter. In the northern part of the country, snow covers the ground from December to April. In the far west, dry winds blow across hot sands. The climate of the United States is varied, to say the least.

## Listen and Write III: A University on a Hill[1]

Directions (instructor to class): "Write this sentence and then prepare to listen: 'A certain university in the Midwest is built on a steep hill.'"

A certain university in the Midwest  is built on a steep hill. In the summer, fat white clouds hang in the sky all day long. Far below, a lake shines in the sun. Baby rabbits sit confidently by a student walk. Students climb the steep hill past the rabbits. The little rabbits, confident that human beings are harmless, do not even take the trouble to hop into the bushes.

## Listen and Write IV: A University with Plenty of Room[2]

Directions (instructor to class): "Write this sentence and then prepare to listen: 'Here is another university in the Midwest.'"

Here is another university in the Midwest.  Over forty thousand students live on the campus, yet there is plenty of room. In the summer, flowers bloom everywhere. A little river runs through the oldest part of the campus. Ducks live along the river and gather by the little waterfall. Students on their way to the library stop on the bridge to enjoy the river, the ducks, and the brilliant flowers.

## FREE WRITING

### A 12 / My Own University[3]

Directions: Write one paragraph beginning, "My own university (name of your previous university) is not like the University of Wisconsin or like Michigan State University." Name some of the differences which give your own university its individuality.

[1] The University of Wisconsin at Madison.
[2] Michigan State University at East Lansing.
[3] university: an institution having schools of law, medicine, business, etc. (A college is not divided into separate schools.)

## FREE WRITING—LETTERS

### A 13 / In Thanks for Hospitality

Directions: Write a note of thanks to a hostess in whose home you have been entertained, preferably very recently. Do the following:

1. Begin by giving your reason for writing.
2. Say why you felt welcomed into the home.
3. Mention one or more definite pleasures of the visit.
4. Include your host and other prominent members of the family in your thanks.

Here is a sample thank-you note.

630 Jefferson Graduate Hall
Bexley University[1]
November 30, 19—

Dear Mrs. Jones,[2]

This is to thank you for the pleasure I had in spending Thanksgiving vacation in your home.

Of the fifteen people at your dinner table on Thanksgiving day, I was the only one who was not a relative, yet you made me feel like a member of the family.

I found the story of the first Thanksgiving touching and your Thanksgiving dinner delightful. I am writing my mother about the turkey, the cranberry sauce, and the pumpkin pie.

You, your husband, and Anne made my first holiday in the United States one I will always remember with pleasure.
Thank you again.

Sincerely,

*Haruko Ide*

It is impossible to write a thank-you note in the simple present tense alone. Yet nothing will please your hostess so much as a brief note from you. Write it. Ask your instructor for a few corrections if you wish, *but send the note.*

---

[1] There is no Bexley University. The addresses in the letters are fictitious.

[2] It is not necessary in a friendly letter to give the address of the person to whom the letter is written. Also, in giving your own address, it is not necessary to give the city and state.

Using a comma rather than a colon after the salutation is another sign of friendly informality.

## A 14 / A Letter to a Friend

Directions: Write a three-paragraph letter, mainly about your new room:

Paragraph 1: Get in touch with your friend
Paragraph 2: The room
        A. The sleeping arrangements
        B. The storage space
        C. The study arrangements
        D. The telephone in the room or down the hall
        E. One more feature
Paragraph 3: A brief paragraph which lets your friend know that **he** or **she** is missed

The following is an example of a letter you might write to your friend:

624 Jefferson Graduate Hall[1]
Bexley University
Wellington, Ohio 40114
September 29, 19—

Dear Knody,
    You are going to hear a lot about this university before I come home, but this time I am going to tell you about my new room.
    It has two of everything except the telephone. The beds are "bunks," one above the other. At bed time, Beth grabs the side of the upper bunk with both hands, takes one good jump, and lands. It is lucky for us that one of us is tall. The closets are too small, so Beth and I each have a big box which we shove under my bunk. Our desks are by the big window, back to back. It is a little hard to stop talking when we first settle down to study (Beth is a very companionable American), but we eventually do stop and begin to study **silently**.
    I wish you were here to meet my new friends and talk everything over, but we can write. Write soon.

Affectionately,
*Sung Hee*

Additional directions: As the "complimentary close" to your letter, translate the ending you would use in your own language or use one of these:

[1] Put your full address on more than one of your letters to friends at home, so that your address cannot be mislaid and lost.

With love (indicates a close relationship)
Affectionately or fondly (girl to girl)
As always/as ever (man to man)

## A 15 / Ordering from a Catalog

Directions: Order something which you find advertised in a catalog, a magazine, or a newspaper.

1. Make a copy of your order for reference, using a sheet of carbon paper and a ball-point pen or a typewriter.
2. In addition to giving the advertiser's order number, add a few descriptive details. This precaution may prevent your order from being incorrectly filled by an inexperienced clerk.
3. Underline any choice offered you (a **blue** decoration, not red, brown, or yellow).
4. Most companies accept a check as readily as a money order when the amount is small. Be sure to mention the form of payment.

The following is an example of the kind of letter which might be written in ordering something from a catalog:

431 Jefferson Graduate Hall
Bexley University
Wellington, Ohio 40114
December 3, 19—

Craft House
Williamsburg Reproductions
Williamsburg, Virginia[1]

Gentlemen:[2]

Enclosed is a money order for $6.25 for a set of three handwoven towels, all with a **blue** decoration, number S137 in your catalog.

Very truly yours,

Celeste Alt

Celeste Alt
(Mrs. Michel Alt)

[1] Williamsburg, the capital of Virginia when this country was still a British colony, has been restored to its former elegance. Copies or adaptations of its furnishings may be ordered by catalog.
[2] The colon (:) is used after the salutation in all formal correspondence.

## A 16 / Sending for Admission Forms

Directions: Write briefly asking for the forms you will need if you decide to transfer to another institution. (It is not necessary to give background information until you see what the forms ask.)

Here is an example of such a request:

329 Jefferson Graduate Hall
Bexley University
Wellington, Ohio 40114
April 14, 19—

Office of Admissions
Graduate Division
Ohio State University
Columbus, Ohio 43210

Gentlemen:

Please send me the forms necessary to apply for admission to your College of Pharmacy.

Very truly yours,

*Chiang Chung*

Chiang Chung

## A 17 / A Letter to the President

Directions: Write a letter to the President of the United States. Note the following:

1. Your letter probably will not be read by the President himself, *but it will be read.*
2. Express your opinion on one issue only, and in one paragraph. The number of letters clearly *for* and *against* each issue are counted and reported.
3. Americans seriously interested in what happens to their country express themselves to their public officials, including the President, as a matter of duty.

The following is a possible letter to the President. Note the use of the colon as a sign of both formality and respect.

763 Jefferson Graduate Hall
Bexley University
Wellington, Ohio 40114
January 2, 19—

The President
The White House
Washington, D. C.

Dear Mr. President:

As a foreign student from Thailand, I want to commend your action in/ protest your action in . . . .

Yours sincerely,

*Thirawat Sagarik*

Thirawat Sagarik

## ADVERBS OF FREQUENCY

### Grammar: the nature of adverbs of frequency

Adverbs of frequency tell how often an action takes place. If the verb is some form of *be*, the adverb of frequency is placed *after* the verb:

| | Verb | Adverb of Frequency | |
|---|---|---|---|
| Pete | is | always | a dependable driver. |
| His friends | are | sometimes | careless. |

If the verb is not some form of *be*, the adverb of frequency is placed *before* the main verb:

| | Adverb of Frequency | Main Verb | |
|---|---|---|---|
| Pete | always | drives | his car on weekends. |
| He | never | drives | it to class. |

## Basic List

The first sentence under each adverb of frequency has some form of *be* as its verb: the second has another verb.

often: many times (synonym for **frequently**)
  I am **often** tired before dinner.
  After dinner, I **often** enjoy the long walk to the library.
rarely: not often (synonym for **seldom**)
  I am **rarely** ill.
  I **rarely** have even a cold.
frequently: many times (synonym for **often**)
  Spring is **frequently** late in this part of the country.
  Spring **frequently** arrives suddenly when it comes.
seldom: not often (synonym for **rarely**)
  I am **seldom** interested in baseball on TV.
  I **seldom** listen to the scores of even the major teams.
  (Beside being synonyms, **rarely** and **seldom** are in equally common
    use in both speaking and writing.)
sometimes: now and then
  I am **sometimes** delighted with midnight TV.
  I **sometimes** watch until 1:00 A.M.
  **Sometimes** a good "talk show" makes me laugh out loud.
  A successful talk show relaxes its listeners, at least **sometimes**.
  (Note that **sometimes** can be placed first and last in the sentence,
    as well as in adverb of frequency positions.)[1]
ever: at any time, even once
  Do you **ever** go to the snack bar between meals?
  Do you **ever** go to Chicago for the weekend?
  (In this text, **ever** is used only in questions.)[2]
always
  **Separate acts:** I am **always** sure to see the University Players—
    every time they produce a new play, I mean.
  **Habit:** I **always** drink two cups of coffee at breakfast.
never: at no time
  The stars are **never** absent from the sky.
  They **never** appear to the naked eye in the daytime, however.

---

[1] For additional adverbs of frequency having "special privileges of occurrence," see p. 28.
[2] *Ever* can be used in statements: "Nothing exciting *ever* happens around here." "They lived happily *ever* after."

**An area of New York's Broadway theater district at night.**
[Carl Centinio, DPI]

### A 18 / Broadway, New York

Directions: Copy the first paragraph as it stands. Make it your introductory paragraph.

Change the second and third paragraphs of questions into statements, putting an adverb of frequency, underlined, after *be*. Make reasonable guesses as to the best adverb to use.

Example:

Question:   Is Broadway of interest to visitors?
Statement:   Broadway is **always** of interest to visitors.

Broadway, one of the widest and most crowded streets in New York, is the heart of the theater district of the whole United States.
Is Broadway brilliantly lighted at night? Are the sidewalks

crowded with people? Are huge[1] crowds on their way to a play
or a movie between 8:00 and 8:40? Is it ever possible to move faster
than the crowd? Are sightseers amused and pleased to be a part
of this crowd? Are eating places crowded after the theater? Are
they crowded at two o'clock in the morning? Are they crowded at
four o'clock in the morning?

Is traffic heavy on Broadway? Are drivers of cars alert?[2] Are
those on foot alert? Is anyone ever relaxed crossing Broadway?

## Oral Practice: not *be*

Directions: When you are asked a question about the President of
the United States, respond individually with what you know or guess
to be the facts, putting an adverb of frequency before the verb.

Example:

Instructor:   Does the President ever work late in the evening?
Student:      The President (or **he**) often works late in the evening.

1. Does the President ever take a walk early in the morning?
2. Does he read the morning newspapers at breakfast?
3. Does he have time to read for pleasure?
4. Does he ever leave the White House for the weekend?
5. Does he take paper work with him?
6. Does he ever leave the country to consult with foreign leaders?
7. Does he think about the rights of people in other parts of the world?
8. Does he ever object to what the newspapers say?
9. Does the President's wife ever help him politically?
10. Do Presidents ever wish to have a second term?

## A 19 / The President at Work

Directions: Change the three following paragraphs of questions into
three paragraphs of statements. Note than an adverb of frequency
has been placed in every question. If your own observation suggests
a different adverb, use it. Underline whatever adverb you decide on.

Does the President of the United States **always** lead a
tremendously busy and varied life? Does he **frequently** appear on
TV? Is he **always** interested in foreign policy? Does he **sometimes**

---

[1] *huge:* very, very large.
[2] *alert:* watchful, ready at any instant for what is coming.

address public meetings? Does he **sometimes** meet with minority groups in the White House? Is he **always** a gracious host to such groups?

Does the President **often** suggest laws for Congress to pass? Is he **frequently** in personal touch with Congressional leaders about the passage of these bills? Does he **seldom** veto[1] bills passed by Congress? Does he **sometimes** consult with labor leaders about certain bills?

Does the President **rarely** have time for small pleasures? However, does he **often** watch at least part of a football game on TV? Does he **frequently** fly to his home state for the weekend?

*Free Writing:* Add a fourth paragraph of statements of your own, giving further activities of the President. Or write a fourth paragraph of questions.

## DICTATION

Dictation is the opposite of Listen and Write. The purpose of dictation is to get on paper every word of a short paragraph read by the instructor. The method of dictation suggested here permits the student to hear every word four times.

Instructor: "I am going to give you a paragraph of dictation. First, I will read the entire paragraph. Don't write. Relax and listen. Then I will begin to read a second time, in phrases. You will write. As soon as I reach the end of a sentence, I will go back and repeat it. When I reach the end of the paragraph, I will go back and read the entire paragraph again. You may not ask for a word during the dictation (this interrupts the concentration of the other students), but you can be sure you will hear every word *four times.*"

### Dictation I: Mrs. Smith at Breakfast

Directions (instructor to class): "Write down this sentence, which will be the first sentence of the dictation: 'Mrs. Smith always drinks coffee at breakfast.' Then listen to the paragraph."

[1] In your statement, the spelling will be *vetoes*. (See Rule 9, p. 262).

Mrs. Smith always drinks coffee for breakfast. She never drinks tea. She sometimes makes pancakes. She often boils eggs. She rarely has fruit at breakfast. She always has orange juice. She always makes toast.[1]

### Dictation II: Mrs. Smith in the Supermarket

**Directions (instructor to class): "Write down this sentence now: 'After breakfast Mrs. Smith always goes to the supermarket.' Then listen to the paragraph."**

After breakfast Mrs. Smith always goes to the supermarket. She almost always looks at the fruit. She often buys oranges. She sometimes buys apples. She never buys grapes. She seldom buys salt. Mrs. Smith always pays cash for her groceries.

### Dictation III: Pete and His Car

**Directions (instructor to class): "Write down this sentence now: 'Pete always has a car.' "**

Pete always has a car. He always parks it in front of his apartment. He never leaves the keys in the car. He always locks all the doors and windows, too. He frequently washes the car on Saturdays. He always looks over the engine first. Sometimes he makes small adjustments. He often buys gas on Saturdays. He always takes a ride on Sundays. Some of his friends always go with him.

## Grammar: adverbs of frequency
## with special privileges of occurrence

A few adverbs of frequency can be placed first or last in the sentence, as well as after *be* and before all other verbs.

## Additional List[2]

generally: synonym for **usually**
　Generally, we have an attendance of 75,000 at our home football
　games.

---

[1] *To the instructor:* Dictation should be corrected immediately, each student correcting his own work from the text, while the instructor circulates casually and encouragingly. The errors which students discover for themselves are the errors which disappear first.

[2] The much-used *sometimes,* which belongs here, was presented in the basic list, p. 24.

We **generally** have an attendance of 75,000 at our home football games.

We have an attendance of 75,000 at our home football games, **generally**.

occasionally: now and then

**Occasionally,** we win by a very large margin.

We **occasionally** win by a very large margin.

We win by a very wide margin, **occasionally**.

usually: habitually, customarily

**Usually,** win or lose, we have a party after a home game.

Win or lose, we **usually** have a party after a home game.

Win or lose, we have a party after a home game, **usually**.


## A 20 / Three Positions for *Sometimes*

Directions: Place *sometimes,* underlined, before a main verb, and first and last in the sentence. Use the three basic sentences below if you wish, but be sure to add two sentences of your own. (This means you will write fifteen sentences in all.)

I study after dinner.

I listen to the news at 7:00 A.M.

I go to the movies.


## Grammar: frequency phrases

Frequency phrases come at the end or the beginning of the sentence:

We have oral practice at least **once a day.**

**Three or four times a week** Bill goes to the telephone and places a long-distance call to Detroit.

Note how the frequency phrases below are listed from the general to the specific:

| | |
|---|---|
| in the morning | once a month |
| on week days | once a day |
| on Sundays | the first of the month |
| every week | at noon |
| every day | at midnight |
| | at 9:00 A.M. |

When two frequency phrases are used in the same sentence, the more general phrase comes first.

Examples:

once a month on Sundays——every day at 9:00 A.M.

## Oral Practice

Directions: Answer the question asked you with a statement ending with one of the frequency phrases in the list above.

1. How often is mail delivered to the dormitories?
2. When is it delivered?
3. Do you carry the key to your mailbox every day?
4. Do you look in your mailbox in the morning or at noon?
5. Does mail ever come at midnight?
6. Does it ever come on Sunday?
7. How often do requests for payment appear in the mailboxes? (requests from clothing stores, for example)
8. When does the student newspaper appear, on week days or on Sundays?
9. How often do you think you should hear from your friends?
10. How often do you write letters?

## Listen and Write after Oral Practice

Directions: Listen while your instructor reads the first question in the above Oral Practice twice. Then write a complete sentence answering the question (not just a few words). When you have written your ten statements, go over your work. Your instructor will then read the questions a third time.

## Grammar: usually

Since *usually* implies habitual action, it is generally used in the simple present tense.

Examples:

Student A:  I **usually go** straight from my last class to the snack bar.
Student B:  So do I. I **usually get** a coke there.

Student C:   I **usually** add an order of french fries to my coke. After all, it's an hour until dinner.

In conversation, a question often contains the limitation as to time or place:

Student A:   What do you drink for lunch?
Student B:   I **usually** drink a coke.


## Oral Practice

Directions: Respond to the questions asked with a statement containing *usually* in one of the various positions in which it can appear.

1. Does Hing get up in time for breakfast?
2. Where does he go for breakfast?
3. Is he on time for his 8:00 o'clock class?
4. Does he have his home work ready to hand in?
5. Does he stay awake in this early class?
6. Where does he sit?
7. Is he glad when the class is over?
8. Does he learn something in this early class?


## FREE WRITING

### A 21  /  My Favorite Newspaper

Directions: Write one paragraph beginning, "I like to read (name of paper, title underlined). I never read it all."
Say how often you read seven of the sections listed below, underlining an adverb of frequency in each sentence and adding a comment of your own here and there.

Example:

I like to read *The New York Times*. I never read it all. I never read the obituaries, for example. I am not interested in reading notices of deaths.

| | |
|---|---|
| the international section | the book-review section |
| the national section | the editorials |
| the sports section | the obituaries |
| the fashion section | the want ads |
| the amusements section | the advertisements |
| the travel section | |

## INTRODUCTORY THERE

### Grammar: introductory there

Introductory *there* is a convenient way to introduce a new subject:

**There** is a concert in the auditorium Saturday evening. Wouldn't you like to go?

| Expletive | Verb | Subject | Place |
|-----------|------|---------|-------|
| There | are | palm trees | in Florida. |
| There | is | a lot of sunshine | **there.** |

When *there* stands first in a sentence, it acts as an introductory word, without meaning, called an "expletive." When *there* stands last in a sentence, it indicates *place*. (See above.)

The following are two ways to say the same thing: Form A is seldom used; Form B is frequently used.

Form A:   A man is at the door.
Form B:   There is a man at the door.

### Oral Practice I

Directions: In chorus, change the statements you are given from *Form A* to *Form B*.

Example:

Form A:   A park is in our city.
Form B:   There is a park in our city.

1. A lake is in the park.
2. A tree is by the lake.
3. A bench is under the tree.
4. Some boats are on the lake.
5. Some boys are in the boats.
6. Some girls are watching the boys.
7. A zoo is in the park.
8. Monkeys are in the zoo.
9. A big cage of monkeys is outdoors.

10. Several monkeys are in a tree in the cage.
11. Several people are on the sidewalk by the cage.
12. A conversation is in progress between a man and a monkey.

## Oral Practice II

Directions: Respond individually to the phrase given you in the following pattern, using *any*,[1] *some*,[2] or *one*. (These words can be used with a noun or alone.)

Example:

Instructor:  signs of spring
Student A:  There weren't **any** signs of spring yesterday.
Student B:  But[3] there are **some** today.

Instructor:  redbird
Student C:  There wasn't **any** redbird here yesterday.
Student D:  But there is **one** today.

1. robins
2. children on roller skates
3. children without sweaters
4. boys playing marbles
5. girls jumping rope
6. adults smiling
7. ice cream man doing business
8. soft wind blowing
9. anyone saying, "Spring is here."

## Oral Practice III

Directions: Continue responding to the phrase given you with *any, some,* or *one*.

1. notice on the bulletin board
2. news about mid-terms
3. anxiety about mid-terms
4. requests for conferences
5. notice from the adviser's office

---

[1] *any*: none, not even one.
[2] *some*: an indefinite number, more than one.
[3] It is permissible to begin a statement with *but*, especially in conversation.

6. letters in my mailbox
7. candy bars in the vending machine
8. speaker in the speech lab
9. good programs on TV
10. opera on TV

## Oral Practice IV

Directions: When you are given a question and a cue word, begin a statement with *there* and insert the cue word or a word of your own.

Example:

Question:    Is there ever a wood-burning fireplace in a city apartment?[1] (occasionally)

Statement:   Occasionally there is a wood-burning fireplace in a city apartment.

1. Is there a lot of room in a city apartment?[2]      (seldom)
2. Are there enough closets?[3]                         (rarely)
3. Is there a kitchen?                                   (always)
4. Is there a refrigerator?                              (always)
5. Is there milk in the refrigerator?                   (generally)
6. Is there orange juice?                                (usually)
7. Are there lamb chops?                                 (occasionally)
8. Is there a living room in an apartment?               (always)
9. Is there a large couch along one wall?                (frequently)
10. Is there a television set opposite the couch?        (almost always)
11. Are there ever blooming plants in the windows?       (often)
12. Is there ever a garden on the roof?                  (sometimes)
13. Are there ever trees in the garden?                  (rarely)
14. Is there ever a lion among the trees?                (never)

## FREE WRITING

### A 22 / A Good Place to Study

Directions: Write one paragraph. Begin, "I have a good place to study." Cover points such as these:

[1] *To the instructor:* The words in parenthesis are merely suggestions for use when the class has difficulty producing an answer.

[2] *apartment:* living quarters for a family or one person in a larger unit called an *apartment building.*

[3] *closet:* an enclosed space for clothing, cooking utensils, etc.

1. Just where is your favorite spot for study—a seldom-used corner of the library, the ignored "study room" in the dormitory, or your own room?
2. What gives you a pleasant sense of being alone? On the other hand, what keeps you from being lonely?
3. How much space do you have for your books and papers?
4. How far are you from a good dictionary?
5. How about a wastebasket?
6. Is there some pleasant way to relax briefly after two hours of hard study?

Finish, "You can see why I go to (name of spot) when I want to concentrate on my work."

## Grammar: <u>do</u>[1] in contrast with <u>make</u>

Since custom, not logic, decides the use of *do* and *make,* the following list is provided.

### List

**do**

We **do** research, all types of work including homework, our best, everything we can, filing, favors, without things. Also (*A 24*) we **do** setting-up exercises, things better, nothing.

**make**

We **make** a living, plans, an effort, progress, requests, things better, appointments, speeches, arrangements, preparations, certain, impressions, decisions. Also (*A 24*) we **make** beds, coffee, pancakes, toast, a beginning, our way, reports, mistakes.

### Oral Practice

Directions: You will be given a word from the *do* list. Respond in chorus, beginning, "We *do* . . . "

Example:

Instructor:   research
Students:    We **do** research.

When the *do* list is finished, go rapidly through the *make* list.

---

[1] This *do* is a main verb, not the *do* used in questions and negatives.

Finally, respond to a list mixed by the instructor.

Example:

Instructor: an effort
Students: We **make** an effort.

Instructor: our best
Students: We **do** our best.

## A 23 / Using *Do* in Contrast with *Make*

Directions: Copy the three following paragraphs, filling the blanks with *does* or *makes*. (The items in the *do/make* lists are roughly in the order in which they appear in this exercise and in *A 24*.)

    Anne _____ her living as a secretary. She works for Dr. Jansen, who _____ research for the Rockefeller Institute. Dr. Jansen _____ his own work exceedingly well. The plans he _____, the effort he _____, and the progress he _____, are all of the greatest value to the institute.

    Anne finds it a pleasure to _____ her best for Dr. Jansen. He never gives her an order. He always _____ requests of her. As a result, Anne _____ everything she can to _____ Dr. Jansen's load a little lighter. She _____ his appointments, she _____ his filing. Sometimes she _____ favors for his associates.

    When Dr. Jansen has to _____ a speech, Anne _____ many of the arrangements. She _____ everything she can to _____ certain Dr. Jansen will _____ a good impression. He does. For his part, Dr. Jansen does not see how he could _____ without his secretary.

## Oral Practice: *get*

Directions: Use the expression given you in a complete statement.

Example:
Instructor: **get up**
Student A: I hate to **get up** in the morning.
Student B: So does Pete, but he **gets up** early.

1. get up
2. get breakfast

3. get a meal
4. get dressed
5. get through with (any type of work)
6. get to
7. get into
8. get busy
9. get away from
10. get back to

## A 24 / Using *Do, Make,* and *Get*

Directions: Instead of writing this exercise, your instructor may wish you to do it orally in class. If you do it orally and any use of *do, make,* or *get* surprises you, write that particular word in your text.

Pete has his own large one-room apartment. From Monday to Friday he _____ up at 6:30. He _____ not make his bed then. He _____ some setting-up exercises. Next he goes into the kitchen and _____ coffee. Then he _____ the rest of his breakfast. He seldom _____ pancakes. He always _____ toast. After breakfast he _____ his bed and _____ dressed for work.

Pete then has well over an hour to _____ part of his homework. First he _____ his calculus. Then he _____ a beginning on his English assignment. He does not _____ through with this second assignment, however.

Pete _____ to the subway by 8:20. He _____ his way through the crowd and _____ into the last car of his train. Then he _____ nothing but hold onto a strap.

In the office, Pete _____ busy and proceeds to _____ a good day's work. Late in the afternoon, he _____ a detailed report to the head of his office on the day's sales. He _____ this work rapidly but accurately. He _____ few mistakes. He seldom _____ the same mistake twice.

Pete _____ from the office a little after 5:00. He _____ back to his apartment well before 6:00. He _____ to his first class by 7:10.

## Grammar: "emphatic do"

*Do* is used not only in forming questions and negatives but also in giving emphasis to affirmative statements:

I **do** wish you could stay a little longer. I **do** hope you can come again soon.

Emphatic *do* occurs most frequently in an affirmative statement made just after a negative statement:

| Negative Statement | Affirmative Statement |
|---|---|
| I don't mind the heat, | but I **do** mind the humidity.[1] |
| Bill never reads a novel, | but he **does** read psychology. |

## A 25 / Certain Affirmations

Directions: Write two paragraphs. In the first paragraph, copy the topic sentence. Then complete each partial negative statement with an affirmative statement containing an emphatic *does*. (The second object should have something in common with the first, yet be different).

Example:

Sergi doesn't like wrestling, . . .
Sergi doesn't like wrestling, but he **does** like karate.[2]

Sergi is a young man of strong likes and dislikes. He doesn't like football, but . . . He doesn't like skiing, but . . . He doesn't like basketball, but . . . He doesn't own a sailboat, but . . .

*Free writing:* Add a second paragraph beginning with the topic sentence, "Sergi has strong likes and dislikes outside the field of sports." Possibilities are geology, biography, ten-speed bicycles, science fiction, old railroad engines, electronic computers.

## Grammar: how future action is expressed

1. *Going to* plus the simple form of the verb is generally used to express future action in conversation:

Question:   What are you **going to see** in Washington, D.C.?
Statement:  I'm **going to see** Lindbergh's plane in the Smithsonian Institution, for one thing.

[1] *humidity:* hot, damp air.
[2] *karate:* a form of self-defense highly developed in Eastern countries.

2. *Will*,[1] plus the simple form of the verb, is generally used to express future action in writing:

Hing **will go** to the college cafeteria in a few minutes for another meal.

The parade **will form** in Marshall Square.

3. Although there is no rule about the matter, *will* generally gives a more formal air to a statement than *going to*:

The President **will** address the nation at 9:00 P.M. tonight.

In this paper I **will** attempt to analyze why agricultural mechanization does not lower the cost of production in El Salvador.

4. The contraction *I'll* is used in conversation:

So long! I'll see you tomorrow.


**Oral Practice I**

Directions: When you are given a question and a cue word, make a statement using the cue in the following pattern:

Example:
Instructor:  Is Bill **going to** be a police-   **(psychologist)**
man?
Student:  No, he isn't **going to** be a policeman. He's **going to** be a
**psychologist.**


1. Is Pete going to be an architect?     (engineer)
2. Is Anne going to be a teacher?     (lawyer)
3. Is Betty going to be a secretary?     (nurse)
4. Is Haruko going to be a newspaper reporter?     (artist)
5. Is Ali going to be a farmer?     (businessman)


**Oral Practice II**

Directions: When you are given a question and a cue phrase, make a statement using the phrase in the following pattern.

[1] For *will* and *shall* as modals, see Section G.

Example:

| | | |
|---|---|---|
| Instructor: | Is Bill going to the movies tonight? | (work on his term paper) |
| Student: | No, he isn't. He's going to work on his term paper. | |

1. Is Pete going to clean the apartment Saturday?    (go sailing)
2. Is Haruko going to make sukiyaki Saturday morning?    (bake cookies)
3. Are Anne and Haruko going to stay home Saturday evening?    (go dancing)
4. Is Ali going to go to bed early Saturday evening?    (after midnight)
5. Are all the students in the university going to get up early Sunday morning?    (sleep late)

## Grammar: "never a future in a time clause"

Whatever logic may suggest, English never uses the future tense in a time clause:

I am going to write a dozen letters when I **get** time.
(not "will get")

I will let you know whenever I **hear** anything.
(not "will hear")

Time clauses (adverbial clauses) begin with a subordinator such as *when, whenever,* or *until* and have a subject and a predicate:

| | Subordinator | Subject | Predicate |
|---|---|---|---|
| I will work hard | until | I | graduate. |
| I will celebrate | when | I | get my degree. |

One type of subordinator answers *when* (adverbial clauses). A second common type answers *who* or *what.*

**when:** at the time that
   I feel happy **when** the weather is fine.
**whenever:** every time that, as often as

Lee makes himself look up the spelling of a word **whenever** he is in doubt.

until: up to the time when

Lee generally keeps on **until** he finishes his assignments.

**Oral Practice: *when, whenever, until***

Directions: When you are given a partial statement, repeat it and complete it individually with a time clause in the simple present tense.

Examples:

Instructor:   I'm going to have a coke . . .
Student:       I'm going to have a coke when I **get** out of class.

Instructor:   I'm going to relax . . .
Student:       I'm going to relax, at least until I **finish** the coke.

Instructor:   I write down a new word . . .
Student:       I write down a new word whenever one **interests** me.

1. I'm going to write a dozen letters when . . .
2. I feel happy when . . .
3. I feel tired whenever . . .
4. I can do my home work rather quickly when . . .
5. Men don't keep their hats on when . . .
6. I hate to write letters when . . .
7. I intend to stay in this university until . . .
8. I intend to keep saving money until . . .
9. (Make up your own statement.)
10. (Make up your own statement.)

**A 26 / The Student Who Makes Progress**

Directions: In the first two paragraphs below, complete the partial statements with a time clause in the simple present tense. Only two subordinators will be needed: *until* and *whenever*, underlined.

The student who makes progress in composition keeps working on each assignment . . . . He remembers to indent . . . . He remembers to put a period (point, full stop) . . . . He makes himself look up the spelling of a word . . . .

In class, he asks a question. . . . If he does not understand the teacher's explanation, he asks additional questions. . . . He keeps making an effort to understand a difficult point. . . .

*Free writing:* Add a paragraph of comment of your own. Is the care in mechanics suggested in the first paragraph important? Is the persistent questioning[1] suggested in the second paragraph respectful? Is there a danger that a persistent questioner will be considered stupid by his classmates? (Whenever one student says he does not understand, several silent students almost certainly do not understand, either.) Number your ideas within the paragraph, as textbook writers sometimes do with (1), (2), (3).

## A 27 / A Familiar Procedure

Directions: Complete the four following paragraphs of partial statements, giving the struggles of a student to assemble his lunch in a crowded cafeteria. The following two subordinators have not been used before:

**as soon as:** the moment after
  Hing will get into line **as soon as** he enters the cafeteria.
**while:** during the time that
  He will carry his briefcase **while** he selects his food.

  Hing will go to the college cafeteria in a few minutes for another meal. He will take off his cap as soon as. . . . He will keep his overcoat[2] on until. . . . In addition, he will carry his briefcase while . . . .
  He will pick up a tray, silverware, and a napkin as soon as. . . . He will decide whether to have meat when. . . . He will not decide whether to have dessert until. . . . He will not get a tea bag and a pot of hot water until. . . . He will put the tea bag into the hot water as soon as. . . .
  After he has his food, Hing will wait in a long line while the students ahead of him. . . . He will get out his own money, ready to pay, while. . . . Promptly, he will put his change in one of his pockets when. . . .
  He will begin to look around for an empty chair as soon as . . . He will put down his tray and his briefcase and take off his

[1] *persistent questioning:* continued questioning.
[2] *overcoat:* a heavy coat worn over a suit in the winter.

overcoat when . . . With special luck, a friend will be at the table with the empty chair, and he and Hing will talk while . . .

## FREE WRITING

### A 28 / A Familiar Procedure of My Own

Directions: Write one paragraph describing a procedure you must go through repeatedly, whether you wish to or not. Begin, "In a few minutes (or hours) I will . . . "

Possible procedures:

1. Drawing a book out of the library.
2. Cashing a check when the bank is crowded.
3. Operating the washing machine in a laundromat.
4. Gradually settling down to an evening of hard study.

Use time expressions such as these to indicate the sequence of your actions: *first, next, then, after this, finally.*

## OUTLINING AND FREE WRITING

So far, little has been said about two of the basic elements of English style, the topic sentence and the paragraph. However, you have been using these two elements ever since the beginning of the course.

*The topic sentence*   The topic sentence announces promptly and firmly what you are going to write about. In this text, whenever you are given the direction *Begin, you are being given a topic sentence.* The topic sentence is the most important sentence in your composition, for it decides the direction your writing will take.

*The paragraph*   When free writing is one paragraph long, the topic sentence begins the paragraph. When the composition is longer, the topic sentence occasionally stands last in the paragraph, acting as a summary. Also, after the opening paragraph, the topic sentence may not be expressed but implied in a group of closely related sentences which form the paragraph. However, for the present we will work with the topic sentence which stands first in a paragraph.

The conclusion   In a one-paragraph composition, the conclusion may be very slight. (See "The Water-Drinking Habit," p. 48). In a longer composition, the last paragraph will restate the main idea, and perhaps, briefly and helpfully, summarize the main points.


## The Outline

The outline is the skeleton of a piece of writing, its bare bones. An outline is useful because it lets you see whether you are moving straight from one point to the next in the logical style which first the English and then the Americans have employed for centuries.

So far, you have not had to wonder when to begin a new paragraph. In the guided exercises, you followed the indentations. In the free writing, you either wrote one paragraph or were told definitely where to begin a new paragraph (the letters). Now your compositions will be longer, and outlining will help with the paragraphing.

When Do You Make an Outline?   Possibly you make an outline before you begin to write. More probably you begin to write and then pause, at a loss. You cannot get down on paper what you want to say next. At this point, outline. Once you can write down your main points, *A, B, C,* and a few of your subpoints, your composition will move forward again.

It is a help, too, to think a little about a composition before you sit down to write. A useful idea is likely to cross your mind while you are doing something entirely unrelated to writing. When this happens, seize any scrap of paper within reach and put the idea down. There is nothing worse than sitting down before a blank piece of "good" paper and saying, "I *must* write something. This is due tomorrow morning."

My New University (the outline)

  I. I like my new university on the whole

II. What I like
   A. The great size of the campus
   B. The sociable dining room
   C. The food, in part
III. Generally speaking, I like my new university

Any outline consists of an introduction, the body of the piece of writing, and the conclusion. The type of outlining employed above is widely used, but any set of symbols is acceptable which makes the relationship of one idea to another clear.

My New University (the composition)

On the whole, I like my new university. Here are three things I especially like.

In the first place, I like the great size of the campus. I do not mind in the least walking twenty minutes to get to my first class, walking back twenty minutes to have lunch, walking another twenty minutes for my afternoon classes, and then walking back again for dinner. In fact, I often walk on the campus at midnight to enjoy the stars and the silent pine trees.

In the second place, I like the big dining room,[1] with no assigned seats. You eat at the big tables with different friends or different strangers at every meal if you wish. Americans are often glad to have a conversation as soon as they find they can understand your English.

In the third place, the food is not so bad, after all. There is a lot of it, more than enough at every meal. However, the seasonings are too simple—salt and pepper, ketchup (a red tomato sauce), mustard, and a few relishes. On the other hand, you can help yourself to three servings of ice cream, and no one minds at all. The ice cream is delicious.

The long distances, the way of dining, and the food are all new to me, but on the whole I like my new university. I intend to stay until I have a master's degree.

Note that an affirmative opinion only needs to be favorable for the most part. The frankness of the writer in saying what he thinks of American seasonings only strengthens his main idea, that he likes his new university on the whole.

[1] This is not the city cafeteria where Hing had trouble assembling his lunch (p. 42).

## FREE WRITING

### A 29 / My New University

Directions: Follow the form of the foregoing composition. Name three things you like (or do not like) about your present university. Or name three things you are only now becoming accustomed to in your new life.

Hand in an outline with your composition, following the three-part form in the example, pp. 44–45.

## The *Five-Paragraph Composition*

The formal five-paragraph composition is an easy step from the one-paragraph composition because it is highly structured:

Paragraph 1: Introduction, topic sentence included
Paragraph 2: First point: begins "First," or "In the first place,"
Paragraph 3: Second point: begins "Second," or "In the second place,"
Paragraph 4: Third point: begins "Third," or "In the third place,"
Paragraph 5: Conclusion: begins "In conclusion," "In summary," "In short," "In brief," "On the whole," or "Generally speaking,"

## FREE WRITING

### A 30 / Back Home

Directions: Begin, "There are three features of my life back home in (name of country) which are very different from life here."

Follow the form for the five-paragraph composition. In particular, try to express your feelings accurately in the conclusion. Do you feel that you cannot enjoy your stay here because of what you are missing? Do you feel that you will appreciate life at home more after being away from it? Or do you feel something else?

Hand in an outline with your composition.

### A 31 / Speaking Politically

Directions: Begin, "I am now going to exercise the American privilege of saying what I think politically."

Still following the five-paragraph format, say what you think of three features of the government here, or, if it seems wise, what you think of three features of the government in your homeland.

Hand in an outline with your composition.

## A 32 / The Work Ahead

Directions: Discuss three problems your country must attack and, to some degree solve, if it is to move toward peace and health by the year 2000.

Hand in an outline with your composition.

## A 33 / My Chosen Field

Directions: Begin by saying what your chosen field is and what your special interest is within the field.

Because there is so much you could say, your ideas are likely to spread in all directions. Limit yourself to three major points which will help an outsider to begin to understand your field. Conclude by saying what your work will probably be when you return home.

Hand in a somewhat detailed outline with your composition.

## A 34 / This Class

Directions: End the writing in the five-paragraph format by answering this question: What would you like to see this class do which it is not doing now, at least not very often?

Hand in an outline with your composition.

## A 35 / (a subject of your own choice)

Directions: Write a composition on a subject of your own choice, with your own title. There is no restriction as to the number of paragraphs.

Write in the English-American style, plunging into your subject immediately and moving straight from one main point to the next. Do not labor over the "introductory paragraph" of generalizations required by some styles. Such a paragraph is not considered necessary in English and will not be read with appreciation if presented.

Hand in an outline with your composition.

## Types of the One-Paragraph Composition

It is not easy to pack three (or more) distinct but related ideas into one paragraph, but it is very good practice. The next three assignments will develop the one-paragraph composition in three ways much used in longer compositions: exposition, description, and example.

*EXPOSITION*   Exposition explains a process or develops an idea first of all by using detail. The following paragraph is an example.

The Water-Drinking Habit

    Americans drink a surprising amount of water. They drink water with their meals, they drink water at the fountains in public buildings, and—what a surprise to European people—even in an intermission during a theater performance Americans stand in a line in front of the drinking fountains patiently waiting for their draught.

Note that in a one-paragraph composition, the conclusion may be as slight as the writer's little joke in calling a drink of water a "draught." (*Draught* is often used for a long, satisfying swallow of beer; it is never used for a drink of water.)

Here is an outline of "The Water-Drinking Habit":

I. Americans drink a surprising amount of water
  A. with their meals
  B. in public buildings
  C. at the theater
II. Conclusion (implied): this custom amuses me

**FREE WRITING**

**A 36 / (exposition—supply a title)**

Directions: Write one paragraph giving details of an American custom which you find surprising and perhaps amusing. Hand in a very brief outline with your paragraph.

*DESCRIPTION*   Description gives a picture of a scene or a person. The following paragraph uses description to give a picture of a college campus.

The Beauty of This Campus

    I like this huge, beautiful campus. There are many lovely places here. On weekends I usually take a long walk around the campus. I like the red brick buildings with their white windows and green ivy. I like the neat and silent chapel and the ornate fountain.

And I love the Memorial Tower playing beautiful music. I like the whole huge campus.

Here is an outline of this descriptive paragraph:

I. I like this campus
   A. the buildings
   B. the chapel
   C. the fountain
   D. the Memorial Tower
II. Conclusion: I like the whole campus

## FREE WRITING

### A 37 / (description—supply a title)

Directions: Describe a scene you enjoy, do not enjoy, or simply see frequently. Hand in a brief outline with your paragraph.

FOR EXAMPLE  Giving an example is a second good way of developing a general statement made in exposition. Common introductory phrases are "For example" and "For instance" (same meaning). The following paragraph shows how example is used.

A Mental Block[1]

   I have a strange mental block about studying. For example, I cannot relax when I am reading something required of me. I feel that I am going to be marked on it. This makes me start to worry about whether I will finish on time, or whether I thoroughly understand the story, and so forth. This makes me tense and prevents me from getting the most out of my reading. How can I get rid of this mental block?

Following is the outline of "My Mental Block." Although outlines are not usually complete sentences, they can be, as shown here. Sentence outlines do not require periods.

I. I have a mental block about required reading
   A. I feel I am going to be marked on it
   B. I worry about finishing on time
   C. I worry about understanding the story

---

[1] mental block: a psychological state that prevents an individual from accomplishing something he is capable of accomplishing.

II. Conclusion
   A. Such worry makes me tense
   B. Worry hinders me in studying
   C. I'd like to know what to do (implied)

## FREE WRITING

### A 38 / My Mental Block

Directions: Give an example of a mental block of your own. Did someone laugh at an effort of yours at the wrong time? Were you merely good at something at which a brother or sister was excellent? (A mental block begins to lose its power as soon as it is squarely faced.) Hand in a brief outline with your paragraph.

### A 39 / Three Topic Sentences

Directions: Write the topic sentences for three one-paragraph compositions which you *might* write. Bring the three sentences to class and read them aloud. After you have the reactions of your classmates, write on one of the three. Hand in a brief outline with your paragraph.

## MAKING CONTRASTS[1]

To contrast is to compare by noting differences. Black, for example, is in strong contrast with white. There is a great contrast, as everyone knows, between life today and life a hundred years ago. Contrasts cannot be made between things totally unlike (lions and houses, for instance).

In a short composition based on contrast, two persons, things, institutions, etc., are compared on a limited number of points.

## FREE WRITING

### A 40 / Three Points of Contrast

Directions: Discuss in class the following outline, which may or may not be the one you use in writing *A 41*. Discuss the points given

---

[1] *To the instructor:* The making of contrasts should be considered before the first important examination of the term.

here. Suggest points you might substitute. Possibly put an entirely new outline on the blackboard.

Turn in an outline with five main points in the composition you finally write.

I. Topic statement: "I am going to discuss briefly three points of contrast between my former university and my present university."
II. Contrast in attendance requirements
III. Contrast in the use of tests
IV. Contrast in the use of student-teacher conferences
V. Comment

## A 41 / The First Meal of the Day

Directions: Contrast breakfast in two countries. Decide on your outline by answering questions like these: What food is characteristic of breakfast in each country? How formal is the serving of the meal? How long does it take to eat it? How long is it until the next meal?

Hand in an outline with your composition.

## A 42 / Two Sports in Contrast

Directions: Contrast soccer with football, tennis with ping-pong, or any other two sports which exhibit strong contrasts. Make use of the following questions:

1. What is the objective of each game?
2. What does one game permit which the other forbids?
3. What do both games permit, that is, how are they alike?[1]
4. Why do you like one game better than the other?
5. How much have you played the game you prefer?

## A 43 / Two Persons in Contrast

Directions: Contrast two strong personalities. Possibilities: two very different friends; two effective but very different teachers; two bosses with opposite methods.

In addition to their contrasts, mention any important points they have in common. Hand in an outline with your composition.

[1] A comparison can give similarities as well as differences.

## ON WRITING A TEST COMPOSITION

In all probability you will be asked to write a test composition
before you feel ready to. Here are a few suggestions:

I. Suggestions
  A. Choose your topic quickly and do not change it. There is not time.
  B. Put your title on good paper immediately, so that you will not
     forget it.
  C. Write and rewrite your opening sentence (the topic sentence)
     until it says just what you want it to. Use scrap paper or the
     back of your test booklet.
  D. List the chief points you want to make on scrap paper (between
     three and five for a one-hour examination).
  E. Privileges
    1. Cross out neatly as often as you need to.
    2. Bring your favorite dictionary, if the rules permit. You probably
       will use it very little, but it is reassuring to have it there.
  F. Requirement
     Try for quantity rather than your best quality on a test composi-
     tion—between two and three hundred words on a one-hour test.
     (The examiners want to be sure you can write a reasonable
     amount of English in a limited amount of time.)
     At some time before the test, find out how many words per page
     you usually write. Then, during the test, write straight ahead
     without word-counting.
  G. Making corrections
     If possible, save the last five minutes to read over what you have
     written and to correct little errors you might have made.
II. Types of topics
  A. Narration
    1. The writer tells what happened.
    2. Example: "When I was thirteen and living in Tel-Aviv, one
       afternoon I climbed a high wall with two other boys."
    3. Caution: Be sure to give time and place in some form in the
       first paragraph.
  B. Exposition
    1. The writer makes a generalization and then supports it with
       evidence.
    2. Example: "In spite of all the quarreling we do, to a surprising
       extent we trust one another. For example, . . ."
    3. Caution: Be sure to give examples or supporting details,
       whether you use the phrase "for example" or not.

C. Comparisons
1. The writer presents ways in which two persons, cultures, institutions, etc., are different or alike.
2. Example: "**X** and **Y** are both good friends of mine, yet they are different in every important respect except one."
3. Caution: Be extremely careful to mention **both** your subjects of comparison under each point you discuss.

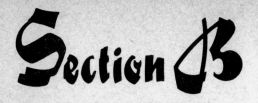

# Section B

---

## The Past Tense and
## The Progressive Present Tense
## Outlining, continued

**Grammar: the nature of the past tense**

The past tense is the narrative tense, the tense which tells what happened. It is much used in conversation:

A: **Did** you **stay** in the dormitory between terms?

B: Oh, no, I **took** a bus to Washington, D.C. I **saw** the Alba Madonna by Raphael in the National Gallery of Art, I **went** to a concert in the John F. Kennedy Center, I **heard** the Supreme Court hand down its latest decisions on Monday morning—I can't tell you everything I **did** between terms.

**Grammar: the past tense and time**

An expression of time must be used with the past tense:[1]

|       | Past Tense |       | Time |
|-------|------------|-------|------|
| Pete  | bought     | a car | yesterday. |
|       |            |       | last summer. |
|       |            |       | after work on Friday. |

[1] For the irregular past-tense forms of often-used verbs, see *For Reference*, pp. 313–316.

Normally, *time* comes last in a sentence.[1] Time does not need to be expressed in months and years:

| | Past Tense | | Time |
|---|---|---|---|
| Pete | learned | to drive | long ago. |
| He | bought | his third car | recently. |

Questions may or may not contain an expression of time:

| Past Form | | Simple Form | | Time |
|---|---|---|---|---|
| Did | Pete | buy | a car? | — |
| Did | he | buy | a car | recently? |

Note that in questions, the past form is *did*. The main verb is in the simple form.

**Oral Practice**

Directions: When you are given a question, respond in chorus. (Each of your statements will end with an expression of time.)

Example:

Instructor:   Did Jack leave the house at 8:15?
Students:    Jack left the house at 8:15.

1. Did Jack get up at 7:00 this morning?
   (Jack got up . . .)
2. Did he leave the house at 8:15?
   (He left . . .)
3. Did he arrive at work by 8:57?
4. Did he do a lot of work before the coffee break?
5. Did Jack leave for lunch at noon?
6. Did he get back to the office in less than an hour?
7. Did he work steadily until closing time?
8. Did he attend classes until 10:00 at night?
9. Did he get back to his apartment an hour later?
10. Did he get to bed by midnight?

[1] For *place* and *time* not in basic (normal) position, see p. 64.

## Grammar: the negative with the past tense

|  | Past Form | Negative | Simple Form | Time |
|---|---|---|---|---|
| Jack | did | not | leave | at 6:00 A.M. |
| He | did | not | arrive | until noon. |

### Oral Practice I

Directions: Give an entirely different impression of Jack by individually giving a negative response to the questions in the previous oral practice. Then add a statement or two of your own.

Example:

Question:      Did Jack leave the house at 8:15?
Statements:   Jack **didn't** leave the house at 8:15. He left at 8:45. He was a half hour late for work, and his boss was not pleased.

### Oral Practice II

Directions: Individually give negative responses to the following questions, adding a statement or two of your own.

Example:

Instructor:   Did you have two dishes of ice cream at dinner last night?
Student:      I **didn't** have two dishes of ice cream last night. I had three: vanilla, strawberry, and chocolate.

1. Did you do your homework at five o'clock this morning?
2. Did you fall asleep over your math assignment last night?
3. Did you spend Saturday morning cleaning your room?
4. Did you refuse an invitation to ride over to the lake Saturday afternoon?
5. Did you forget to take your bathing suit?
6. Did you forget to take your tennis racket?
7. Did you drink a lot of **warm** Coca-Cola?
8. Did you take a row boat out on the lake?[1]
9. Did you have a dull Saturday?

---

[1] *row boat:* a small wooden boat moved by hand with oars.

## WH-QUESTIONS

**Grammar: the nature of wh-questions—when, where, who, what, which, why, how, how often, how much. For convenience, the how questions have been placed with the wh-questions.**

Up to this point, you have worked with *yes/no* questions, which gave you precisely two choices: you could make an affirmative statement, or you could make a negative statement.

yes/no question: **Did** John go to Boston?
Affirmative statement: John went to Boston.
Negative statement:    John did **not** go to Boston.

Now you will begin to work with *wh*-questions, each of which permits any number of answers:

*wh*-questions: **Where** did John go?
Affirmative statements: John went to Boston. He went to Central America. He went to Paris.
Negative statements:    John did **not** go to Boston. He did **not** go to Central America. He did **not** go to Paris.

(Where else could you say John went or did not go?)

**Oral Practice I**

Directions: When you are given a *wh*-question, respond individually with a complete statement.

Example:

Question:    What time did your alarm clock ring this morning?
Statement:   It rang at 6:30.

Question:    What time did you get up?
Statement:   I got up at 7:00.

1. What time did you leave the dormitory this morning?
2. Where did you put your keys?
3. Where did you put your identification card?
4. Where did you put your money?
5. How did you carry your books?
6. How cold (or hot) was it?
7. What did you wear on your head—something or nothing?
8. Which building did you go to?

9. Which room did you enter?
10. Whom (who) did you speak to?


**Oral Practice II**

Directions: When you are given a statement, change it individually into a *wh*-quesiton.

Example:

Statement:   Chang got to breakfast at 8:29 this morning.
Question:    When did Chang get to breakfast this morning?

1. Chang left the dormitory at 8:35 this morning.
   (**When did . . .**)
2. He put his keys in his pocket.
   (**Where did . . .**)
3. He put his identification card into his breast pocket.
   (**Where . . .**)
4. He put his money into the same pocket.
   (**Where . . .**)
5. Chang carried his books in his briefcase.
   (**Where/How . . .**)
6. He went to the International Building.
   (**Where/Which** building . . .)
7. He took the campus bus.
   (**What . . .**)
8. He went to room 5.
   (**Where/Which . . .**)
9. He said "Hi" to Miss Liu.
   (**What . . .**)
10. Then he sat down.
    (Then **what . . .**)


# BASIC ENGLISH WORD ORDER

## Grammar: the importance of word order in English

The order in which the elements in a sentence follow one another affects the meaning of the sentence in English:

| Subject | | Object |
|---|---|---|
| The tiger | killed | the cow. |
| The cow | killed | the tiger. |

The elements in both of the sentences above are *the tiger*, *killed*, and *the cow*. The vast difference in meaning comes only from the order of the words in the sentences. The actor (the subject) comes before the verb. The receiver of the action (the object) comes after the verb.

| Subject (actor) | Verb (action) | Object (receiver) |
|---|---|---|
| The tiger | killed | the cow. |

## Oral Practice

Directions: When you are given a question about an American drugstore, answer individually, using basic English word order. For example,

| Subject | Verb | Object | |
|---|---|---|---|
| I | remember | my first visit | to an American drugstore. |

1. What did you expect to find?
2. What did you go in to buy?
3. What were you astonished to find?
4. Did you have trouble finding a clerk?
5. Did you ever see a druggist?[1]
6. What were the short-order cooks frying?
7. What did you buy first?
8. What did you buy in addition?
9. What was "on sale" at a reduced price?

---

[1] By law, at least one druggist, a registered pharmacist, was on duty to fill medical prescriptions. He was probably working in the back of the store.

10. What did you buy at the counter by the door?
11. Did you write home about this strange American institution?
12. What do you often buy in a drugstore now?

## B 1 / A Trip to a Zoo

Directions: First orally and then in writing, answer the five following paragraphs of *wh*-questions. Write *we* whenever you and a companion acted together. In paragraph 3, *feed* is an irregular verb. Check the past-tense form in a dictionary or in *For Reference,* p. 314. If you wish to make a negative statement, you can say, "There was no baby elephant."

When was the last time you went to a zoo? What country were you in? What was the name of the zoo? Whom did you go with? Did you get there by car, by bus, or on foot?

How was the weather? Was there a big crowd? Did you ride around the grounds in a little train? Did you walk for a long time?

Where were the monkeys—outdoors or indoors? What did they do? How long did you watch them? Where were the lions? What did they do—sleep, yawn, or roar? What did you feed the elephants? Was there a baby elephant?

Where did you find a refreshment stand? What did you drink? What did you eat? Did you eat standing up or sitting down?

What time did you get home? Did you enjoy your trip to the zoo?

## On Departing from the Facts

In writing *B 1,* you probably departed from the actual facts of your life. If you did not, you soon will. When you have an exercise to write, simply seize upon something you can say easily in English and use it. An affirmative statement does not have to be "the truth."

## Grammar: putting place and time last

The following formula expresses the basic word order of English:

S + V + (object) + (adverbial of place) + (adverbial of time)

A sentence *must* have a subject and a verb. It is likely to have, in addition, one or more of the other elements in the formula: *object, place, time:*

| Subject<br>(actor) | Verb<br>(action) | Object<br>(receiver) | Place | Time |
|---|---|---|---|---|
| Jack | fought | Bill | behind the gym | after class. |
| Mr. Chen | read | his paper. | — | after dinner. |
| The wind | howled. | — | — | — |

## Oral Practice

Directions: Individually, answer a pair of questions, a *where* question and a *when* question.

Example:

Instructor:  Where do you buy textbooks?
Student:     In the college bookstore.

Instructor:  When do you buy textbooks?
Student:     At the beginning of the term.

1. Where do you buy aspirin?
   When do you use it?
2. Where do you buy sunglasses?
   When do you wear them?
3. Where do you buy stamps?
   When do you use them?
4. When do you usually go to the movies?
   Where do you go?
5. Where do you go to pay your tuition?
   When do you pay it?
6. When does the first class of the day begin?
   Where do you have your first class?
7. When do you study best, in the morning or at night?
   Where do you study best, in the library or in your room?
8. When do you read for pleasure?
   Where do you read—in a big, soft chair, in bed, or under a tree?

## B 2 / Lost in the Subway

Directions: As you change the five following paragraphs of questions into statements, note that you are writing in basic English word order.

When were you lost in the subway? Was the dim light of the underground station a little depressing that day? Did the group on the platform look a little depressed, too? Was there almost no conversation?

Did a train arrive with a rush? Did two doors slide open almost at your feet? Did you step into the car without reading the sign in the window? Did the doors close swiftly?

Did the train gather speed immediately? Did it rush forward in the darkness in a manner almost alarming? Did you realize after a few minutes that the train was going in the wrong direction? Did you have a thoroughly unpleasant moment then? However, did you remain quiet and simply step out of the car at the next stop?

Did you then read all signs carefully? Did you find the proper track quite easily? Did you have to wait five minutes, three minutes, or not at all for your train? Did you check the sign in the window before stepping into a car this time?

How many minutes did it take to get back to your starting point? Did your mistake make you late? Did it put you in a bad temper? Why do you have no trouble with the subway now?

## B 3 / A Ride Past the Statue of Liberty

Directions: Do this exercise orally; possibly write it. Answer the questions individually. If a question seems too long, ask your instructor to repeat it or shorten it. Your object is further practice in basic English word order.

When was the first time you took the ferry ride[1] past the Statue of Liberty? How did you get to South Ferry?[2] How long did you have to wait for a boat—fifteen minutes, a few minutes, or not at all?

Was your boat one of the big ones? Did you find a good seat near the railing? Did you have a fine view of the statue? How was the weather that day?

Did the harbor swarm[3] with boats? Did you notice a very small tugboat pulling a very large ocean liner? Did you notice a flat-bottomed freighter loaded with rusty iron ore?

Did the statue look strong and serene?[4] Did you see why Americans sometimes say "her" and "the Lady"?

[1] A *ferryboat* carries passengers over a narrow stretch of water, in this case, the part of New York Harbor between Manhattan Island and Staten Island.

[2] *South Ferry:* the station on the Manhattan side.

[3] *swarm:* to move about in great numbers.

[4] *serene:* at peace with herself.

Did some sea gulls float effortlessly over your head? Did they stay with the boat almost to Staten Island? Did they seem to enjoy the ride? Did **you** enjoy your ride past the Statue of Liberty?

**The Empire State Building.**
[David Herman, DPI]

## B 4 / A Visit to the Empire State Building

Directions: Change the six following paragraphs of questions into statements in writing. Note the use of capitals in the first three paragraphs.

Where is the Empire State Building?[1] How tall is it? On a clear day, does the Observation Tower provide a splendid view of the city? When did you visit the Tower?

Is the Observation Tower on the eighty-sixth floor? Does a special elevator rise from the first floor to the eightieth without a stop? Does a second elevator take sightseers to the eighty-sixth floor?

[1] The Empire State Building is in New York City on Fifth Avenue at 34th Street. It is an office building 102 stories tall.

Does a strong railing encircle[1] the Observation Tower? Is it safe to lean against the railing and look out over the city? Did you see Central Park to the north? Did you see the UN to the east? Did you circle the Tower and look for the Statue of Liberty to the south? Did you see the George Washington Bridge spanning[2] the Hudson River far to the north?

Did the people far below on the street seem six inches tall? Were the automobiles the size of toys? Did the great distance make the traffic and the people silent?

On the way down from the Tower, did your special elevator drop from the eightieth floor to the first without a stop? Did your ears hurt? Did your stomach tighten? Did you hold your breath? Or did you enjoy the prolonged drop?

When are you going to watch the sun set from the eighty-sixth floor of the Empire State Building?

## Grammar: place and time not in basic position

Attention can be drawn to *place* and *time* by shifting them away from their normal position at the end of the sentence:

**Last night** I had a leisurely dinner. **Tonight** I had a sandwich and a cup of coffee.

**In my own country,** I spent an hour over lunch. **Here,** I am likely to eat in twenty-five minutes.

However, until basic English word order is firmly established in your writing habits, it is best to put *place* and *time* at the end of the sentence.

## STARTING CONVERSATIONS THROUGH ICEBREAKING

*Icebreaker:* (1) a strong ship for breaking a passage through ice, (2) figuratively, any means that permits strangers who would like to talk to begin talking.

American students are often delighted to talk with a foreign

---

[1] *encircle:* surround.
[2] *spanning:* crossing the river from one bank to the other.

student if they feel he can carry on a conversation. Your "breaking the ice" will show that you can, and want to, converse in English. It is easiest to break the ice in pairs, probably in the college dining room.

Example:

A or B: Do you mind if we sit here?
C or D: (Americans) of course not, do sit down.
A or B: (before a deadly silence can develop): Is this a typical American dish?
C or D: Yes, but it isn't a very good example . . . (There is nothing like a little grumbling[1] about the food to break the ice.)

Following is an example of how you might try icebreaking with students from other countries:

Example:

A: Lunch wasn't like this in (name of your country).
B: It certainly wasn't like this in **my** country.
A: May I ask where you are from?

Icebreaking with classmates is easy: you can simply introduce yourself, as in this example:

A: I'm Akbar Akbarzadah. Just call me Aka.
B: I'm Keiko Negoro. Most people call me Kay.

## FREE WRITING

### B 5 / A Little Icebreaking

Directions: Tell how you "broke the ice," to the satisfaction of both a stranger and yourself.

If you have never written conversation, you may want to use the dialog form of the first example below. If you have had practice in writing conversation or would like to investigate the punctuation required for conversation within a narrative, follow the second example, called "narrative form."[2]

---

[1] grumbling: mild fault-finding.
[2] For a full list of the conventions used in writing conversation, see Section I, p. 236.

A Little Icebreaking
(dialog form)

|        |                                                              |
|--------|--------------------------------------------------------------|
| I:       | May I sit down here?                                         |
| Stranger: | Sure.[1] Please.                                            |
| I:       | My name is Keiko. I'm from Japan.                           |
| Stranger: | My name is Sue. I'm from Detroit.                           |
| I:       | It's very hot today, isn't it?                             |

(The talk drifts along comfortably on the subject of the weather, eventually reaching the fact that Keiko does not have either an air conditioner or an electric fan in her room.)

|      |                                                                      |
|------|----------------------------------------------------------------------|
| Sue: | Then you can't study well in your room, can you?                    |
| I:   | I usually study in the library.                                     |
| Sue: | That's good. But can you sleep well?                                |
| I:   | It isn't too bad. I always fan myself with a Japanese fan when I go to bed. |
| Sue: | Oh, a Japanese fan! I've seen a beautiful fan in one of my books, but I haven't seen one actually. |
| I:   | I'll show you mine. Why don't you come to my room after dinner?     |
| Sue: | Thank you, I'd like to very much.                                   |

A Little Icebreaking
(narrative form)

At the Language Center picnic I was very glad to see the pretty lake and the neat park, but in a few minutes I became sad because the lake reminded me of my home. When everyone began swimming or playing softball, I went walking along the lake alone, singing Japanese songs loudly.

Suddenly two girls and a boy in the camping area spoke to me and asked, "Where are you from?"

I answered, "I'm from Japan. I am here studying English."

They said, "That's great."

I said, "My name is Michiko. It's a really nice day for a picnic, isn't it?"

They said, "Yes. Our names are Bill, Sue, and Linda."

At that time something came to my mind. I remembered what

---

[1] *Sure* is often used in informal conversation. *Surely* is used in standard writing.

I had learned in class about icebreaking. "It's a good chance to try," I thought. "They look friendly, and they want to talk to me."

So I said, "Are you camping here?" They said they were. Then I said, "Do you mind if I see your camping car?"[1]

They said, "Sure, please come with us." They took me to their parents and introduced me to them. Then the parents showed me their camping car. How interesting it was! It was like an apartment, with an electric stove, a refrigerator, a small dining table, places to sleep, and a very small bathroom.

Then we talked and talked. Finally I said it was time to eat, so I had to go. They invited me to dinner with them. It was a delicious dinner—fresh corn, fresh tomatoes, melon, ham, sausage, and home-made peach pies.

Later I knew why the children were interested in me. They were interested in the world. Their father had been in Germany for three years and in Alaska for two years. He sometimes takes the children to Chinese restaurants.

It was an unusual experience for me because I am a little shy. I enjoyed my adventure and learned how to do icebreaking. It was not only an unusual experience but also practice for me.

## OUTLINING AND FREE WRITING, continued[2]

Variations in outlining will be presented in the next five topics for free writing:

1. **B 6**  "A Brief Report on the Library": The writer outlines by means of subtitles
2. **B 7**  "A Teacher in My Past": The writer uses the contents of the outline given
3. **B 8**  "A Trip to Remember": The writer provides the subpoints for the outline given
4. **B 9**  "In Preparation": The writer provides the subpoints
5. **B 10**  "How to . . .": The writer lists the steps in a process

---

[1] *camping car:* a trailer, a special kind of small house which can be attached to the back of a car, permitting a family to travel without staying at hotels.

[2] For the first work in outlining and free writing, review Section A, pp. 43–45.

## An Hour in the University Library

Directions: (instructor to class) "This course ends with 'The First Term Paper.' Now, while there is no pressure to write at length, take a leisurely hour by yourself to explore the basic kinds of help and pleasure the library has to offer you. Let's read together through the next assignment, *B 6*, 'A Brief Report on the Library.' "

*The Card Catalogue*   In the library, go first to those formidable-looking rows of files called the author/title/subject catalogue. Look up an English writer whom you have already studied (last name first). See how a book you have read looks on a title card. Then turn past the rest of the author's title cards and take a look at what has been written *about* him, biographies, criticism, etc.

*The Foreign-Language Newspapers*   Ask where the foreign-language newspapers are kept. It is a fine thing to see a paper in one's own language in an American library when one is only a few weeks away from home.

*The New York Times*   Next, ask whether the library carries *The New York Times* on microfilm. If it does, and the library has the complete set, ask for any date you wish after September 17, 1851. Let the librarian demonstrate the simple process of running the viewing machine. Then watch the chosen day's news unroll, page by page, before your eyes at the rate you decide.

*The Encyclopedias*   Next, locate the encyclopedias. Take down the volumes dealing with "Interior Decoration" in both the *Encyclopaedia Britannica* and the *Encyclopedia Americana*. You may be surprised at the beauty of the colored pictures and the difference in the way the two authorities present the same subject.

*The Reader's Guide to Periodical Literature*   Finally, locate the long row of thick green volumes called the *Reader's Guide to Periodical Literature*. Every title appearing in approximately 150 magazines is listed here. The title appears a second time under the subject the writer discusses. One of the first lessons in "The First Term Paper" will be on the *Reader's Guide*, Section M, pp. 288-290.

## FREE WRITING

### B 6 / A Brief Report on the Library

Directions: Write five paragraphs. Make your first paragraph this topic sentence: "I am not well acquainted with the university library yet (it is a very complex institution), but here are three features I have already investigated briefly."

Write a paragraph under each of the three following subtitles, underlined. Put the subtitles in the center of the line, in the style of a term paper.

1. The Foreign Language Newspapers. Which papers will you return to? Why?
2. *The New York Times*. What interested you most on microfilm? If the library does not have the *Times* on microfilm, what did you glance at in some issue of the *Times* of a certain date?
3. The Encyclopedias. Which encyclopedia do you think you will consult first when you need information? Why?

As your fifth and final paragraph, write a few sentences summarizing your general impression of the library.

### B 7 / A Teacher in My Past

Directions: Make your first paragraph this topic sentence: "One of my best teachers in elementary (or secondary) school was _____."
Then make use of the following outline. (You need not use subtitles in this informal writing.)

I. The introductory facts (one paragraph)
   A. Where you were living
   B. How old you were then
   C. The subject studied
II. The teacher (one or three paragraphs)
   A. What he/she firmly required
   B. On the other hand, what he/she freely permitted
   C. The effect of this combination of firmness and freedom on the class
III. The teacher and you (one paragraph)
   A. The satisfaction you had in this class
   B. What you accomplished
   C. The influence of this teacher which possibly remains with you today

## B 8 / A Trip to Remember

Directions: Think of a trip you have taken. Write of it with pleasure on scrap paper. Then, before you make your good copy, fill in the following outline and hand it in with your writing.

  I. Introductory information
    A.
    B.
    C.
 II. Outstanding experiences
    A.
    B.
    C.
III. Conclusion
    A. What the trip did for you
    B. What features you will add if you repeat the trip

## B 9 / In Preparation

Directions: Before you write, complete the outline begun below, listing practical steps which a student might take who intends to study extensively in the United States. (Note that subpoints under capital letters are numbered 1, 2, 3.)

  I. While still at home
    A. Listen to broadcasts in English
      1. The newscasts of the British Broadcasting Company
      2. The American Sunday forums on TV
      3. British and American plays on TV
    B.
    C.
    D.
    E.
 II. After arrival at the university
    A. Don't overload yourself with courses the first term
    B.
    C.
    D.
    E.
III. (writer's choice)

## B 10 / How to . . . (complete the title)

Directions: Give detailed instructions for doing something which you yourself know how to do very well. Hand in an outline with your composition.

In the example below, note how the introduction has been expanded well beyond the single sentence recommended for earlier practice. Note, too, what a clear outline of the process is produced by numbering the steps. Finally, note that a concluding paragraph can give new information, perhaps implied before.

Falling Backward in Judo

Since judo is first of all a technique for self-defense, it is necessary to learn how to fall safely. There are three ways to fall: sideward, forward, and backward. However, since the backward fall is the basic fall of judo, and the one American students fear most, I shall give directions for the backward fall here.[1]

1. Stand straight on the mat.
2. Bend the knees until the thighs touch the lower legs.
3. At the same time, pull your jaw toward your chest, so that your head will not strike the mat.
4. Then throw yourself backward bravely. Do not hesitate.
5. As your back touches the mat, strike the mat with both hands strongly, bracing yourself with both forearms. Thus you will guard yourself from the fall.

After a student can fall backward, sideward, and forward safely, he is ready to study the techniques of throwing other persons down.

# THE PROGRESSIVE PRESENT TENSE

## Grammar: the simple present tense in contrast with the progressive present tense

| Simple Present | Progressive Present |
|---|---|
| I read every day. | I am reading now. |
| I sleep every night. | I am not sleeping now. |

[1] The commands are in the second person (you). The rest of the composition follows the normal procedure of writing in a single person, in this case the third: *judo, three ways*, etc.

The progressive present tense is formed with *be* and the *ing*-form of the main verb. Note the contrast in the following examples between the habitual action of the simple present and the temporary action of the progressive present:

Simple present: Tom **plays** tennis very well.
Progressive present: He **is playing** with Helen now.

Simple present: Dr. Simpson **teaches** psychology.
Progressive present: He **is teaching** an advanced course this term.

Simple present: Jack **visits** us once in a while.
Progressive present: He **is visiting** his relatives in California this month.

Simple present: The hotel **serves** good meals.
Progressive present: The hotel **is serving** breakfast from 8:00 to 9:30 until Labor Day.

## Grammar: uses of the progressive present tense

When the progressive present is used in conversation, the expanse of time indicated is likely to be brief:

It **is beginning** to snow.
The tea kettle **is boiling** now.
Isn't the doorbell **ringing?**

When the progressive present is used in writing, the expanse of time is likely to be longer and the situation more formal than in conversation:

Science **is** continually **making** new discoveries.
Congress **is considering** additional curbs on pollution.
Abstract painting **is passing** into a new phase.

The progressive present can express action taking place wholly in the future:

**Are** you **going** to go[1] out of town for Thanksgiving?
**Are** you **taking** a heavy coat?

The action in the progressive present need not be in progress at the actual moment of speaking:

[1] *going to:* See Section A, p. 38.

A (over a coke):   **Are** you **working** hard this term?
B:                 Oh, yes, **I'm carrying** a very heavy schedule.

English never uses the progressive present for completed action, no matter how long the action continued in the past:

Wrong:  I **am studying** English five years in my own country.
Right:  I studied English five years in my own country.

Wrong:  I **am swimming** every day last summer.
Right:  I swam (went swimming) every day last summer.

## Oral Practice I

Directions: Use the following pattern with each sentence given you:

Example:

Instructor:   Paul is writing a **letter**.
Student:      Paul is writing a letter **now**.         (progressive present)
              He wrote a letter **yesterday**.           (past tense)
              He writes a letter **every day**.          (simple present)

1. Jim is using his dictionary.
2. Betty is writing an exercise.
3. We are practicing English.
4. Pete is looking out of the window.
5. Frank is thinking about his vacation.
6. It is raining.
7. Professor and Mrs. Simpson are taking a walk. (They . . .)
8. I am reading the *Washington Post*.
9. I am reading an editorial.
10. I am enjoying the political cartoon on the editorial page.

## Oral Practice II

Directions: When you are asked a question in the simple present tense, respond with a statement containing an adverb of frequency. When your instructor follows up his first question with a question in the progressive present tense, respond with a negative statement.

Example:

Instructor:   Do you ever walk to class?
Student:      I **sometimes** walk to class.

Instructor:   Are you walking to class now?
Student:      I am **not** walking to class now.

1. Do you ever sing? Are you singing at this moment?
2. Do you ever smoke? Are you smoking at this moment?
3. Do you ever play cards? Are you playing cards now?
4. Does the student on your right ever sleep in class? Is he/she sleeping now?
5. Do Mr. and Mrs. Smith sometimes watch TV at midnight? Are they watching TV at this moment?
6. Do you ever ride a bicycle? Are you riding a bicycle now?
7. Do you frequently read articles about space travel? Are you reading such an article now?
8. Does the student on your left ever eat a chocolate bar in class? Is he/she eating a chocolate bar now?
9. Do you generally have lunch on the steps in front of the International Building? Are you lunching there now?
10. Do you ever go wading¹ in the little river on the campus? Are you wading there now?

## B 11 / Signs of Spring on the Campus

Directions: Change the two following paragraphs of questions into statements, inserting an *ing*-form wherever there is a blank in the question. Use each word in the two lists below once.

| *Paragraph 1* | *Paragraph 2* |
|---|---|
| blowing | explaining |
| sauntering² | listening |
| shining | looking |
| singing | sighing³ |
| sunning | sitting |

Is it hard to be in class today? Is the sun _____? Are birds _____ outside the classroom windows? Is a spring breeze _____? Are students without a class _____ slowly across the campus? Are boys and girls _____ themselves on the grass in front of the library?

¹ *go wading:* to walk in shallow water.
² *sauntering:* walking along slowly and happily.
³ *sighing:* to let out a long, deep breath because one is sad.

Are you in class? Are you _____ in your usual seat? Is the teacher _____ the uses of the progressive present tense? Is the student on your right _____ to the teacher? Is the student on your left _____ wistfully[1] out of the window? Are you _____ as you look out of the window, too?

## B 12 / Signs of Fall[2] in the City

Directions: Change the two following paragraphs of questions into statements, inserting an *ing*-form, underlined, wherever there is a blank in a question. Use each word in the list below once.

| | |
|---|---|
| blowing | holding |
| congratulating | hurrying |
| falling | lifting |
| flying | turning |
| hiding | walking |

Is it a fine fall morning in the city? Are the leaves of the maple trees _____ red? Is a brisk wind _____? Are the brown leaves of the oak trees _____ to the ground? Are a few men _____ onto their hats? Is the wind _____ leaves, dust, and scraps of paper into the air?

Are birds _____ south in great flocks?[3] Are squirrels _____ nuts in the hollows of trees?[4] Are people _____ briskly down the street? Are they _____ each other on the beautiful weather? Are boys and girls, almost late, _____ to school?

## B 13 / My Next Trip

Directions: Change the following paragraphs of questions into paragraphs of statements. Note that the progressive present tense in this exercise expresses action taking place wholly in the future. As you write, substitute some ideas of your own for those in the exercise, but stay in the progressive present tense for the sake of concentrated practice.

[1] *wistfully:* longingly.
[2] *fall:* autumn.
[3] *flocks:* groups of animals of one kind.
[4] *hollows of trees:* holes in trees large enough to hold nuts.

Are you taking your next trip to Canada, Mexico, or the West Coast of the United States? Are you going in June or July? Are you traveling by car, train, plane, or bus?

Are you taking one, two, or three pieces of luggage with you? Are you taking a light-weight woolen coat? Are you taking a raincoat that will be useful in various types of weather? Are you planning to avoid laundries by using wrinkle-free synthetics? Are you going to take a thoroughly comfortable pair of walking shoes?

Are you doing any reading in preparation for your trip? Are you planning to be away a full six weeks? Are you planning to come home tired out but happy?

## B 14 / Lee Chang as an Exercise Writer

Directions: As you change the three following paragraphs of questions into statements, decide whether you want to make Lee Chang a willing or an unwilling learner.

Examples:

| | |
|---|---|
| Unwilling learner: | He is looking out of the window. |
| | He is looking at the ceiling. |
| Willing learner: | He is not looking out of the window. |
| | He is not looking at the ceiling. |

Remember that *or* implies choice. Lee can be sitting at only one of the three locations suggested. Make two of your three *or* statements negative.

Is Lee Chang writing his English assignment now? Is he writing B 14? Is he sitting at a desk? Or is he sitting at a card table? Or is he writing in the breakfast nook in the kitchen?

Is Lee looking at the ceiling? Is he looking out of the window? Is he listening to his radio? Is he smoking? Is he drinking Coca-Cola?

Is his textbook lying open to the assignment? Is he writing an exercise in the progressive present tense? Is he writing with a pen? Is he skipping every other line? Is he indenting every paragraph? Is he considering leaving the exercise unfinished?

## FREE WRITING

## B 15 / At This Moment

Directions: Begin, "It is now _____ A.M./P.M. in (name of your home city)." Say what widely different types of people are doing at the moment you name. Write one paragraph in the progressive present tense.

Example:

It is now noon in Columbus, Ohio. Office workers are pouring into the sandwich shops. Bus drivers are moving cautiously along High Street. Nurses are delivering trays to patients in Grant Hospital. . . .

## Grammar: verbs seldom used in the progressive present

Certain verbs, the following among them, are seldom used in the progressive present tense.[1] They express a habitual situation rather than a temporary action.

| | | |
|---|---|---|
| believe | like | see |
| belong | love | seem |
| cost | mean (intend) | smell |
| forget | need | taste |
| have (possess) | own | want |
| hear | prefer | understand |
| know | remember | |

Examples:
I **like** beer. (You like it or you do not like it.)
I **belong** to the International Club. (You are a member or you are not a member.)
The abbreviation M.D. **means** Doctor of Medicine. (This is an agreed-upon fact.)
Pete **has** (possesses) a car. (He owns a car or he does not.)

*Exceptions*   It is possible to use some of the verbs in the above list in the progressive present tense. Such use implies future time, as in the following examples:

I **am seeing** him tomorrow.
We **are hearing** chamber music tomorrow night.
We **are having** (entertaining) guests Saturday evening.

Nevertheless, this statement still stands: Certain verbs are seldom used in the progressive present tense.

---

[1] Occasionally a verb from this list is used in the progressive present tense: "I *am taking* tennis lessons twice a week now."

## Oral Practice

Directions: When you are asked a question, answer individually with a full statement. (Each question contains a verb seldom used in the progressive present tense.)

1. What do you **believe** in?
2. What do you **belong** to? (Name one organization.)
3. What does a sports car **cost**?
4. Do you ever **forget** to take your change when you pay a cashier?
5. Do you **hate** hot weather?
6. Do you **love** cold weather?
7. Do you **have** a cold?
8. What do you **hear** about the mid-term examinations?
9. What do you **know** about atomic physics?
10. Do you **like** hamburgers?
11. Do you **own** an airplane?
12. Do you **need** anything from the drugstore?
13. Do you **prefer** to fly or go by bus? Why?
14. Do you **remember** your first day at school? What happened?
15. Do you **see** many good movies?
16. Does it **seem** too warm in here?
17. Does it **smell** like spring?
18. Do those cigarettes **taste** fresh?
19. Do you **understand** the new math?
20. Do you **want** to learn more about it?

## B 16 / Unimportant Facts about Me

Directions: Complete the following partial statements, each of which contains a verb seldom used in the progressive present tense. If you find yourself at a loss to complete a certain statement, use an ending from the list following the exercise.

I believe in. . . . I sometimes/never. . . . I always/seldom. . . . I know. . . . I love. . . . I like. . . . I need. . . . I own. . . . I prefer bicycling to. . . . I distinctly remember. . . . I do not see. . . . I thoroughly understand. . . . I want very much to. . . . I seem to smell and taste. . . .

Possible endings

| | |
|---|---|
| being on time | a notebook |
| forget my keys | riding a motorcycle |
| hear the 6:00 P.M. news | my first ride in a taxi in this country |

the multiplication table
my family
cats
a Master's degree

many operas
this exercise
finish my homework in the next ten minutes
the fragrant cup of hot tea I am going to have soon

## Dictation: Briefcases

Directions: (instructor to class): "I am going to give you a short dictation for practice with verbs that are seldom used in the progressive tense and that require an *s* after the verb with a third person singular subject. Write down this sentence now: 'Lee understands the word *briefcase.*' "

Lee understands the word **briefcase**. He owns an old one. He wants a new one. He needs a new one. He prefers the tan ones to the black ones.

A briefcase sometimes costs thirty dollars. It often costs six or seven dollars. It seldom costs as little as two dollars. A student needs a briefcase of some type.

## Grammar: the <u>ed</u> ending in the past tense

Regular verbs form the past tense by adding *ed* to the simple form—or merely *d* if the simple form ends in *e*, as *arrive* and *use* do: use, use*d*; arrive, arrive*d*.

The *ed* ending has three different sounds in spoken English, in spite of always being spelled *ed*:

| *ed*[t] | *ed*[d] | *ed*[id] |
|---|---|---|
| asked | realized | started |
| crossed | waved | ended |
| helped | turned | needed |
| washed | arrived | invited |
| lurched | cheered | rented |
| boxed | called | pointed |

## Dictation I: The Past Tense *ed*

Directions: Follow the procedure for taking dictation given in Section A, p. 27. On the fourth reading, underline *ed* and add any *ed* which you find you have failed to write.

When I realized I was lost, I asked a policeman for directions. The policeman pointed across the street and waved his hand to the right. I crossed the street and turned to the right. The policeman's directions helped me. I walked three blocks and arrived at the right address in ten minutes.

### Dictation II: The Past Tense *ed*

The crowd cheered when the football team appeared. The captain called his men around him. They formed a circle with their heads toward the center. The captain talked for perhaps two minutes. Then the circle opened up, and everyone walked to his position. The crowd cheered, and the game started. It ended in victory for our side.

## Grammar: the irregular past tense

The three principal parts of irregular verbs must be learned, the past tense being the second part given in the dictionary and the past participle the third:

| Simple Form | Past Tense | Past Participle |
|---|---|---|
| eat | ate | eaten |
| run | ran | run |
| shake | shook | shaken |

The principal parts of irregular verbs are to be found in every dictionary; nevertheless, a compact list of such verbs is offered in *For Reference,* pp. 312-316, as a convenience in the checking of spelling.

### Oral Practice

Directions: Complete the partial statements given you individually. Each contains an irregular verb in the past tense.

Example:

Instructor:   The police **shot** at . . .
Student:      The police **shot** at the escaping thief.

1. Two thieves **broke** into . . .
2. They **stole** . . .
3. The police **burst** into . . .

4. They **fought** . . .
5. One thief **fell** . . .
6. The second thief **fled** . . .
7. The police **caught** only . . .
8. The owner's dog **barked** at . . .
9. Then he **bit** . . .
10. Then he **lay** down near his master . . .

### Listen and Write: Mr. Huntington's Wives

Directions (instructor to class): "Listen to the following selection twice. Then write down the English still in your mind. Write the first sentence now: 'Mr. Huntington's first wife was the most beautiful woman in town.' "

Part I: The First Wife

    Mr. Huntington's first wife was the most beautiful woman in town. She had beautiful hair, and her nose was perfect. Her housekeeping was perfect, too. In addition, she was a member of six clubs and president of three of them. Mr. Huntington knew he was a lucky man. Mr. and Mrs. Huntington were happy.

Part II: The Second Wife

    Unfortunately, Mrs. Huntington died. Many months later, Mr. Huntington began to see the widow, Mrs. Jones. Mrs. Jones was not the most beautiful woman in town. She weighed a little too much, and something about her nose was not quite perfect. However, she was an excellent cook, and she loved to laugh. She laughed at Mr. Huntington's jokes, and she cooked him excellent dinners. Mr. Huntington and Mrs. Jones were married. They are happy.

## PLACE AND TIME IN NARRATIVE WRITING

*Place* and *time* must be given as you begin a piece of narrative writing (an account of events in the past).

Example:

Marcus remembers his boyhood with pleasure. He sailed his own small boat on the Bay of Naples. He climbed the hill where Vergil lived two thousand years ago. He bicycled with his club to the base of Mt. Vesuvius and the excavations at Pompeii.

*Place* and *time* must be given, and promptly, but they need to be given only once. *Time* does not need to be given in years. *Boyhood* in the example is definite enough.


## FREE WRITING

General direction: Write on one or more of the following topics. Turn in a simple outline with each topic you write on, one which accounts for your paragraphing.


### B 17 / I Was Late That Day

Directions: Be sure to give *place* and *time* as you introduce your narrative.


### B 18 / When I Was New

Directions: Begin, "I did not have a great deal of difficulty when I was new in (name a city), but one day . . ."


### B 19 / A Responsibility Successfully Carried

Directions: Use the following questions as a general guide:

1. Something had to be done, and the responsibility fell to you. Why?
2. What were the difficulties of the situation? How did you deal with them?
3. What permanent difference did this successful effort make to you and perhaps to others?

# Section C

---

## The Articles
## Noncounts
## Quantifiers

### TERMS AND FACTS[1]

1. Count nouns singular (*a* or *the* required):[2]

**a** star   **an** idea   **the** sun

2. Count nouns plural (*the* or nothing required):

**The** guests are arriving.
**The** guests **at a wedding reception** may be late.
**Guests** are always welcome at our house.

3. Noncount nouns (*the* or nothing required):

coffee   furniture   money   traffic

Noncount nouns refer to things which cannot be counted in English. Always singular in form, they take and omit *the* precisely as plural count nouns do:

**The** coffee is boiling.
**The** coffee of **Colombia** grows high in the Andes.
**Coffee** is a mealtime drink.

---

[1] These terms and facts are meant for reference only. The actual work on the articles begins with *the*, p. 84.
[2] Or some other marker of the noun: *that* star, *my* idea, *one* sun.

4. Quantifiers   Quantifiers answer "How many?" for count nouns and "How much?" for noncounts:

| *How many?* | *How much?* |
|---|---|
| **some** guests | **some** money |
| **a few** guests | **a little** money |
| **few** guests | **little** money |

## THE ARTICLE THE

### Grammar: the used alone with count nouns

The is definite. It specifies a particular one or a particular group. The by itself can identify a noun when the speaker and his hearer agree easily and completely as to who or what is under discussion:

| **the** parade | (the one we are watching) |
|---|---|
| **the** band | (the one marching by) |
| **the** Mayor | (our mayor) |
| **the** sun | (the earth's sun) |
| **the** university | ("my" or "our" university) |
| **the** Common Market | (the organization) |

In other words, speaker and hearer both understand what is meant.

The is retained when adjectives are used before a noun:

the **little** lady
the **little Norwegian** lady

When *a* is used the first time a specimen is mentioned, *the* is generally used thereafter:

Our neighbors have **a** cat and **a** dog.
**The** dog is friendly with everyone.

### Oral Practice

Directions: Give short answers in chorus, all together, to the questions asked.

Example:

Instructor:   Pete has a job and a television set. Which pays his rent?
Class:        **The** job.

1. Pete owns a car and a dog. Which does he drive?    (car)
2. Pete buys gasoline and sandwiches near his office. Which does he eat?    (sandwiches)
3. Pete owns a stamp collection and an alarm clock. Which wakes him in the morning?    (alarm clock)
4. Betty owns a wrist watch and a dictionary. Which does she wear?    (wrist watch)
5. Betty likes candy and she likes her cat. Which does she pet?    (cat)
6. Betty likes novels, and she likes the movies. Which requires a ticket?    (the movies)
7. Mrs. Smith owns a fur coat and a sweater. Which is warmer?    (fur coat)
8. Mrs. Smith baked a cake this morning. She also baked bread. Which did she serve with the meat?    (bread)
9. Mr. Smith buys a newspaper and a cigar every morning. Which does he smoke?    (cigar)
10. Mr. Smith owns both a car and a sailboat. Which does he drive to work?    (car)

## Dictation: The Campus

Directions (instructor to class): "I am going to give you a paragraph of dictation making frequent use of *the*. As usual, you will hear every word four times. Write down the first sentence now, and then prepare to listen: 'Let me show you around the campus.'"

Let me show you around the campus. The Foreign Student Center is in the middle of the campus. The building devoted to classes for teachers is nearby. The library is somewhat farther away, across the little river. The Memorial Tower is near the library. The Student Union comes next. Now we are close to the business section of the town. Almost all of the shops display goods to attract the forty thousand students.

*After the dictation:* Open your texts and first insert any *the*'s you may have missed. Mark each *the* which you heard with a capital *C* for "correct." Afterward add any capitals you need to in the proper nouns, such as "Memorial Tower."

General direction: In every exercise on the articles, insert the article wherever it is grammatically possible. Occasionally, an article can be either used or omitted without producing a significant difference in meaning. Therefore, in order to eliminate unproductive class discussion and to get as much practice as possible, in every exercise insert the article *wherever it is grammatically possible.*

### C 1 / From Copenhagen to New York

Directions: Before you write this exercise, put a mark in your text wherever you intend to insert *the*. (The useful mark called a caret [∧] has already been inserted in the first sentence.)

After you have finished writing the exercise, read it aloud, outside of class, underlining *the* and looking sharply to see whether all *the*'s you are saying are also on the paper.

I left ∧ Danish capital, Copenhagen, ∧ first of May. We flew in one of airplanes of Icelandic Airline Company over Swedish-Norwegian border to biggest Norwegian city, Oslo. From Oslo, plane headed for Iceland. While we were flying over north Atlantic Ocean, we saw British fishing boat, Johnny, riding waves. When we had rested and admired raw but beautiful Icelandic landscape, airplane took off for Canadian airport, Gander. I had seen a lot of unusual things by time I entered plane for final trip to American city, New York.

### FREE WRITING

### C 2 / A Plane Trip of My Own

Directions: Write one paragraph beginning, "Here is a plane trip of my own." After you have finished, underline the *the*'s you find you have used.

### Grammar: <u>the</u> with the noun described by the phrase following

The hearer may not be sure who or what the speaker means until he adds a descriptive phrase[1] to *the* and the noun:

Speaker:   Do you know the boy?
Hearer:    Which boy?

---

[1] Or a restrictive clause (Section K): *The* President *who followed George Washington* was John Adams.

Speaker:  **The boy in the bright red sportshirt.**

Speaker:  Are you coming to the lecture?
Hearer:  Which lecture?
Speaker:  **The lecture on our changing environment.**

## Oral Practice I

Directions: Begin each sentence "Abdul is studying" and complete the sentence. Use *the* only if you are given a descriptive phrase.

Example:

Instructor:  history of France
Student:  Abdul is studying **the history of France.** (descriptive phrase)

Instructor:  history
Student:  Abdul is studying **history.** (no descriptive phrase)

1. history
2. history of ancient Greece
3. science of electronics
4. electronics
5. science
6. science of space exploration
7. music
8. music of twentieth century composers
9. art
10. art of the American Indian
11. Spanish
12. English

## Oral Practice II

Directions: Think of the different cities you have known. When you are given a phrase, say "I remember" and complete the statement with a descriptive phrase.

Example:

Instructor:  clean streets
Student:  I remember **the clean streets of Salt Lake City.**

Instructor:  dusty streets
Student:  I remember **the dusty streets of my grandmother's village.**

1. beautiful streets
2. dirty streets
3. narrow streets
4. steep streets
5. crooked streets (not straight)
6. quiet streets
7. badly lighted streets
8. noisy streets
9. tree-lined streets
10. dangerous streets

## C 3 / Streets

**Directions:** Copy the complete statements. Complete the partial statements with a descriptive phrase, underlining as in the example.

Example:

Partial statement:     I remember with particular pleasure the sleepy
                       streets . . .

Complete statement:    I remember with particular pleasure **the sleepy
                       streets of my college town.**

All sorts of streets are interesting. I remember with
particular pleasure the wide streets. . . . Narrow streets are
picturesque.[1] I used to spend hours exploring the picturesque
streets. . . . Crooked streets slow down traffic, but I hope
that the city will not straighten. . . . Busy streets are stimulating.
It is a pleasure to walk down the crowded streets of . . .
at noon. Noisy streets can arouse one's energy. I like the noisy,
untidy. . . . However, enough is enough. All streets should
be quiet by midnight, even. . . .

## Prepositions of Time and Place: In, On, At

| Time | | Place | |
|---|---|---|---|
| in | *Largest units:* | in | *Largest units:* |
| years | in 1776 | countries | in Thailand |
| months | in May | states | in California |
| seasons | in the spring | cities | in New Orleans |

[1] *picturesque:* interesting enough to be the subject of a picture.

*Special expressions:*

in the morning
in the afternoon
in the evening
in the daytime
in a minute
in time (not late, effort
   implied: "We reached
   the airport just in
   time.")

on  *Smaller units:*
(*days of the week*)

on Wednesday
on July 4, 1776

on  *Surface contact:*

on Fifth Avenue (no building number)
on the fortieth floor
on the desk
on the wall

*Special expressions:*

on weekends
on holidays
on time (not late, effort
   not implied: "The plane
   was **on time,** as
   usual.")

at  *The exact time:*

at 11:30 P.M.
at one o'clock

at noon (12:00 A.M. )
at midnight (12:00 P.M. )

at  *A specific address:*

at 630 Bourbon Street
at 19 Hanover Square

on Broadway at 116 Street (the intersection of two streets)

*Special expressions:*

at night

## FREE WRITING

### C 4 / The Climate of (name of country)

Directions: Write one paragraph. Begin, "The climate in (name of
country) is varied." Or begin, "The climate in (name of country) is
delightful." (Or write of the various seashores or lakes of your country.)

Useful phrases:

in the northern part of
in the southern part of
in the eastern part of
in the western part of

along the coast
in the mountains

in the spring
in the summer
in the fall (autumn)
in the winter (The seasons are not capitalized in modern English.)
the orange-growing region
the olive-growing region
the cattle-raising region

## C 5 / Where They Live

Directions: Make your first paragraph this statement: "Three good friends of mine live and work in widely different parts of the world." Write a short paragraph on each friend. Refer to the foregoing table of prepositions of time and place.

## C 6 / Time in (name of country)

Directions: Begin, "The time schedule in (name of country) is quite different from that in the United States." How long do people take for meals? Do they go home for lunch? How many hours a day do they work? How often do they have a day with no work? And so forth.

Write one paragraph. When you have finished, underline the *in*'s, *on*'s, and *at*'s you find you have used.

## Grammar: plurals without <u>the</u>

Plurals used in a general sense do not require *the:*

Children play. (children in general, all children)
Children love a surprise. (all children)
Children are delighted with small gifts. (all children)

**Oral Practice I: Plurals without *the***

Directions: Think of that astonishing place, the university bookstore. When you are asked what it sells, respond with a complete statement without *the*. (Your instructor will supply a word if you need one).

Example:

Instructor:    What clothing does a university book store sell?
Student:       Sweaters—it sells sweaters.

| | |
|---|---|
| 1. What other clothing does a bookstore sell? | (raincoat, shirt, jacket) |
| 2. What does the bookstore sell to brighten a dormitory room? | (toy dog, plastic snake) |
| 3. What does it sell to those who like music? | (record) |
| 4. What does it sell to smokers? | (cigarette, pipe, lighter) |
| 5. What does it **give** to smokers? | (match) |
| 6. What does it sell to those who have trouble waking up? | (alarm clock) |
| 7. What does it sell to take the place of a letter? | (greeting card) |
| 8. What kinds of greeting cards have you in the bookstore? | (birthday card, thank-you card, get-well card) |
| 9. What does the bookstore sell at the counter by the cash register? | (candy bar) |
| 10. Oh, yes, what else does a bookstore sell? | (book) |

**Oral Practice II: Plurals without *the***

Directions: Begin each statement, "This country needs more . . ."[1] Then add the phrase given you. (You will be using an adjective before the plural.)

Example:

Instructor:    clean streets
Student:       This country needs more clean streets.

1. public-spirited citizens
2. neatly dressed teen-agers

---

[1] *More* acts as a substitute for *some*.

3. hard-working students
4. well-trained doctors
5. critical watchers of TV programs

Instructor: What else does this country need?

## Oral Practice III: Plurals without *the*

Directions: Begin each statement "I like" or "I don't like." Then add the phrase given you.

Examples:

Instructor:   long assignments
Student:      I like **long assignments.**

Instructor:   burned hamburgers
Student:      I don't like **burned hamburgers.**

 1. present-day hair styles
 2. American dating customs
 3. frank discussions about politics
 4. freedom of the press (newspapers and TV)
 5. big family celebrations
 6. careless drivers
 7. shoestring french fries[1]
 8. American breakfasts
 9. TV horror movies
10. friends who write every week

## NONCOUNT NOUNS[2]

### Grammar: the nature of noncount nouns

Noncount nouns refer to things which cannot be counted in English, such as chalk, gold, clothing, information, cream, and furniture.

---

[1] *shoestring french fries:* fried potatoes whose thickness is that of a shoestring.

[2] *To the instructor:* Because noncount nouns representing things we can see occur so frequently in English, they must be presented before extensive exercises can be given on the articles. (See also the footnote p. 93.)

The article *a/an* is never used with noncounts, although non-counts are singular in form and take verbs singular in form.

**Chalk is** the instructor's friend.

**Gold is** the most valuable of metals.

Accurate **information makes** wise decisions possible.

*The* is used (and omitted) with noncounts *precisely as it is with plural count nouns:*

| Count Nouns | Noncount Nouns |
| --- | --- |
| **The instructors are** in a meeting. | May I have **the sugar?** |
| **The** trees **on our street** are old and huge. | **The** information **in a telephone book** is accurate. |
| **Men** fight. (no **the**) | **Money** talks, they say. (no **the**) |

All of the noncounts in the following list are used in this section, but the list is not complete. In the blank space at the end of the list add other noncounts as they come to your attention.[1]

## List I: common noncounts[2]

| | | |
| --- | --- | --- |
| affection | conservation | ice cream |
| air | cream | information |
| art | dirt | ink |
| bread | dust | jewelry |
| butter | exercise | literature |
| cake | food | luck |
| cement | fruit | machinery |
| chalk | furniture | meat |
| china (dishes) | gasoline | milk |
| clothing | gold | money |
| coffee | hay | music |
| condition | ice | news |

---

[1] *To the instructor:* A few frequently used "abstract" noncounts such as *information* and *exercise* are included in this list. Also included are some frequently used nouns which have both a noncount and a count sense, such as *cake* and *noise*.

[2] A list of only abstract noncounts occurs on p. 118.

| | | |
|---|---|---|
| noise | science | tea |
| oil | silver | temptation |
| orange juice | silverware | toast |
| pepper | smoke | traffic |
| poetry | snow | trouble |
| pollution | soap | water |
| psychology | soup | writing |
| salt | spirit | wine |
| sand | sugar | |

## Oral Practice I: recalling noncounts

Directions: Recall your knowledge of noncounts by answering the following questions in complete statements. (Your instructor will supply a word if you need it.)

Example:

Instructor:   What is used to write on a blackboard?
Student:      **Chalk**—**chalk** is used to write on a blackboard.

| | |
|---|---|
| 1. What covers a beach? | (sand) |
| 2. What covers a ski slope? | (snow) |
| 3. What covers four-fifths of the earth? | (water) |
| 4. At a meal, after you ask for salt, what do you usually ask for next? | (pepper) |
| 5. What word includes everything we eat? | (food) |
| 6. What word includes oranges, bananas, and grapefruit? | (fruit) |
| 7. What word includes ornaments, such as rings and necklaces? | (jewelry) |
| 8. What is the most valuable of metals? | (gold) |
| 9. What metal is next in value? | (silver) |
| 10. What makes a motor car run? | (gasoline, oil, water) |

## Oral Practice II: recalling noncounts

| | |
|---|---|
| 1. Name a popular American dessert. | (ice cream, cake) |
| 2. What do most Americans drink at breakfast? | (coffee) |
| 3. What do most Asians drink? | (tea) |

4. What does everyone drink at a public drinking fountain? **(water)**
5. What is controlled by red and green lights above city streets? **(traffic)**
6. When you drop a slice of bread into a toaster, what soon pops up? **(toast)**
7. When you ask questions and are given facts, what do you have? **(information)**
8. When you interfere in a fight, what are you asking for? **(trouble)**
9. What do you find in every factory? **(machinery)**

**Oral Practice III: *the* used alone with noncounts**

Directions: It is fifteen minutes before dinner time. Say which items are already on the table and which are still somewhere in the kitchen. Use *the* with the noncount.

Example:

Instructor: butter
Student: **The butter** is still in the refrigerator.
Instructor: salt
Student: **The salt** is already on the table.

1. salt and pepper
2. soup
3. hot bread
4. sugar
5. coffee
6. cream
7. meat
8. ice cream
9. silverware
10. china

**Oral Practice IV: *the* with the noncount described by the phrase following**

Directions: Begin each sentence "Marie is taking a course in . . ." and complete the sentence. Use *the* only if you are given a descriptive phrase.

Example:

Instructor:   conservation
Student:      Marie is taking a course in conservation.

Instructor:   conservation of our natural resources
Student:      Marie is taking a course in **the** conservation of **our natural resources.**

1. psychology
2. psychology of Freud
3. poetry of Walt Whitman[1]
4. poetry
5. art of ancient Greece
6. art
7. literature
8. literature of ancient Egypt
9. writing
10. writing of the short story

## FREE WRITING

### C 7 / A Few Unkind Words about (name of city)

Directions: Make your first paragraph this topic sentence: "Here are a few unkind words about (name of city)." Complete the partial statements in the second paragraph with whichever of the following words and phrases you find appropriate.

air
    polluted
    filthy
    unbelievable (pollution)
water
    insipid[2]
    tasteless
the area surrounding the city
    disfigured by junk yards
    lined with hamburger stands, pizza parlors, and motels
traffic and noise
    appalling[3]

---

[1] *Walt Whitman* (1819–1892): an American poet of the outdoors.
[2] *insipid*: without enough taste to be pleasing.
[3] *appalling*: shocking, dismaying.

almost intolerable
certainly inexcusable

Traffic is a problem in every modern city, but the traffic. . . .
No one expects the purest of air in the center of a large city,
but the air. . . . The pollution caused by smoke alone. . . . Everyone
prefers his usual drinking water, but surely the taste of the water. . . .
The area around a city should be pleasing, if not beautiful, but
the. . . . Noise is a problem wherever there are jets, but the
noise. . . . Why doesn't everyone get out of (name of city)?

## Grammar: units of measure for noncounts

Noncounts cannot be counted, yet we frequently speak of a
portion of a noncount: a slice of cake, a piece of furniture, a
gallon of gasoline. The variety of such units of measurement is
almost endless.

### Oral Practice

Directions: Put the following noncounts on the blackboard and see
how many different units of measure you can produce for each: bread,
coffee, gold, ink, meat, milk, soap, water. Use such phrases as a slice
of, a cup of, a bar of, a quart of, or a gallon of.

### FREE WRITING

### C 8 / The Fortunate Mrs. Kilroy

Directions: Write one paragraph describing the life of an imaginary
Mrs. Kilroy. Begin, "Mrs. Kilroy always has cream in her coffee. Her
clothing . . ." Run your eye down the list of noncounts on p. 93 and
see how many you can somehow connect with a luxury-loving
woman. Underline the noncounts you use. Possibly use a few negatives: Mrs. Kilroy is not interested in machinery.

### A CHINESE-AMERICAN WEDDING RECEPTION

### Oral Practice: the used alone with count nouns[1]

Directions: Answer the following questions. Any guess which begins
with the will be acceptable for this practice, but the facts will appear
in the next three exercises.

[1] For grammar, see p. 84.

1. Who are the two most important persons at any wedding reception?   **(bride and groom)**
2. Who pays for a Chinese-American wedding reception?   **(groom's father)**
3. What begins two hours late?   **(dinner)**
4. Who may not speak at some Chinese-American weddings?   **(bride)**
5. Given this perfect opportunity, whom do the men at the reception tease?   **(bride)**
6. Who finally grows angry?   **(groom)**
7. In the middle of the dinner, who introduces the bride to each guest?   **(groom's parents)**
8. Who, then, offers sweet tea to each guest?   **(bride)**
9. Who drinks the most wine?   **(men)**
10. Who drinks a little wine?   **(women)**
11. Who drinks no wine?   **(children)**
12. After the reception, in their new home, who offers precious tea to their closest relatives and friends?   **(bride)**

**General directions for C9, C10, and C11:** In the next three exercises, insert a caret [∧] in your text wherever you intend to write *the*. Underline *the* when writing.

### C 9 / Part I

A Chinese wedding reception is an exciting affair, even in the United States.[1] Reception, paid for by groom's family, is held in one of big restaurants specializing in Chinese parties.

Groom's father rents an entire floor of restaurant. Room contains twenty or thirty tables seating twelve persons each. Outside restaurant hangs a huge flower sign, reaching to second story, at least. Inside, another flower sign spells out names of bride and groom.[2]

Invitations read "seven o'clock," but last guests do not arrive until nearly nine o'clock. Everyone understands that dinner will be late, but by nine o'clock everyone is fully ready for feast.

---

[1] The article *the* is a part of some names: *the* United States, *the* Soviet Union, *the* Indian Ocean. See pp. 128–129.

[2] One *the* is enough: *the* bride and groom.

## C 10 / Part II

There are no fewer than twelve meat dishes at typical
Chinese wedding dinner. Men drink wine. Women drink a little
wine, too, but generally women, and, of course, children,
drink soft drinks.

In middle of dinner, bride and groom and groom's parents
come to guests, and groom's parents introduce newly married couple
to everyone. Bride offers sweet tea to guests. As guests take
offered cups, head of each family puts a red envelope on tea tray.
It contains a little money for bride, in addition to gift already
made to bride and groom.

## C 11 / Part III

In some places, there are special customs in regard to
bride. In first place, she may not drink tea; she must drink wine.
In second place, men at wedding have privilege of teasing bride.
She cannot answer, no matter what they say, for a bride may
not speak on her wedding day. Finally bridegroom grows angry,
and men agree that their joking has gone far enough.

Dinner ends with a sweet dish and wishes of everyone
for many children and a long, prosperous, and happy life for
newly married couple. After dinner, in their new home,
bride and groom offer special, precious tea to their closest
friends and relatives.

## FREE WRITING

### C 12 / A Happy Party in (name of country)

Directions: Write of a large, happy party which is part of the culture
of your country. Divide what you have to say into three main parts,
according to the following outline.

I. **The occasion**
   Why is the party being given? Who are the host and hostess? Who
   are the guests? Approximately how many guests are present? How
   are the women dressed? The men? Do children attend?
II. **The entertainment**
   What is the entertainment? Music? Food? Dancing?

What types of dances? Are there hired entertainers?
III. **The end of the party**
   How long does the party go on? What brings it to an end?
   Who are the last persons to leave?

## THE SPELLING OF PLURALS[1]

1. Most plurals are formed by adding s to the singular:
   wedding—weddings; letter—letters; place—places
2. A few plurals are exceptions to this rule:
   kimono—kimonos (Rule 9, p. 262)
3. A few plurals are completely irregular:
   woman—women; man—men; child—children
4. Singulars ending in a hissing sound add es to form the plural:
   wish—wishes; sandwich—sandwiches; (Rule 10, p. 282)

### Dictation: A Private Japanese Wedding (plurals without *the*)

Directions: Put on the blackboard two phrases you will need in this dictation: "Japanese kimonos" and "in the Shinto way." Then prepare to listen. As usual, you will hear every word four times. The dictation will contain a number of plurals.

   Most weddings in Japan are held in the spring and in the fall. Japanese kimonos are too hot to wear in the summer and too cold to wear in the winter. Letters of invitation are sent out about two months before the day of the wedding.
   Weddings celebrated in the Shinto way are private. Only the parents, sisters, brothers, and close relatives of the bride and groom attend. After the wedding, all of the friends of the two families attend the big, formal wedding reception.

## A JAPANESE WEDDING RECEPTION

### C 13 / Part I

Directions: When writing, turn the nouns in parentheses into the plural form, underlined. In this exercise, the nouns to be pluralized are in parentheses.

---

[1] Detailed work on spelling will be given, with dictation, in Sections E through L.

First of all the (guest) invited to a Japanese wedding
reception seat themselves in the chosen room of one of the large
(hotel). Most of the (woman) are wearing satin (kimono). Then
the bride and groom come into the hall with their two (matchmaker).[1]

The (matchmaker), always a husband and wife, introduce
the bride and groom to the (guest). They tell a little about
their (background). They name their (school). They mention
the (position) of the bridegroom, past and present. Then one
person, selected beforehand, shouts, "Your health!" and the (guest)
all drink wine. (Relative) and (friend) extend their best (wish)
to the young couple.

## C 14 / Part II

Directions: Underline the nouns you pluralize.

Occasionally, the wedding dinner begins with tiny sandwiches
and cake, ice cream, and coffee. In some circle, Japanese dish
are not eaten at wedding. The food consists of Western dish
only. The guest sit at the table two or two and a half hour.

At the end of the dinner, both the bride's father and the
groom's father express their thank to the guest. Before the guest
go home, the bride and groom, the two matchmaker, the
bride's parent, and the bridegroom's parent stand in a row at
the entrance to the hall and bow politely to all the departing guest.

## MATCHMAKING IN MODERN JAPAN

General directions: In the next three exercises, underline the nouns
you pluralize.

## C 15 / Part I

Are matchmaker used in arranging modern Japanese marriage?
Yes, they are. There are various way of using the service
of a pair of matchmaker. Here is one way.

The matchmaker, always a husband and wife, are well
known to both set of parent. The parent of a girl old enough to marry
gives several of her picture to the matchmaker. Relative show their
friend these picture, too, but relative are never matchmaker themselves.

[1] *matchmaker:* one who seeks to bring about a marriage.

The girl's parent give her background, height, weight, school, and number of brother and sister to their friend. The friend pass the information along to the matchmaker. (The girl learns as many fact about the young man as he does about her.) Question of suitability are all settled before the first meeting. But will the young couple like each other?

## C 16 / Part II

The first meeting of a prospective couple[1] still takes place in some circle in the presence of the two mother. The second time the young couple go out alone. Usually they go to a movie, a restaurant, or an art gallery. After three or four meeting, they must decide. The girl tells her mother **yes** or **no**. The boy tells his mother, too.

Money and gift go to the matchmaker the day after the wedding. These reward are never discussed. The parent of the bride simply are generous.

## C 17 / Part III

The relationship between the matchmaker and a happy young couple continues for year. The young husband and wife visit their matchmaker at New Year's. They tell them of the birth of a child. They send gift at the end of each year and in the middle of the year. Ten year after a happy marriage, the two are still sending gift to their matchmaker.

## FREE WRITING

## C 18 / The New Way

Directions: Discuss the degree of freedom permitted the young people of today in a country you know well. Hand in an outline covering the points below or other points suited your subject.

  I. How the subject of marriage is initiated
 II. Preliminary steps
III. Possible financial arrangements
IV. Opportunity for choice of mate
 V. Opportunity to become acquainted with mate decided upon
VI. Your comment

---

[1] *couple:* keep the singular form, but use *they* as the pronoun.

# THE ARTICLE *A*[1]

## Grammar: the nature of the article <u>a</u>

1. The article *a* indicates a portion of something which can also be thought of as plural:

cable cars, **a** cable car
buses, **a** bus
young San Franciscans, **a** young San Franciscan

The fact just stated can be put in other ways:

**A** is used when any one of a group is meant, not a special one.
**A** is used when a sample represents the whole.
**A** is nondefinite. (**The,** in contrast, is definite.)

2. *An* is the form of *a* used when the following noun begins with the *sound* of a vowel:

an apple    an exercise    an island    an owl    an umbrella
an honor    an hour (the **h** is not pronounced)

3. *A* is used when the following word begins with the *sound* of a consonant:

a university    a uniform    a union
a unique experience    a European city    a united front
a one o'clock class (the first sound is **w**)
a home (the **h** is sounded)

4. As with *the, a* is retained, even when one or more adjectives come before the noun.

a little lady
a lively little old lady

### Oral Practice I

Directions: In the sentence given you, change the plural noun *used as subject* without an article to a singular noun used with *a* or *an.*

[1] In explanations, *a* will be considered to include *an* wherever appropriate.

Examples:

Instructor:   Tigers hunt silently.
Student:      **A** tiger hunts silently.

Instructor:   Cats like soft beds.
Student:      **A** cat likes soft beds.

1. Children like zoos.
2. Lions roar near mealtime.
3. Lions like raw meat.
4. Monkeys peel bananas easily.
5. Monkeys climb trees easily.
6. Children love to watch monkeys.
7. Adults love to watch monkeys.
8. Polar bears like water.
9. Polar bears sit in pools of water in the summer.
10. Polar bears almost fan themselves in the heat. (Use "itself" in the singular.)

**Oral Practice II**

Directions: Make a complete statement using *a* or *an* before the cue given you.[1]

Examples:

Instructor:   What fell on Sir Isaac Newton's head?        (apple)
Student:      An apple—an apple fell on Sir Isaac Newton's head.

Instructor:   What did Mr. Smith carry to work this morning?  (umbrella)
Student:      An umbrella—Mr. Smith carried an umbrella to work this morning.

1. What did Betty refuse to carry this morning?  (umbrella)
2. What is Betty?                                (only child)[2]
3. What type of school gives graduate work?      (university)
4. What is Harvard?                              (university)
5. What is Yale?                                 (university)
6. What do many students have at one o'clock?    (one o'clock class)
7. What did the Mayor give Mr. Smith yesterday?  (honor)
8. What did the Mayor call Mr. Smith's plan?     (imaginative plan)
9. How long did the Mayor talk with Mr. Smith?   (hour)

[1] cue: a signal or hint as to what is expected.
[2] only child: the one child in the family.

10. What does everyone wear in the army? **(uniform)**
11. What does a marching band also wear? **(uniform)**
12. What do nurses wear on duty? **(uniform)**
13. What do workers form when they organize? **(union)**
14. What does every political leader call for? **(united front)**
15. What will you probably begin before you leave class today? **(exercise)**
16. Name a bird which can see in the dark. **(owl)**
17. What do you call a piece of land entirely surrounded by water? **(island)**
18. What did the newspapers call the first landing on the moon? **(unique experience)**
19. What is sleep often called? **(universal need)**
20. What is work sometimes called? **(universal need)**

## C 19 / A Girl's Handbag

Directions: First insert a caret in your text wherever *a* is grammatically possible. Underline *a* when writing.

Girl's handbag contains jumble of objects. Almost certainly it contains lipstick. It also contains comb and small mirror. If the girl is student, the handbag inevitably contains pen. If the girl has job, the handbag may contain checkbook. If she prefers to go without raincoat on dark morning, girl at least carries folded plastic rain hat in her handbag. The handbag is not easy to close some mornings.

## C 20 / A Good Place to Go

Directions: Insert *a* or *an,* underlined, in the following paragraph when writing.

Good place to go for pleasant evening is the Little Place. Smiling host shows his guests to comfortable booth. Smiling waiter brings menu. Light supper does not destroy limited budget. Violinist and pianist play now and then on small platform at one end of the room. The Little Place is unusually good place to take date.

## FREE WRITING

## C 21 / On Saturday Evening

Directions: Begin, "A place students like to go on a Saturday evening in (name of city) is (name of place)." Write one paragraph.

After you have finished, underline the *a*'s and *an*'s you find you have used.

## C 22 / A Picture I Know Well

Directions: Begin, "In _____ is a picture I have often studied with pleasure." Write one paragraph. After you have finished, underline the *a*'s and *an*'s you find you have used.

## C 23 / My New Office

Directions: Underline *a* and *an* when writing the five following paragraphs. (Note the number of plurals without *the* which this student writer has used.)

My new office is lovely place. There is title on the door printed in beautiful black letters. Inside is big room, where draftsmen draw plans for new buildings.

Partitions[1] divide the big room into number of small rooms. Each beginning draftsman has desk and drawing board in one of these small rooms. The desk is good one. Even beginning draftsman has such items in his drawer as drafting pencil, eraser, and dusting brush.

There is waiting room, of course. It has magazine rack and reading lamp by each comfortable armchair. On certain wall are big pictures of the company's finished product, for example, architectural drawing of Rocky River High School.

My new office has model room. This room is full of models of our projects—model of bridge, for example. The room has very nice piano. Piano is unusual in model room. Sometimes obliging fellow worker plays for all the rest of us. Music puts us in working mood.

In the back, is my room. It has big drawing board, drawing shelves, and supply file. In the desk are twenty-five articles, such as roll of sketching paper, roll of tracing paper, and small bottle of very black ink, called India ink. There is beautiful plant in the window. I am draftsman, but I am girl.

## LIFE AT AN AMERICAN RACETRACK

General direction: As you read aloud in class or write the various sections of "Life at an American Racetrack," look for noncounts.

---

[1] *partitions:* walls which generally go only part way to the ceiling of a larger room.

The American student who furnished this information used non-counts easily and naturally.

## Oral Practice I: Introducing an exercise boy (insert *a/an*)

I am exercise boy at the Thistledown Racetrack near large city in the Midwest. I am college freshman, as well as exercise boy. Here is something about racetrack with average of thirteen hundred horses.

## Oral Practice II: The electric walker (insert *the*)

Electric walker, a fairly recent innovation,[1] is most efficient way to give horses at a race track daily exercise they must have. Walker is a heavy pole, with five arms sticking out at top. (Arms resemble rotating blades of a helicopter.) Five horses at a time are hooked by their halters to arms. Electric current is turned on. Base begins to revolve. Horses begin to move in a circle along with revolving arms. Pace[2] is a walk. If even one horse stops, walker stops.

While horses are walking, grooms clean stalls, leaving enough hay and water for next twenty-four hours. After thirteen minutes, exercise boy, or someone else, takes horses off walker and puts them into their stalls. Horses begin to eat at once.

## Oral Practice III: A workout (insert *the*)

Horses which kick electric walker get out of using it. They are exercised individually. Also, horses being put into condition to race are exercised individually. Here is a typical workout.

Exercise boy has a very small, light saddle. He does not sit down in saddle. He half stands and grips reins steadily and hard. (Horse will run away if it gets slightest chance.)

Exercise boy makes horse gallop for a mile or even two. Trainer decides exercise. (A gallop consists of a succession of leaping strides, with all four feet off ground at same time.) Galloping is heavy work, but it is good exercise for a horse because it builds up his muscles and wind.[3] While horse is galloping, exercise boy counts number of times it stumbles and tells trainer. If a horse stumbles more on a dry track than a muddy one, naturally trainer and owner will plan to race it on a muddy track.

[1] *innovation:* a new way of doing something.
[2] *pace:* rate of movement.
[3] *wind: breathing.*

As a treat, at end of gallop, exercise boy loosens reins just a little, and horse begins to run.

### C 24 / A Racehorse as a Personality

Directions: Write the three following paragraphs, inserting *a* and *an*, underlined.

Racehorse has personality, just as person has. Racehorse is highly bred and extremely nervous. If he is not given chance to exercise every day, he goes wild. Horse denied exercise because of injury may bite the first man who comes within reach of his teeth.

Racehorse wants his own way. For example, around mealtime, he just doesn't want to leave his stall. Anyone who goes into stall when horse is in this mood may easily get kick.

Horse often likes the men who care for him. He doesn't bite them

**Jockey Ron Turcotte riding the racehorse Secretariat in an early-morning workout.**
[N.Y.R.A.—Bob Coglianese]

without extremely good reason. Instead he reaches out and licks arm
or cheek with long, wet tongue. Sometimes he walks up to favorite
exercise boy and rubs against him, little like cat. Horse responds
to affection more readily than many animals.

### C 25 / A Horse of My Own

Directions: Write the two following paragraphs, inserting *a* and *an*,
underlined.

I have horse of my own. I call her Pretty Girl. She is intelligent
animal, but she is not thoroughbred[1] horse. I could never enter her
in race, even if I wanted to. But I do not want to. She is companion,
for my own pleasure. I took her swimming day or two ago.

### C 26 / The Race

Directions: Write the four following paragraphs, inserting *the*, underlined.

A horse knows when he is going to race.[2] How does he know?
His breakfast was scanty.[3] (He is angry about that.) He does not
have a saddle on his back. He is being led, not ridden, to grandstand.[4]
He is led under grandstand into an unusual, special stall.

Horse is nervous. Sometimes he does not know what to do
when starting gate flies open and track is before him. If he does not
begin to run instantly, other horses are already ahead of him.

During a race, a horse with spirit,[5] when he sees another horse
just ahead of him, will try to pass him. Sometimes jockey[6] holds
him back to save his energy for last stretch. Eventually a horse gets
to run as fast as he can.

Exercise boy, watching owner's favorite jockey riding horse he
has exercised day after day, says nothing. Secretly, he is planning
for day when he will be a jockey himself, and his horse will be first
one to cross finishing line.

[1] *thoroughbred*: of pure stock.
[2] *verb phrase*: "going to race" (no *the*).
[3] *scanty*: not enough.
[4] *grandstand*: the principal place for people to sit at a racetrack.
[5] *spirit*: pride (List II, p. 118).
[6] *Jockey*: one who rides horses in races as an occupation.

## FREE WRITING

### C 27 / A Pet of My Own

Directions: Write of a pet you have understood and enjoyed. Write three paragraphs, using and adding to the following suggestions.

Paragraph 1: How did you acquire your pet? What was his age? Your age? His appearance?

Paragraph 2: What special relationship developed between you two? What did you do together?

Paragraph 3: What ended the relationship, if it is ended?

### C 28 / The Animals of (name of country)

Directions: Write of not more than three animals common to your country, either pets or work animals. Have a brief introduction; devote a paragraph to each animal; write a concluding paragraph if one seems needed.

### C 29 / A Special Possession

Directions: Write of some possession which was a highly satisfactory part of your life as a child or a teen-ager.

Paragraph 1: What was the possession? What did it look like? How did you acquire it?

Paragraph 2: What activities did you engage in with this possession?

Paragraph 3: Where is the possession now? What will you remember about it permanently?

### C 30 / Test: A Summer Session Bedroom

Directions: In this exercise, insert *a, an,* and *the,* but do no underlining. This is a test of how automatically you now use the articles and plurals without *the.* (Your instructor may wish the class to read the first two paragraphs aloud and then write only the last two paragraphs.)

I am attending summer session of large American university. In fall and spring semesters, boys live in dormitory where I am living, but during summer session it is occupied by girls.

It is amusing to girl to see how rooms are planned to resist rough treatment which boy gives his study-bedroom. Floor is not cement, but it is made of something as hard as cement. Dirt cannot show on its speckled[1] tan and brown surface. There is not even small rug on floor. Straight chair (there is only one) is heavy and solid. Varnish[2] is half worn off its seat. Many boys have used this chair without doing it serious damage. Desk is long shelf, with drawers placed conveniently under shelf. Over desk are other shelves for books.

There is no student lamp. Instead, two long tubes providing fluorescent lighting[3] are fastened under bookshelves. Light is both soft and bright. When boy leaves, there is no temptation to pack lamp along with his personal belongings. Fluorescent tubes are fastened solidly to wall just under bookshelves.

There is no door to closet, but closet is satisfactory one, with hooks along walls and plenty of coat hangers to slide along rod placed across closet.

All in all, this study-bedroom, planned for boy, is comfortable room for girl attending summer classes at certain large American university.

## QUANTIFIERS

### Grammar: the nature of quantifiers

Quantifiers answer the question "How many?" for count nouns and "How much?" for noncounts. In the following list, note when the same word is used for both counts and noncounts and when the words differ.

*Same Terms Used*

| Count | Noncount |
|---|---|
| some | some |
| a lot of, lots | a lot of, lots |
| all, almost all, most | all, almost all, most |
| hardly any, not any | hardly any, not any |
| no (adjective), almost no | no (adjective), almost no |
| none | none |

---

[1] *speckled:* very small spots of different colors next to each other.
[2] *varnish:* a hard, clear protective coating used to cover wood.
[3] *fluorescent lighting:* a tube, rather than a bulb, gives off light.

*Examples*

**All** children like a surprise.        **All** gold has a high commercial value.

**None** (of the passengers) **are**[1] on a long trip.

**None is** a mailman.[2]        None of the news **is** encouraging this morning.

*Different Terms Used*

| Count | Noncount |
|---|---|
| many, not many | much, not much |
| a few, very few | a little, very little |
| few[3] | little |
| both (two) | — |
| several (more than two) | — |
| each (one) | — |
| one (of the passengers) **is** | — |

*Examples*

**A few** (of the) passengers read.        **A little** (of the) information was misleading.

**Several** (of the) passengers looked out of the windows.

**One** (of the passengers) **is** a salesman. One **is a** writer.

**Few** countries desire war.        **Little** care is generally taken to prevent war.

## Grammar: <u>some</u>

*Some* indicates an indefinite amount. As the first table of quantifiers shows, *some* is used both with plural count nouns and with noncounts.

---

[1] When *none* directs the reader's attention to the group as a whole, the verb is plural. ("None of the passengers *are* on a long trip.")

[2] When *none* directs the reader's attention to a single unit, the verb is singular. ("None of the passengers *is* a mailman".)

[3] *Few* and *little* put emphasis on the smallness of the amount.

There are **some** cigarettes on the coffee table. (count noun)

There is **some ice cream** in the refrigerator. (noncount)

## Oral Practice

Directions: Haruko and Marie are planning a small party for Sunday afternoon. Each time you are given an item, say, "They will need . . ." and complete the statement. Use *a* with singular items and *some* with plural and noncount items.

Examples:

Instructor:   teapot
Student A:   They will need **a** teapot.

Instructor:   tea
Student B:   They will need **some** tea.

Instructor:   teacups
Student C:   They will need **some** teacups.

1. dust cloth
2. small tables
3. silverware
4. napkins
5. dozen bottles of coke
6. tea and coffee
7. teapot and coffeepot
8. sugar
9. cream
10. sandwiches
11. sandwich tray
12. big tray of small cakes
13. ice cream
14. chairs and cushions

## Grammar: <u>any</u>

*Any* represents the whole in general. (*Some* represents part of the whole.) *Any* is frequently used in negative statements and questions:

There aren't **any** cokes in the refrigerator.

Isn't there **any** ginger ale, either?

*Some* is also used in negative questions:

Isn't there **some** tomato juice, at least?

Less frequently *any* is used in affirmative statements and questions:

You can get **any** book you want at the library.

Can you get **any** record you want, too?

**Oral Practice I: responding to *some* and *any* in questions**

Directions: You will be asked a question that may contain *some* and may contain *any*. Answer in chorus according to the fact, using *some* or *any*.

Examples:

Instructor:   Are there any lights in this classroom?
Class:        There are **some** lights in this classroom.

Instructor:   Is there **some** dust on the floor?
Class:        There isn't **any** dust on the floor.

1. Are there some windows in this classroom?
2. Are there some chairs?
3. Are there any students sitting in the chairs?
4. Is there some cake on the teacher's desk?
5. Are there any pictures on the walls?
6. Is there some coffee on the teacher's desk?
7. Are there some maps on the walls?
8. Is there some money on the teacher's desk?
9. Are there any notebooks in the room?
10. Is there some ice on the windows?
11. Is there any news about examinations?

**Oral Practice II: *a few, a little, a lot of*[1]**

Directions: Answer the questions asked about the purchases Haruko and Marie made Saturday morning at the supermarket, the post office, and the bookstore.

Examples:

Instructor:   How many oranges were there in the supermarket?
Student A:    **A lot**—there were **a lot of** oranges in the supermarket.

[1] For grammar, see p. 111.

| Instructor: | How many oranges did the girls buy? |
|---|---|
| Student B: | A few—they only bought **a few**. |

Instructor:   How much orange juice was there in the supermarket?
Student C:   A lot—there was a lot of orange juice in the supermarket.

Instructor:   How much did the girls buy?
Student D:   A little—they bought only **a little**.

1. The supermarket was having a big sale on the girls' favorite cookies.[1] How many did the girls buy?
2. Potato chips were not on sale. How many did the girls buy?
3. The girls needed soap, but not a lot of soap. How much did they buy?
4. Haruko and Marie like their bread very fresh. How much do they buy at a time?
5. The girls do not use many eggs. How many did they buy?
6. Salt and pepper last a long time. How much did the girls buy?
7. The girls write a lot of letters. In the post office, how many stamps did they buy?
8. By the time the girls reached the bookstore, they were almost out of money. How many paperbacks[2] did they buy?

## Oral Practice III: a variety of quantifiers

Directions: Haruko and Marie's party Sunday afternoon was a success. Use a variety of quantifiers to show that the guests had a good time.

Example:

Instructor:   How much of the food provided did the guests eat?
Student A:   They ate **a lot of** the food.
Student B:   They ate **all** of the food.

1. How much tea did the guests drink? How much coffee?
2. There were a dozen bottles of Coca-Cola for eight girls. How much of the Coke disappeared?
3. The sandwiches were very good but very small. How many were left after the party?
4. The cookies were plentiful and delicious. How many of them were left after the party?
5. The eight girls ate two quarts of ice cream. Was this **a lot** or **a little** for each girl?

[1] *cookies*: small, flat, sweet cakes.
[2] *paperbacks*: inexpensive books without hard covers.

6. One girl was trying to lose weight. How many of the rich little cookies did she eat?
7. The guests talked, laughed, and played the guitar for two hours. How many of them enjoyed the party?
8. After the guests left, how many of the hostesses got busy with the dishes? (washing, cleaning up)

### Oral Practice IV: a variety of quantifiers

Directions: It is difficult to make a statement true of a whole group "Men work." Is this strictly true? Is it not more accurate to say *"Most* men work"? In order to keep the statements given you from being too broad, too inclusive to be true, put a variety of quantifiers before the plural nouns and the noncounts.

Examples:

Instructor:   Modern office buildings are handsome.
Student:      **Some** modern office buildings are handsome.

Instructor:   Chalk is white.
Student:      **Most** chalk is white.

1. Women are talkative.
2. Women listen well.
3. Women are careful drivers.
4. Men take chances.
5. Sand is white.
6. Wine is sweet.
7. Old buildings have charm.
8. Beautiful china is made in France.
9. Boxers keep in condition to fight at all times.
10. Exercise is healthful.
11. Men are good cooks.
12. Women are good cooks.

### C 31 / By Bus

Directions: First orally and then in writing use a variety of quantifiers to tell how the passengers on a bus endured an early morning ride.

When writing, turn the four paragraphs of questions into four paragraphs of statements, underlining the quantifiers.

When was the last time you took a bus? Where did you wait? Where did you want to go?

How much was the fare? What coins did you drop into the coin box? Was the driver glad to see you? Did he say something cheerful about the weather?

How many seats on the bus were empty? How many men read the morning paper? How many men scowled[1] at sheets of figures? How many women held shopping bags on their laps? How many passengers looked into space? How many slept? What did you do?

Which door did you leave by? How many passengers blocked your way? How far did you have to walk? Did you arrive at your destination on time? Did you arrive breathless?

## FREE WRITING

### C 32 / The Difference between Men and Women

Directions: Write one paragraph beginning, "Men and Women often react differently to the same situation." If the opposite sex pretends to find one of your comparisons outrageous, very well. A few mock disputes will make the class hour lively.

Examples:

Almost all women are cautious drivers;[2] some men take a chance.

A lot of men enjoy sailing alone; few women do.

Not many men cook regularly; a great many women do.

## ABSTRACT NONCOUNTS

### Grammar: the nature of abstract noncounts

The student describing life at an American racetrack used several noncounts of the type generally called "abstract":

horses being put into **condition** to race

a horse denied **exercise** because of injury

---

[1] *scowled:* frowned angrily.
[2] Note the use of the semicolon [;]. Two independent statements are linked without a connective such as *and* or *but*. In *For Reference*, see p. 307.

a horse with **spirit** when he sees another horse just ahead of him

horses respond to **affection**

Abstract noncounts refer to concepts such as *exercise* and *spirit*, emotions such as *affection*, and conditions such as *peace*. Such noncounts take and omit the articles precisely as plurals and the noncounts in the earlier list do (p. 93).

## List II: abstract noncounts[1]

The following list is not complete. In the blank space at the end of the list, add other abstract noncounts as they come to your attention.

| | | |
|---|---|---|
| advice | health | poetry |
| courage | ignorance | poverty |
| curiosity | inflation | progress |
| determination | intelligence | scenery |
| education | leisure | shopping |
| environment | literature | spirit |
| freedom | love | success |
| friendship | luck | technology |
| fun | peace | transportation |
| happiness | persistence | weather |

Note that major fields of study are not capitalized in English:

| | | |
|---|---|---|
| biology | forestry | secondary |
| electrical | physics | education |
| engineering | psychology | zoology |
| food service | | |

**Oral Practice I**

Directions: Give complete answers to the following questions, each of which contains a noncount from the foregoing list or the list on p. 93.

1. Where can you go on this campus for **advice?**
2. Which helps most in passing courses, **intelligence** or **persistence?**
3. What does cigarette smoking do to **health?**
4. What does factory **smoke** do to the surrounding **environment?**

[1] A third list, noncount nouns used also in a count sense, is on p. 120.

5. How frequently do **ignorance** and **poverty** go together?
6. Name one modern means of **transportation**. Name another.
7. Name one ancient means of **transportation**.
8. Is **technology** able to control the **weather?**
9. What sport arouses the greatest **enthusiasm** in your country?
10. What are the rewards of **success** in this sport?
11. What is "**freedom** of the press"?
12. What is **inflation?**
13. How much **enthusiasm** do you feel for modern music? For modern painting? For modern furniture?
14. Name a country with beautiful **scenery**. Name a favorite scene of yours within this **scenery.**
15. Does **success** bring **happiness?**
16. Does a lot of **leisure** bring **happiness?**
17. Name one of the benefits of **education**. Can you name another?
18. What is your idea of a weekend of **fun?**

**Oral Practice II**

1. How much **advice** do you take from strangers?
2. How much **courage** does it sometimes take to say **No?**
3. How much **curiosity** does a scientist need?
4. How much **determination** does an inventor need?
5. How much **fun** do you get from watching American football?
6. How much **freedom** do you think students should have in the dormitory?
7. How much **luck** have you been having lately?
8. How much **progress** are you making in understanding English over the telephone?
9. How much **determination** does it take to get a Master's degree?
10. How much **shopping** do you intend to do when your next check from home arrives?

# WORDS USED AS BOTH NONCOUNT AND COUNT NOUNS
## Grammar

Various nouns generally used as noncount nouns are also used as count nouns:

Everything passes; **art** alone endures. (noncount)

Sculpture is one of the **arts**. (plural)

Skillful cooking is **an art**. (singular)

A noncount noun represents a whole:

**Success** should follow effort.

A count noun represents *part* of a whole:

In his lifetime, Martin Luther King was **a success**.

The following list gives only a few of the numerous words used in both a noncount and a count sense. In the blank space at the end of the list, add other examples as they come to your attention.

## List III: noncount nouns also used in a count sense

| | |
|---|---|
| art | science |
| cake | success |
| condition | tea |
| democracy | trouble |
| exercise | writing |
| experience | wine |
| fear | |
| food | |
| fruit | |
| history | |
| meat | |
| noise | |
| opportunity | |

### Oral Practice

Directions: You will be given a sentence and a cue phrase. Use the phrase in a sentence of your own.

Examples:

Instructor:   **Tea** is my favorite mealtime drink.          (a **tea**)
Student:       Jasmine is **a delicious tea**.

Instructor:   A boxer has to get into **condition** for a fight.   (**conditions**)
Student:       The **conditions** in a boxer's training camp are not for me.

1. Pete likes **cake**.                                    (a **dark cake**)
2. **Democracy** implies a right to the secret ballot.     (a **democracy**)
3. **Exercise** promotes health.                           (a few **exercises**)
4. **Experience** is a good teacher.                       (my **experiences**)
5. **Fear** freezes effort.                                (a **fear**)
6. **Food** is necessary to man and beast.                 (a **food**)
7. **Fruit** is a pleasant addition to any meal.           (a **fruit**)
8. **History** sometimes repeats itself.                   (a **history**)
9. **Noise** represents one of the great discomforts       (loud **noises**)
   of modern living.
10. **Opportunity** is said to knock only once.            (an **opportunity**)
11. **Science** does not always benefit man.               (a **science**)
12. However, **science** frequently benefits mankind.      (a helpful **science**)
13. **Wine** is made from grape juice.                     (a **wine**)
14. **Trouble** comes to everyone.                         (the **troubles** of)
15. **Writing** is hard work.                              (the **writings** of)

Occasionally the noncount form of a word differs sharply in meaning from the count form:

I have plenty of **change**—small coins—but no bills.        (noncount)
There is going to be **a change** in the weather.            (count)

A modern office building makes use of **glass**.             (noncount)
May I have **a glass** of water?                             (count)
My new **glasses** make it easy to see at a distance.        (count)

Modern business uses tons of **paper**.                      (noncount)
**The papers** contain important news tonight.               (count)
**A paper** is on the floor.                                 (count)

## FREE WRITING

### C 33 / Changes in (name of country)

Directions: Write of three changes of any type in your country which have taken place in the last ten years.

Use an underlined and capitalized subtitle for each of these changes. Put the subtitle in the center of the line, in the style of a term paper.

### C 34 / The Well-Rounded Student

Directions: Write one paragraph. Give three ways in which a student can broaden his outlook and thoroughly enjoy himself, in addition to doing good work in his courses.

*General direction:* Use part of the suggestions in the three following assignments either to write three short compositions or one longer composition called "The System of Education in (name of your country)."

## C 35 / The System of Elementary Education in (name your country)

Directions: Write two paragraphs. Give the information suggested below and additional appropriate information.

Paragraph 1: At what age do children start to school? **Must** they go? For how many years? For how many hours a day? For how many weeks a year? What about girls?

Paragraph 2: What is taught? How is it learned?

## C 36 / The System of Secondary Education in (name your country)

Directions: Write three paragraphs. Give the information suggested below and additional appropriate information.

Paragraph 1: How does one get into secondary school? Who pays for the schooling? What about girls?

Paragraph 2: What subjects are taught? How are they presented?

Paragraph 3: What is a graduate prepared to do?

## C 37 / The System of Higher Education in (name your country)

Directions: Write on college or university education in your country, using the three subtitles given below or substituting others more appropriate to your situation.

Underline the subtitles or use all capitals, centering your titles in the style of a term paper:

THE ELIGIBLE

THE VARIETY OF DEPARTMENTS

THE PREPARATION PROVIDED FOR A CAREER

## A CERTAIN SMALL TOWN

The following exercises are the most advanced work in this text on the articles. A few brief directions before an exercise suggest what to do with certain less frequent uses of the articles. A number followed by an asterisk (*) indicates that more examples of the article just used can be found at the end of this section under "Less Frequent Uses of the Articles," p. 127.

## C 38 / An Old-Fashioned American House, Part I

Directions: Insert a/an, underlined. In paragraph 1 write "such <u>a</u> small town" (1*), and "<u>a</u> dozen families" (2*).

Fifty years ago most people in the smaller towns in the United States lived in house. Perhaps only dozen families in town of ten or twelve thousand lived in apartment. Here are few facts about American house in such small town.

The house had yard. It had front yard and back yard. Even very small back yard had flower bed. The back yard usually had clothes line for the family washing. During the summer the back yard had set of metal chairs and metal table under big umbrella. There was usually garage in the back yard, too.

## C 39 / An Old-Fashioned American House, Part II

Directions: Insert a/an, underlined. In paragraph 2 write "<u>a</u> plate, <u>a</u> glass, and <u>a</u> napkin" or write "<u>a</u> plate, glass, and napkin" (3*). In paragraph 3 write "breakfast" (no article) (4*).

Every house in small town had living room. The older houses also had dining room. Set of beautiful dishes in "china closet" was often ornament of this room.

In the center of the room was large dining table. In most households the table was covered with white linen tablecloth at all times. Few young women, however, left their polished tables bare; they set centerpiece of flowers on it. For meal, housewife put plate, glass, and napkin at each person's place. Then she added knife, fork, and spoon.

The newer houses had "breakfast nook." This was table and two benches in corner of the kitchen. The family always had breakfast here and often quick lunch. The breakfast nook was right for "midnight snack," too. Important meal, though, on holiday or birthday took place in the dining room.

## C 40 / An American Housewife

Directions: Insert a/an, underlined. In paragraph 1 write "<u>a</u> necessity" and "<u>a</u> luxury." (These two words are count nouns, not adjectives.) In paragraph 2 write "one day <u>a</u> week" (2*).

After World War II, housewife in small town had lot of mechanical help. Housewife always had gas or electric stove. She always had refrigerator, too. Very modern refrigerator sometimes had deep-freeze compartment. Automatic washing machine became almost necessity, but automatic clothes dryer remained luxury.

Housewife in such home did most of the work herself. Perhaps woman came in one day week to clean. Such woman was never called servant. She was not even called maid. Housewife simply said, "Mrs. X, who helps me one day week."

Family could live comfortably in old house in small American town.

## C 41 / A Certain Small Town

Directions: Insert *the,* underlined. In paragraph 1 write *"The* nearest city" (5*). In paragraph 2 use quotation marks only the first time you write "*the* Square," but use *the* every time, for it is part of the name. Write *"the* elm trees" (6*).

Here is a certain small town in Midwest as it was fifty years ago. Town had a population of 9,192. Town was not a suburb. Nearest city was forty miles away. Town was a county seat, governmental center of villages and farms surrounding it.

Center of town was a square unit called "Square." Square was large; elm trees were old and beautiful. In middle of Square was Courthouse. Dark stone Courthouse, built to last, sat firmly among beautiful old trees. Courthouse was center of life of county. County treasurer and county recorder had their offices there. County farm agent (there was only one) had his office on lowest floor of building. On rare occasion when a crime had been committed in county, trial was held in Courthouse.

## C 42 / Saturday Night in a Certain Small Town, Part I

Directions: Insert *the,* underlined. In paragraph 2, the apostrophe used in *week's work* is called "the possessive of measure" (7*).

Busiest night of week in small town we are speaking of was Saturday night. Most important stores of town, grouped on four sides of Courthouse Square, stayed open for benefit of farmers in surrounding countryside.

Farm family, week's work finished, drove into town in family car.

Dress department in largest department store was busy. All of tables were full in most popular ice-cream parlor. Rest of ice-cream parlors were almost as full. Moving picture theater (there was only one) was having biggest attendance of week.

## C 43 / Saturday Night in a Certain Small Town, Part II

Directions: Insert *the,* underlined. In paragraph 1 write "On the streets, the crowd . . ." (6*). Write "in the spring . . ." (8*). In paragraph 3 write "The mother (small *m*). "Mother" capitalized becomes a name for an individual.

On streets, crowd moved up and down. Tired housewives, through with shopping, exchanged news of week on small, hard, chairs set near entrance of chief ten-cent store. Motionless farmers stood on sidewalk and talked about weather and crops they had planted in spring. Talk was same as that of week before. It was same, too, as that of week to come.

By 10:30 each family had gathered at family car. Head of house drove. Smallest child sat between his father and mother. Rest of children sat in back of car. By 11:00 o'clock car turned into family driveway. Car was put into garage.

Everyone went into house. Someone put on lights. Some of children went into kitchen and to refrigerator. Everyone said "Good night." Mother put littlest child to bed.

## C 44 / Women's Clubs

Directions: Insert *a, an, the,* underlined. In paragraph 2 write "one of the . . ." In paragraph 3 write "the Parent-Teacher Association" and "the PTA" (9*).

Most persons living in small towns in Midwest belong to variety of organizations even today. Some persons belong to half dozen organizations of various types. Almost everyone belongs to one of numerous churches and to one of organizations within that church. Women, in particular, belong to number of other organizations called "clubs."

More than dozen card clubs for women meet in afternoon in town of ten or eleven thousand. Woman who belongs to one of card clubs may belong to one of garden clubs, too. Some women who belong to card club and garden club may belong to one of book clubs and one of music clubs, besides.

In addition, mothers with children in school belong to Parent-Teachers Association (there is only one). PTA is one of most faithfully attended clubs in town. It meets once month. There is program. Later there is coffee hour. During coffee hour, mother meets and comes to know teachers of her child.

## C 45 / Men's Clubs

Directions: Insert *a, an, the,* underlined. In paragraph 2 write "<u>a</u> secret social and benevolent organization." (An article is retained before adjectives.) Write either one or three *the*'s with the series, "Masons, Odd Fellows, or Elks" (3*).

Men have fewer hours to give to time-consuming activities of clubs than women have, but most men in small town belong to club or two.

One of clubs is likely to be secret social and benevolent organization, such as Masons, Odd Fellows, or Elks. (George Washington and Benjamin Franklin were two early Masons in America.)

Businessman is likely to belong, also, to either Kiwanis[1] Club or Lions. Such businessmen's organizations may meet as often as once week in one of private dining rooms of town's leading hotel for lunch. They have good lunch, hear good program, and continue their fund-raising program for worthy organization, such as local hospital (there is only one).

## C 46 / The 4-H Clubs

Directions: Insert *a, an, the,* underlined. In paragraph 1 copy the motto of the 4-H club just as it stands. Do not add *the*'s. In paragraph 2 write "<u>the</u> county fair." (A county has only one fair a year.) In paragraph 3 use *a/an* in naming the four different types of meals.

Some of most interesting clubs in Midwest are not in towns but in country. These are 4-H Clubs, developed by farm agent in each county for pleasure and profit of farm boys and girls. (Four H's of title stand for motto, "Head, Heart, Hands, and Health.")

Here is one of 4-H Club projects for ten-year old boy. Select pig two months old. Weigh pig. Record weight. Feed and care for pig twice day. When pig is fat and almost proper weight to sell, exhibit pig at country fair. With luck, receive first prize, blue ribbon given for best young pig.

---

[1] *Kiwanis* is a coined name, meaning "to trade."

Here is one of projects for sixteen-year old girl. Cook oven meal, broiler meal, stew-pot meal, and skillet meal. Set table attractively. Receive compliments of family. Wash dishes and clean up kitchen each time. Keep recipe file[1] of all dishes cooked.

## FREE WRITING

### C 47 / A Certain Small Town in (name of country)

Directions: Write about a certain small town in your own past. Did you live there? Did your grandparents live there? Did you go there on long-ago vacations? What stands out in your mind when you think of this small town now?

First, try writing down whatever comes into your mind. Then see what main points you have or wish to develop. Turn in a brief outline with your composition.

## Less Frequent Uses of the Articles

1. A follows **such** in reference to something just mentioned:

   such a home
   such a small town
   such an opportunity

2. A is used with units of measure:

   one day a week
   ninety miles an hour

   half a dozen, a half dozen (either way)
   a dozen eggs

3. Native speakers and other advanced users of the articles do not always insert an article every time it is grammatically possible. "A plate, a glass, and a napkin" indicates a group of three objects with great precision, but "a plate, glass, and napkin" also indicates three objects of the same type and also is grammatical. However, if a contrast is intended, the article is repeated:

   A boy and a girl may not see a social problem from the same angle.

4. Use no article when **breakfast, lunch,** and **dinner** refer to the three meals eaten every day. However, use an article to point out a special meal:

[1] recipe file: a cook's box of directions for preparing dishes she has made or may make.

I had **an** excellent lunch yesterday.
**The** lunch I had this noon was a sandwich and a cup of coffee.

5. **The** is used in forming the superlative degree:

    **the hardest** test of the term
    **the worst** hurricane ever to strike the east coast
    **the most** important news of the week

6. **The** is often used when a specimen, although mentioned for the first time, is closely related to another specimen introduced earlier:

    Here is a certain small town. **The** streets . . .

7. An article is used with the possessive of measure:

    **an** hour's steady effort
    **a dollar's** worth
    **the year's** record
    **the month's** bills

8. **The** is used with the four seasons when a time phrase indicates a particular span of time:

    in **the** spring
    during **the** summer
    throughout **the** fall (autumn)
    for **the** winter

    **The** is not required when the names of the seasons take the place of a proper noun:

    My favorite season is **spring,** but I like **fall,** too.

    The names of the seasons are not capitalized in present-day English.

9. **The** (not capitalized if often used before the names of organizations):

    the PTA      the Masons      the Kiwanis Club

    **The** is part of the name of a university when **of** is included:

    **the** University **of** Texas at El Paso
    **but:** Princeton University

10. **The** may or may not be used with names of countries and geographical units:

    Countries:
    **the** Netherlands       England
    **the** Soviet Union      Thailand
    **the** United States     Australia

Oceans:
**the** Pacific Ocean      **the** Atlantic Ocean       **the** Indian Ocean

Rivers:
**the** Nile    **the** Rhine     **the** Hudson     **the** Danube

Lakes:
Lake Superior     Lake Placid     Great Salt Lake

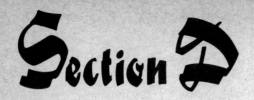

# Section D

---

## Adverbials
## The Progressive Past Tense

### ADVERBIALS

#### Grammar: the nature of adverbial clauses and phrases

Adverbial clauses and phrases[1] tell *when* something happened, *why* it happened, or *in spite of what* it happened:

**After the concert,** the audience rose to its feet.
(The adverbial phrase tells **when**.)

The audience rose **because it wished to honor the singer.**
(The adverbial clause tells **why**.)

The audience was delighted, **even though the singer was new to the city.)**
(The adverbial clause is saying "in spite of.")

#### Grammar: the subordinators <u>before</u>, <u>until</u>, and <u>after</u>

before: earlier than
  The alarm clock rang **before** Lee woke.

until: up to the time when
  It rang **until** Lee woke.

---

[1] A clause contains a subject and a verb; a phrase does not.

after: later than
It ceased **after Lee woke.**

| Main Clause | Adverbial Clause |
|---|---|
| (independent) | (dependent) |
| The alarm clock rang | **before Lee woke.** |
| It rang | **until Lee woke.** |
| It ceased | **after Lee woke.** |

Without a subordinator, an adverbial clause would be a sentence. (Lee woke.) With a subordinator, such as *before, until, after,* the clause becomes firmly attached to the main clause and dependent on it.

Very often, particularly in conversation, time is indicated by a phrase rather than a clause:

| | Adverbial Phrase |
|---|---|
| The alarm clock rang | **before 7:00.** |
| It rang | **until 7:00.** |
| It ceased | **after 7:00.** |

**Oral Practice**

Directions: When you are given a sentence beginning with *before, until,* or *after,* put the adverbial which follows *after* the main clause. (Time clauses are placed before and after the main clause with equal frequency.)

Examples:

Before he took off his coat, Lee turned on the news.

Lee turned on the news **before he took off his coat.**

Until the broadcast ended, Lee listened intently.

Lee listened intently **until the broadcast ended.**

1. Before he left for lunch, Peter decided to try a new place.
2. After he saw the menu, he was sorry.
3. Before he finally ordered, he read the whole menu.

 4. After he ordered, he was sorry.
 5. Until his sandwich came, he drank hot coffee.
 6. Until he finished the tasteless sandwich, he was unhappy.
 7. After the sandwich, he refused dessert.
 8. Until late afternoon, he grumbled about the new place.
 9. After he left the office, he decided to try another new place.
10. After an excellent dinner, he forgot about the lunch.


## D 1 / Women Drivers

Directions: Copy the two following paragraphs, putting *before, until,* or *after,* underlined, into the blanks. (Use either *before* or *until* in the first sentence.)

_____ Lee came to the United States, he had seldom seen women driving cars. _____ he came to the United States, he saw innumerable women driving. He was fearful for his own safety and that of the general public _____ he had observed women driving for three or four weeks.

He noted that women fastened their seat belts immediately _____ entering a car. He noted that a woman looked over her shoulder more than once _____ backing out of a parking space. He noted with approved that women waited at an intersection _____ they clearly had the right of way. _____ observing women drivers at length, Lee became their champion.


## Grammar: <u>although</u>

*Although* means in spite of the fact that, not withstanding that. *Although* introduces an element of surprise into the main clause:

|  | The Surprise (main clause) |
|---|---|
| Although we started early, | we arrived late. |
| Although we had a map, | we got lost. |
| Although Betty stirred the soup, | it burned. |

The main clause can be placed first in the sentence, reserving the element of surprise for the end of the sentence:

We arrived late, **although we started early.**

Whether it is first or last in the sentence, the *although*-clause is in opposition to the main clause.

### Oral Practice

Directions: Listen to the two statements given you. Make one statement beginning with *although.*

Example:

It was snowing. The stranger wore no coat.

**Although** it was snowing the stranger wore no coat.

1. It was in bad shape. Pete repaired the car.
2. There were several applicants. Pete got the job.
3. It is dirty work. Pete likes repairing cars.
4. It is clean work. Pete does not like writing compositions.
5. She does not play cards well. Mrs. Smith often wins.
6. He plays cards very well. Mr. Smith often holds poor cards.
7. Her parents play cards every week. Betty does not know one card from another.
8. Jacques and Hans are roommates. They do not like each other.
9. They argue a lot. They do not listen to each other.
10. They consider separating. They stay together.
11. The politician made promises. He lost the election.
12. They said little. The voters were thinking.

## Grammar: <u>although</u> in contrast with <u>because</u>

because: due to the fact that
  **Because** it was the end of the month, Mr. Smith had to finish a certain report before he went home.
although: in spite of the fact that, notwithstanding that
  **Although** he was tired, Mr. Smith worked on.

### Oral Practice

Directions: Listen to the two statements given you. Make one statement, using *because* or *although.*

1. I must find out my bank balance. I need to write a check.
2. I can still write a check. My bank balance is low.

3. Betty can fry eggs. She doesn't know much about cooking.
4. The clock stopped. I didn't wind it.
5. The apartment is comfortable now. The superintendent turned on the heat.
6. People are wearing winter coats. It is spring by the calendar.
7. I seldom read for pleasure. I don't have time to.
8. I looked up the word. I was unsure of the spelling.
9. I looked up the word. I was almost sure of the spelling.
10. I always do the free writing. It isn't easy.
11. I like my major. It deals with my greatest interest.
12. I like my major. The work is difficult.

## Grammar: even though

*Even though* is slightly more emphatic than *although* and *though*. The general meaning of the three terms, however, is the same.

### Oral Practice

Directions: Listen to the two statements given you. Make them into one statement using *even though*.

Example:

Pete went without a tie. The occasion was formal.

Pete went without a tie, **even though** the occasion was formal.

1. I passed the test. I did not study.
2. Someone opened the classroom windows wide. It was cold outside.
3. Five thousand persons entered the contest. Only one could win.
4. I forgot to take my package. I had paid cash.
5. I forgot my appointment with the dentist. I needed to see him.
6. Betty ate a big piece of chocolate cake. It was fattening.
7. She enjoyed it. It was fattening.
8. Pete watched a horror film to the end. He disliked it.

### D 2 / Sung Hee and Required English

Directions: Copy the two following paragraphs, putting *although*, *even though*, *though*, or *because*, underlined, into each blank.

_____ Sung Hee was from a conservative Eastern country,

she was a modern young woman. She came to the United States _____ she wanted to study Western art. Within three days she was furious _____ her department ordered her to take ten weeks' work in English before she took any work in art. _____ she remained angry, she did not study well. _____ she did not study well, she failed.

The second term, _____ Sung Hee still thought her department unjust, she got down to work. Almost at once she began to improve _____ she was an intelligent young woman.

_____ she never came to enjoy writing English, at the end of the term, Sung Hee, her adviser, and her composition teacher were happy _____ she passed.

## D 3 / Lee Chen and Required English

Directions: Copy the two following paragraphs, putting *although, even though, though,* or *because* into each blank.

_____ Lee Chen's main interest in civil engineering, his department made him begin with a course in composition. Lee was far from pleased _____ he wanted to spend all his time in his major field.

However, _____ Lee does all school work well, he soon began to work on this course. _____ he found English spelling unreasonable, he wasted no energy on complaints. Instead, _____ some spelling rules work, he made use of them. Moreover, _____ his teacher was pleased with his well-planned papers, he worked with confidence. _____ Lee sometimes thought he would never learn to write standard English, he did.

## Punctuation: adverbial clauses

An introductory adverbial clause is regularly followed by a comma:

When the car hit a lamppost, the lamppost toppled over.

No comma is normally required when the adverbial clause follows the main clause:[1]

The lamppost toppled over when the car hit it.

---

[1] However, see footnote, p. 176.

An adverbial clause can be placed within a sentence, just before the verb:

The lamppost, **when the car hit it,** toppled over.

### Dictation: The Beach Party

Directions: When the following paragraph of dictation is read for the fourth time, place a comma after each introductory adverbial clause.

Example:

When some one suggested a day at the beach, everyone was in favor of the idea.

Before we reached the beach, we were far too hot. When we reached the beach, we rushed into the water. After we swam around a little while, we felt fine. The boys stayed in the water until the girls finished unpacking the lunch. Then, before the girls could call them, the boys came out of the water with a rush.

### D 4 / On a Cold Morning

Directions: First orally and then possibly in writing, put *although* or *until* into each of the following blanks.

Use either *although* or *until* in the second sentence. Discuss in class which subordinator implies that Lee did not yet know about the painful condition called "frostbite."

_____ it was only fourteen degrees above zero that January morning, Lee wore no cap. He kept insisting to himself that he did not really feel the cold _____ his ears began to grow numb.[1] Then, _____ he was close to the university campus, he could not wait until he reached it. He stepped inside a drugstore, _____ he had no purchase to make, and waited _____ his ears began to grow warm again. _____ this experience taught Lee something about winter in the United States, he thinks he will wait _____ it is a little colder before he buys a woolen cap.

### Grammar: additional subordinators

These subordinators are introduced in the oral practice following:

---

[1] *numb*: deprived of feeling.

**as soon as:** the moment after

**by the time that:** at the end of the time named

**whenever:** every time that

Two more subordinators are introduced in the next dictation:

**just as:** at the same moment that

**ever since:**[1] from the time named to the present

## Oral Practice

Directions: Listen to the two statements given you. Join the first statement to the second with *as soon as.*

Example:

Max and his uncle got off the bus. They saw the ball park.

Max and his uncle got off the bus **as soon as** they saw the ball park.

1. Max and his uncle entered the ball park. The gates were open.
2. They went to their seats. They located an usher.
3. Uncle Sol bought two bags of popcorn. He saw a vendor.[2]
4. Uncle Sol bought two hot dogs. He and Max finished the popcorn.

Directions: Join the two sentences given you. Begin with *by the time.*

5. They finished the hot dogs. They were not very hungry.
6. They finished some ice cream cones. They were not hungry at all.
7. The seventh inning was over. They were glad to stretch their muscles.

Directions: Join the first statement to the second with *whenever.*

8. Both men groaned. The other side made a home run.
9. Both men cheered. Their side made a home run.
10. Now, Max talks like an experienced baseball fan. Someone mentions the game.

## Dictation: My Uncle Met Me

Directions: When the paragraph is read for the fourth time, make sure you have placed a comma after each introductory adverbial clause.

---

[1] *Since,* which answers both *when* and *why,* will be discussed in Section E.

[2] *vendor:* a seller, a peddlar.

As soon as I came off the plane, I saw my uncle. Just as I saw my uncle, he saw me. By the time we got my bags out of customs, I was hungry. Ever since my uncle introduced me to broiled steak[1] and hot apple pie, I try new American dishes with confidence. Whenever I recall my first day in this country, I remember my uncle's kindness.

### D 5 / Crossing a Busy Street

Directions: Put the list of additional subordinators (p. 136) into the blanks in the following paragraph. Use each subordinator, underlined, once and one of the subordinators twice. (It is helpful to check each subordinator off the list as you use it.)

_____ I try to cross (name a street with heavy traffic), I have trouble. Yesterday, _____ I stepped off the sidewalk, the traffic policeman stopped me by blowing his whistle. I went back to the edge of the street and waited. _____ the officer lifted his hand, I started across again. _____ I reached the middle of the street, the light turned yellow. _____ I reached the opposite sidewalk in safety, I was almost tired. However, _____ I was almost hit by a car, I cross all streets carefully.

## Grammar: the subordinator <u>as</u>

The subordinator *as* can be used in place of a number of other subordinators:

**because**
   The meeting adjourned **as** there was no further business.
   The government fell **as** it was not able to lower taxes.

**while**
   **As** the Guard was changing at Buckingham Palace, the crowd outside the iron fence watched every move.

**in comparisons**
   Lee is **as** tall as Lou. (See **Comparisons**, Section L.)

**in expressions of time**
   Come **as** soon as you can. Stay **as** long as you can. Come **as** often as you can.

---

[1] *broiled steak:* tender steak cooked over a very hot fire.

in often-used similes:[1]
   **as** good **as** gold      **as** hard **as** nails      **as** easy **as** rolling off a log
   **as** simple **as** ABC


## THE PROGRESSIVE PAST TENSE

### Grammar: the progressive past tense introduced

In the most frequent use of the progressive past tense, one action is going on in the background (progressive past) at the same time a second action, on which attention is focused, is going on in the foreground (simple past).

| Foreground Action | Background Action |
|---|---|
| The dancers stood frozen | while the clock was striking. |
| Mrs. Smith read a detective story | while the cake was baking. |

### Grammar: <u>while</u> with the progressive past tense

Native speakers do not always follow the custom, but it is helpful to use *while* consistently with the progressive past tense and *when* with the simple past.

**while:** during the time that (an expanse of time)
**when:** at the time that (a point of time)

#### Oral Practice

Direcions: Listen to the two statements given you. Use *while* with the second statement if the verb is in the progressive past tense. Otherwise, use *when.*

Examples:

The doorbell rang. I was talking on the phone.
The doorbell rang **while I was talking** on the phone.

I was talking on the phone. The doorbell rang.
I was talking on the phone **when the doorbell rang.**

---

[1] *simile:* a statement that one thing is like another.

1. We listened intently. The President was speaking.
2. We turned the TV off. The President finished.
3. We discussed the message. We were having refreshments.
4. A heated debate developed. We were arguing about the President's third point.
5. The students waited in the lounge. The desk clerk was sorting the mail.
6. Each student looked first for personal letters. He got his mail.
7. No one spoke. He was reading his personal letters.
8. The photographer wanted a picture. He saw a band of wild horses.
9. He crept close. The horses were resting.
10. He got his picture. The horses were fleeing.

## Dictation: A Secretary's Morning

Directions: As you take the dictation, note the use of *when* and *while*.

When Anne came into the office this morning a big pile of mail was waiting on her desk. While she was opening the letters, the office boy arrived with more mail. When Dr. Jansen came in, everything was in orderly piles. While Dr. Jansen was reading the most important letters, Anne did some filing. When Dr. Jansen was ready, Anne began to take dictation.

## D 6 / Getting Breakfast

Directions: Copy the following paragraph, putting the simple past or the progressive past, underlined, of the verbs in parentheses into the blanks.

When Mrs. Smith (go) _____ into the kitchen yesterday morning, the first thing she did was to put the coffeepot on the stove. While the coffee gradually (come) _____ to a boil, she put two eggs into a pan of cold water over low heat. While the water around the eggs (heat) _____, she dropped two slices of bread into the toaster. While the coffee (boil) _____, the eggs (come) _____ to a boil, and the bread (toast) _____, Mrs. Smith (pour) _____ out two glasses of frozen orange juice. Breakfast (be) _____ ready in seven minutes, as usual.

## D 7 / A Chance Meeting

Directions: Copy the following paragraph, putting *while* or *when*, underlined, into each blank.

_____ I saw Kemal, my good friend from Turkey, coming down the street, I was pleased. _____ we reached each other, we stopped to talk. Traffic rushed by us _____ we were talking. We even exchanged news _____ a fire engine was sounding its siren. _____ we were talking, Kemel felt in his pockets. _____ he found what he wanted, he pulled it out. _____ he gave it to me, I saw that it was a pack of his best Turkish cigarettes.

## FREE WRITING

### D 8 / A Long Day's Shopping

Directions: Write about the long, determined search you once made to find precisely the article you wished. Be sure to mention place and time within the first paragraph.

## Grammar: additional uses of the progressive past tense

It is possible to use the progressive past tense effectively in a succession of sentences, if you start from the simple past and return to the simple past:

Anne and Haruko **paused** on a low stone bridge and **considered** the Sunday afternoon scene in the park. Two sailors were rowing a flat-bottomed boat on the miniature lake. Two small boys were scrambling grimly up a rough gray rock. On the top of the rock, a young man was getting ready to take a snapshot of a smiling girl. "Where," Haruko **asked** Anne, "are the restless Americans?"

It is possible, but not usual, to use the progressive past for both actions in a sentence:

While Mrs. Smith **was making** the salads,
Betty **was setting** the table.

While the guests **were enjoying** the main course,
Mrs. Smith **was worrying** about the dessert.

The progressive past tense is used less extensively in English than in some other languages. In English, past action in progress is likely to be indicated, not by the verb form, but by an adverbial phrase which suggests extended time. Extended time is the opposite of "at this moment." In such cases, the verb is in the simple past tense:

| *Simple Past* | *Extended Time* |
|---|---|
| I **did** not **sleep** | the whole night. |
| Lee **practiced** ping-pong | all summer long. |
| The bus **appeared** regularly | every hour on the hour. |

## D 9 / One Morning at School

Directions: Copy the topic sentence and complete the two paragraphs of partial statements.

The teacher was very late one morning in a long-ago classroom of mine. When he/she finally came into the room, one of the boys. . . . A second boy. . . . A third. . . . A pair of boys. . . .

As for the girls, one of them. . . . Another. . . . A third. . . . The rest. . . .

*Free writing:* Add a third paragraph, telling what the teacher did first, next, and next. (The teacher's actions will be in the simple past tense.)

## Grammar: extended-time phrases

The following are examples of adverbial phrases which suggest that action in the past went on for some time:

| | |
|---|---|
| for two minutes | during the big sale in the College Shop |
| long after midnight | for half an hour |
| in the fourth grade | from 9:00 to 12:00 Saturday |
| all weekend | between classes |
| for seven years | during spring vacation |

## Oral Practice

Directions: Complete the partial statement given you with an extended time phrase—one of your own or one from the list above.

Example:

Instructor:    practiced in the speech lab
Student A:    I practiced in the speech lab **for a full hour.**
Student B:    Fine. I only had time **for twenty minutes.**

1. talked with my adviser
2. talked with friends in the hall
3. took mid-term exams
4. studied English in my own country
5. bought a sweater
6. had guests
7. learned the multiplication tables
8. visited Niagara Falls
9. laughed at an American joke
10. left the party

## D 10 / Using Extended-Time Phrases in Writing

Directions: Make statements in writing based on the oral practice just completed. Use all ten of the extended-time phrases listed on p. 142. (It is helpful to check each phrase off the list as you see it.)

1. How long did you talk with your adviser?
2. When did you talk with your friends in the hall?
3. When did you take mid-term examinations?
4. When did you learn the multiplication tables?
5. How long did you study English in your own country?
6. When did you get your new sweater?
7. How long did you have guests?
8. When did you visit Niagara Falls?
9. How long did you laugh at the American joke?
10. When did you leave the party?

## FREE WRITING

## D 11 / A Successful Party

Directions: Tell what everyone was doing at the moment when you arrived at a party. Begin, "The party was in full swing when I arrived." Proceed to tell what individuals and small groups were doing to amuse themselves, including the host and hostess (progressive past tense). Then tell how you and your particular friends amused yourselves (simple past tense). Close, "Decidedly, it was a successful party."

Before you make your final copy, consider what you want to do about paragraphing.

**Listen and Write: The New Textbook**

Directions: Before hearing Part I twice, be sure you know the meaning of *contents*[1] and *index*[2] as they apply to books. Then write down the first sentence and prepare to listen.

Part I

   After dinner, Lee settled down in his easy chair to become acquainted with his new textbook. Before he did anything else, he turned to the Contents in the front of the book. He read the titles of chapters until he knew a little about the book. Then he turned to the back of the book. It had an index. Lee was pleased.

Part II

   After looking over the book briefly, Lee began to read the assignment, Chapter 1. As he read, he marked the main ideas. After he finished, he went back and reread the marked parts until the main ideas of the chapter were clear. The next day, when Dr. Simpson gave his lecture, Lee understood him very well.

**Dictation: The First Registration**

Directions (instructor to class): "This is a new kind of dictation. I will read a *partial* statement twice. You will write it down and then complete it with words of your own. Let's do the first sentence together now."

1. Lee Chen decided to come to the United States because . . .[3]
2. He decided to share an apartment rather than live alone because . . .
3. When it was time to register for courses at the university, . . .
4. When Lee found he could see a foreign student adviser, . . .
5. Before he talked with his adviser, . . .
6. However, after he talked with his adviser, . . .
7. After Lee wrote the same information on numerous cards, . . .
8. After he paid his bill, . . .
9. Whenever Lee remembers his first registration in this country, . . .

---

[1] *contents*: the listing of ideas or chapter titles in the front of a book.
[2] *index*: the detailed alphabetical listing of separate items in the back of a book.
[3] *To the instructor*: Have a few students read their first statements aloud to the class. When all nine statements are complete, ask for volunteers to read their statements aloud.

**Grammar: adverbs of manner**

Adverbs of manner answer the question *how*: How did the witness answer?

boldly

nervously

willingly

Most frequently adverbs of manner are formed by adding *ly* to an adjective, as in the three adverbs above.
Occasionally adverbs of manner do not end in *ly*:

Go **slow.** (a direction to motorists)

He walked **fast.**

She worked **hard.**

She worked **well.**

Occasionally adjectives end in *ly*:

a **friendly** greeting          a **manly** attitude

**brotherly** advice              **womanly** patience

**fatherly** comfort             **lovely** roses

**Oral Practice: Forming *ly*-adverbs**

Directions: Change the sentence you are given so that the adjective becomes an *ly*-adverb of manner.

Examples:

Instructor:  Tigers are fierce fighters.
Student:     Tigers fight **fiercely.**

Instructor:  Anne is an accurate typist.
Student:     Anne types **accurately.**

1. Anne is a careful typist.
2. Also, she is a rapid typist.
3. Dr. Simpson is a successful teacher.
4. In addition, he is a fair grader.
5. Mr. Smith is an enthusiastic gardener.
6. Mrs. Smith is an enthusiastic cook.
7. Betty is an enthusiastic basketball player.
8. Lisa is a professional dancer.

9. The senator is a brilliant speaker.
10. Jack Holmes is a skillful broadcaster.

## D 12 / Planning a Community Project

Directions: Copy the following paragraph, putting this list of adverbs of manner into the blanks. Use each adverb once.

| | | |
|---|---|---|
| actively | eventually | promptly |
| attentively | inconclusively[1] | thoughtfully |
| clearly | obviously | vigorously |

    Dr. and Mrs. Simpson recently invited a few neighbors to spend the evening in their home to consider the problem of (name a current problem) in their community. Everyone arrived _____. The leader set forth the facts of the situation _____. Everyone listened _____. Then the problem was discussed _____. _____ one definite action was open to everyone present. _____ a committee was formed to (name one definite action). Usually such meetings end _____. This one ended with the group planning to work _____.

## FREE WRITING

## D 13 / A Pressing Problem

Directions: Write on some pressing problem, either in American society or in your own society.

    Because your subject is complex, simplify what you attempt by making your first paragraph your topic sentence. Then use the following or similar statements to introduce your subtopics:

Conditions are serious.

Solutions so far are unsatisfactory.

A radical but practical possibility is to . . .

It will be difficult to put this approach into effect, since . . .

However, it is my belief that . . .

## D 14 / Danger

Directions: Modify the following outline to fit your circumstances and hand it in with your composition. (Change *your* to *my* and *you* to I.)

---

[1] *inconclusively*: not settling anything.

I. Introductory facts
  A. Where
  B. When
  C. What you were doing
II. The danger
  A. Its sudden appearance
  B. Your reaction
  C. Your successful escape
III. Afterward
  A. How you felt
  B. What you learned

## D 15 / No Danger

Directions: Tell of a time when you thought you were in danger but proved to be in no danger at all. Modify the following outline to fit your circumstances and hand it in with your composition. (Change *your* to *my* and *you* to *I*.)

I. Introductory facts
  A. Place
  B. Time
  C. What you were doing
II. The apparent[1] danger
  A. The circumstances
  B. Your reactions
  C. The solution
III. Afterward
  A. How you felt
  B. How any witnesses to your fears reacted
  C. Why this "danger" cannot disturb you now

[1] *apparent*: seemingly real but not real.

# Section E

---

## The Present Perfect Tense
## but and however
## Spelling: Rule 1

**Grammar: the difference between the past tense and the present perfect tense**

| *Past Tense* | *Present Perfect Tense* |
|---|---|
| The past tense presents a specific action:<br>I bought another ballpoint pen yesterday. | The present perfect summarizes experience:<br>I have come to like this type of pen. |
| The past tense places an action definitely in the past:<br>I came to the United States on June 9. (This action is finished.) | The present perfect began in the past, generally comes up to the present, and often implies connection with the future:<br>I have been in this country since June 9. (I am still here.)<br>I have seen Rockefeller Center. (This experience is now part of my background.) |
| The past tense uses an endless variety of time signals:<br>last year<br>in the Middle Ages<br>five minutes ago | The present perfect uses a small, well-defined set of time signals:<br>**for/since**<br>**already/yet,** etc.<br>**again and again,** etc.<br>adverbs of frequency |

| Time is definitely stated, if not in the sentence under consideration, then in a sentence nearby. | Time need not be stated: I have finished my work. I have seen that play. Juan has traveled in Portugal. |

## Grammar: the present perfect tense in questions

The present perfect tense is much used in asking questions:

How long **have** you **been** in this country?
**Have** you **done** your homework?
**Has**[1] Marie **come** in yet?

However, the past tense, rather than the present perfect, is often used in conversation in discussing an agreed-upon event, such as a vacation:

**Did** you **see** Niagara Falls on your trip?
**Did** you **get** down to Washington, D.C.?

## Oral Practice I: using the past tense first and then the present perfect

Directions: Answer the first question in the past tense. Answer the second in the present perfect.

Example:

Instructor:  What sort of coat did you bring with you to this country?
Student:  I **brought** a light woolen coat.

Instructor:  What sort of coat have you bought since?
Student:  I've (have) **bought** a heavy woolen coat, a regular winter coat. (Or "I **haven't bought** a coat since I came to this country.")

1. Your room contained the bare essentials of living when you took it. What **were** they?
   What **have** you **done** to make your room more comfortable?
2. **Did** your room **express** your individual taste when you took it?
   What **have** you **added** to express your own taste?
3. **Did** all American food **taste** strange at first?
   What **have** you **grown** accustomed to? What **have** you **grown** to like?
4. **Did** you **come** from a more formal culture than the American?

[1] *Has* is the form of *have* used after third person singular subjects.

What forms of American informality **have** you **accepted** easily? What **have** you not **accepted** yet?

5. What **was** your favorite type of recreation at home?
**Have** you **found** an equally satisfactory type of recreation here?

**Oral Practice II: using the present perfect
first and then the past**

Directions: Ask a fellow student what countries he has lived in. Other members of the class will then call out questions about these countries.

Example:

Student A:   What countries have you lived in, Mr. B?
Student B:   I have lived in Austria, Roumania, and the United States.
Student C:   Where did you live in Roumania?
Student D:   Did you go hunting there?
Student E:   What did you generally shoot?
Student F:   Did you ever go through the wine cellars in Oradea? I have been there myself.

**Oral Practice III: "No, but . . ." with the present perfect**

Directions: When you or your instructor asks one of the questions below, a student will respond in the following pattern:

Example:

Student A:   Have you been in Ireland?
Student B:   **No, but** I have (I've) been in Wales.

1. Have you been in Egypt?
2. Have you been in Ghana?
3. Have you been in Greenland?
4. Have you been in India?
5. Have you been in Cuba?
6. Have you seen the St. Lawrence River?[1]
7. Have you seen the Gulf of Mexico?
8. Have you seen the Great Salt Lake?[2]

[1] *The St. Lawrence River:* An important Canadian river, which briefly divides New York state from Canada.
[2] *Great Salt Lake:* A lake in the state of Utah. No one sinks in this lake. See footnote, p. 162.

## E 1 / The Lunch-Counter Habit[1]

Directions: As you write this exercise, note that the statements in the past tense give a single fact, while the statements in the present perfect summarize experience.

Example:

| | |
|---|---|
| Single fact: | I ate at a table in Korea. (past tense) |
| Summarized experience: | I have now drunk many cups of coffee . . . (present perfect tense) |

**You may find some negatives useful:**

I have not learned to eat in a hurry.

Did you eat at a table, or did you eat at a lunch counter in (name of country)? Have you acquired the lunch-counter habit since coming to this country?

Have you now drunk many cups of coffee while sitting on a high stool? Did you climb onto a stool and have a cup of coffee yesterday? Have you learned to pile catsup, chopped pickle, and raw onion on the same hamburger? What did you put on a hamburger yesterday? Have you learned to like french-fried potatoes? Did you have an order of french fries with your hamburger yesterday?

Have you fallen into the bad habit of eating in a hurry? Did you eat in a hurry yesterday?

## E 2 / A Variety of Experiences

Directions: Copy the topic sentence. Then complete the partial statements.

I have had a variety of experiences in my past. I have missed an important plane connection in _____. I have eaten huge and excellent sandwiches in _____. I have endured a talkative guide in/on _____. I have been cheated in _____. I have been treated with the greatest courtesy in _____. I have spent a delightful day with perfect strangers in _____. All in all, I have had a wide variety of experiences in my comparatively brief life.

---

[1] When you eat in public on a high stool at a shelf narrower than a bar, you are eating at a lunch counter. Such eating is common in crowded cities at noon.

## FREE WRITING

### E 3 / (a topic of your own choice)

Directions: Use one of the statements you made in *E 2* as the topic sentence in a short composition. Make up your own title. The topic sentence, in the present perfect tense, will summarize one of your experiences. Follow this general statement with an example, a brief narrative in the past tense.

## TIME SIGNALS

### Grammar: time signals <u>for,</u> <u>since,</u> and <u>ever since</u>

for:  indicating extent in time, "as long as"
    **for** a week
    **for** nine days
    **for** a thousand years

since:  from the point of time named to the present
    **since** June
    **since** New Year's
    **since** the founding of the republic

    Note: Since in these examples is used as a preposition with a noun or a noun phrase as its object. Since can also be used alone as an adverb of time: "I wrote my first composition in a great hurry. I have taken more time **since**."

ever since:  since emphasized, the speaker implying that he regards the extent of time named as lengthy.
    **ever since** that experience
    **ever since** I found out

### Oral Practice I

Directions: When a student is asked a question, he will respond with a statement using *for.* A second student will then give the same information using *since* or *ever since.*

Example:

Instructor:    Aki, how long have you been in this country?
Aki:           I've been in this country for **two** months.

Instructor:    Mohammed, how long has Aki been in this country?
Mohammed:   He's been here **since June.**

1. How long have you been in this university?
2. How long have you lived at your present address?
3. How long have you been attending classes today?
4. How long have you been in this class today?
5. How long have you studied English seriously?

**Oral Practice II**

Directions: Form one sentence in the present perfect tense from the following pairs of sentences, using *for* or *since*.

Examples:

Hing owns a color camera.[1] He bought it in April.
Hing has owned a color camera **since** April.

Mark belongs to a judo class. He joined it last week.
Mark has belonged to a judo class **for** a week.

1. Betty knows Hamlet's "To be or not to be." She memorized it last week.
2. Mrs. Smith knows the new neighbors. She called on them a week ago.
3. We know our mid-term grades. We learned them on Tuesday.
4. Mr. Brown is a candidate for mayor. He announced his candidacy the first of July.
5. Pete has a new car. He bought it a week ago.
6. Haruko has a scholarship. She received it in May.
7. Gene is with his brother in Princeton. He went there several days ago.
8. George goes to a Sunday evening discussion group. He joined it in March.
9. It is surprisingly cold. The temperature dropped yesterday afternoon.
10. I know dormitory life. I move into a dorm in January.

**E 4 / Using *For*, *Since*, and *Ever Since* in Writing**

Directions: First orally and then in writing, state the information given in the sentences below through the present perfect tense. Underline, *for, since,* and *ever since* when writing.

[1] *a color camera:* A camera which takes pictures in color.

Examples:

Bill read *The New York Times* in 1965, and he reads it now.
Bill has read *The New York Times* **since** 1965. In fact, he has read it **ever since** he was a high school senior.

Anne began to do morning exercises three months ago, and she still does them.
Anne has done morning exercises **for** three months.

1. I liked hard candy when I was six, and I like it now.
2. I wanted to see Paris after I graduated from high school, and I want to see it now.
3. I wanted a larger apartment a year ago, and I want a larger apartment now.
4. I disliked practicing the piano when I was nine, and I dislike it now.
5. My brother owned a boat when he was in the fourth grade, and he owns one now.
6. I intended to read Galsworthy's *Forsyte Saga* five years ago, and I intend to read it now.
7. I began to like ballet ten years ago, and I like it now.
8. (your statement)
9. (your statement)
10. (your statement)

## Grammar: time signals <u>just</u>, <u>recently</u>, and <u>so far</u>

just: only a moment before (adverb of frequency position)
     I have **just** finished telephoning Marie.

recently: not long ago, but a little further back in time than **just** (much used at the end of sentences)
     The senator has been much in the news **recently**.
     It has been unusually rainy **recently**.

so far: up to the present moment (first or last in the sentence)
     **So far**, I have not had a reply to my request.
     The human race has survived, **so far**.

### Oral Practice

Directions: When you are given a statement, repeat it, putting *just* in the middle of the sentence.

Example:

Instructor:    The President has made an important announcement.
Student:      The President has **just** made an important announcement.

1. My favorite news analyst has commented on the President's announcement.
2. We have heard the news.
3. The plane has left.
4. I have finished my homework.
5. The store has closed.
6. I have paid my bills.
7. I have had a letter from my family.

**Directions: When you are given a sentence, repeat it and put re-
cently first, last, or in the middle of the sentence.**

Examples:

**Recently** Congress has been very busy.

Congress has **recently** been very busy.

Congress has been very busy **recently**. (most used position)

  8. I haven't read a novel.
  9. I haven't written my relatives.
10. I have read a lot about space exploration.
11. I haven't been to the movies.
12. The President has appeared on TV.

**Directions: When you are given a statement, repeat it, putting so far
either first or last in the sentence.**

Examples:

**So far,** I haven't had a cold this term.

I haven't had a cold this term, **so far.**

13. I have passed all my courses.
14. Life has treated me very well.
15. I haven't dropped my new watch.
16. I haven't left my briefcase on a bus.
17. I haven't lost any of my textbooks.
18. I haven't had a response to my application.
19. My last composition is my best writing in English.
20. The great powers have reached a very limited number of agreements.

*Summary of Positions*   *Just* is placed in the middle of the sentence; *so far* is placed first or last in the sentence; *recently* is placed first, last, or in the middle of the sentence.

## E 5 / Using *Just, Recently,* and *So Far* in Writing

Directions: Copy the following paragraph, filling each blank with one of the three time signals in the title, underlined.

_____ I have not had to write a term paper in English. However, my instructor in United States history has _____ made such an assignment. I have thought about the matter for more than a week, but _____ I have not been able to decide on a topic. However, to give myself a sense of accomplishment, I have _____ bought a hundred index cards. This has been my only act toward writing the paper, _____.

## Grammar: already and not yet

already: before now (affirmative)
> **Already** may be used before the main verb, or, without change of meaning, at the end of the sentence.
>
> I have **already** visited Mexico City.
> I have visited Mexico City **already**.

not yet: not up to the present moment
> Ivan has not finished college **yet**.
> In formal writing, **yet** is often placed before the main verb:
> Ivan has not **yet** written his first book.

## Oral Practice

Directions: Listen to the question. Make a statement in the present perfect. Use *already* or *not yet*.

1. Have you graduated from high school?
2. Have you graduated from college in your own country?
3. Have you received the Master's degree in this country?
4. Have you read several books in English?
5. Have you read a thousand books in English?
6. Have you seen the President on TV?
7. Have you visited an American factory?
8. Have you visited an American farm?
9. Have you purchased the **Encyclopaedia Britannica**?

10. Have you bought an American alarm clock?
11. Have we done some work on the present perfect tense?
12. Have we finished working with this tense?
13. Have we had oral practice on the coordinator **but?**
14. Have we contrasted the perfect tense with the past tense?
15. Have we worked on the articles?
16. Have we learned everything about them?

## FREE WRITING

### E 6 / Using *Already* and *Not Yet* in Writing

Directions: Write two short paragraphs. In the first, mention memorable sights you have already seen. In the second, mention sights you have not seen yet but intend to. Say what impressed you, or what you expect will impress you.

Examples:

I have already seen the Empire State Building. It was amazing to see New York City spread out eighty-six stories below me.

I have not climbed the stairs inside the Statue of Liberty yet. When I do, I will see all the ships in New York Harbor coming and going far below me.

## Grammar: frequency expressed by an extended-time phrase

When a repeated action is expressed by an extended-time phrase rather than by an adverb alone, the phrase is placed at the end of the sentence. The following phrases are typical:

all my (your/his/her) life

a few times, several times, many times

more than once, once or twice

for a long time, for years

again and again, over and over

On rare occasions, the phrase is placed at the beginning of the sentence, with a change in basic word order:

| Verb Phrase | Verb | Subject |
|---|---|---|
| Again and again | came | a cry for help. |

**Oral Practice**

Directions: Listen to the statement, which will contain an extended-time phrase. Respond with a statement in the present perfect.

Example:

Instructor:　Jacques and Hans have had serious disagreements **several times**, yet they are still rooming together. Why, do you suppose?

Student A:　They have settled their differences.

Student B:　They have agreed to disagree.

Student C:　They haven't been able to find separate rooms.

Student D:　They haven't meant as much as they said.

1. Mr. Smith is forty and a quiet businessman. There is something he has wanted to do **all his life.** What do you suppose it is?
2. Mrs. Smith loves to dance. There is something she has wanted to do do **for years.** What do you suppose it is?
3. Mrs. Smith is her own cook. What tasks has she performed **over and over?**
4. Betty helps her mother faithfully, if not enthusiastically. What tasks has she performed **again and again?**
5. Betty loves the movies. What has she done **a few times,** even on school days?
6. No one likes to do his duty every single minute. What have you wanted to do, just **once or twice?**
7. Some persons have the same dream **many times.** Do you know of such a person? Do you know the dream?

## THE PRESENT PERFECT TENSE WITHOUT TIME SIGNALS

### Grammar

The present perfect tense can be used without a time signal of any kind:

I have read that book.

Lee has entered graduate school.

Spring has come.

### Oral Practice

Directions: When you are given a question, begin your response, "No, but . . ." Use the present perfect without a time signal.

Examples:

Instructor:   Have you been in Ireland?
Student A:   No, but I have been in Wales.

Instructor:   Have you seen the Alba Madonna in Washington, D.C.?
Student B:   No, but I have seen the Mona Lisa in the Louvre.

1. Have you seen Whistler's portrait of Madame X in New York?
2. Have you seen Rodin's great statue, "The Thinker," in Cleveland?
3. Have you been in the Fairmont Hotel in San Francisco?
4. Have you been in Sweden?
5. Have you been in Rome?
6. Have you floated on a canal in Venice?
7. Have you seen an American prizefight?
8. Have you seen the Irish marching on St. Patrick's Day?
9. Have you seen an elephant help build a house?

## E 7 / Varied Weather

Directions: Change the following paragraph of questions into statements without time signals.

Have you experienced varied types of weather in your travels?
Have you worn a woolen suit in comfort in England in August? Have
you added a sweater to the suit in Scotland? Have you disregarded
the misty rains on long walks in Ireland? Have you braced yourself
against the winds sweeping in from the North Sea in Denmark?
Have you moved slowly on hot afternoons in Rome in August? In
general, have you adjusted to these varieties of weather without
much difficulty?

## THE PRESENT PERFECT TENSE
## WITH ADVERBS OF FREQUENCY

### Grammar

Adverbs of frequency (Section A, p. 23) are often used with the
present perfect tense. You may want to put the following list on
the blackboard so that you can review these adverbs with your
books closed.
Before the main verb:

often, frequently     rarely, seldom     always     never

First in the sentence, last, or before the main verb:

sometimes    occasionally    generally    usually

## Oral Practice I

Directions: Answer the following questions with a statement containing an adverb of frequency.

1. How often has the weather been pleasant during the past thirty days? Always? Often? Rarely?
2. How often has it rained? Frequently? Seldom? Never?
3. How often has it snowed? Frequently? Occasionally? Never?
4. How often has the football team won this season? (Or the soccer, tennis, or track team?)
5. How often have you attended the home games?
6. In your own country, what was your favorite sport?
7. Did you frequently attend games there?
8. How often did you play on a team?
9. How often did you have a large crowd watching?
10. How often did your team win?

## Oral Practice II

1. Have you ever looked up a word in an English dictionary? Has Bill ever looked up a word in an English dictionary?
2. Have you ever located a strange city on a map? Has Bill ever used a road map?
3. Have you ever used the card catalog in the library? Has Bill ever used the encyclopedias?
4. Have you ever written a term paper in English? Has Marie ever written a term paper in French?
5. Have you ever begun a composition with a topic sentence? Has Marie ever forgotten to begin a composition with a topic sentence?
6. Have you ever forgotten to divide a composition into paragraphs? Has Marie ever forgotten about paragraphing?
7. Have you ever made a short outline? Has Pete ever made a long outline?
8. Have you ever studied for three hours without stopping? Has Pete ever studied for five hours without stopping?
9. Have you ever studied all night? Has Pete ever studied all day Saturday?

## E 8 / How Often?

Directions: Write one paragraph. Begin, "If you are interested in my nonacademic past, here are a few facts." Change the questions into statements, each containing an adverb of frequency, underlined.

Have you ever been in a street fight? Have you ever danced the tango? Have you ever traveled by jet? Have you ever had a coffee break?[1] Have you ever visited a museum of modern art? Have you ever eaten pink "cotton candy"[2] in an American amusement park? Have you ever seen palm trees growing in the United States? Have you ever ridden all night on a bus?

## E 9 / In Thailand

Directions: Copy the three following paragraphs, putting what you guess to be an appropriate adverbial, underlined, into each of the blanks. (Usah, an active fifteen-year-old boy, lives in the city but gets out into the country in Thailand.)

Has Usah ever seen a pagoda[3] in Thailand? Has he ever seen the Emerald Buddha[4] sitting serenely on its golden throne? Has he ever admired the magnificent bell tower nearby?

Has Usah ever gone into the jungle in Thailand? Has he ever watched a monkey club a coconut tree? Has Usah himself ever climbed a coconut tree? Has he ever opened a fresh coconut with a heavy knife? Has he ever drunk the sweet milky liquid inside?

Has Usah ever seen a sacred white elephant in the city? Has he ever seen a working elephant pull a log? Has he ever seen an elephant help build a house?

## E 10 / Marcus

Directions: Use the following three paragraphs to demonstrate your knowledge of different types of adverbials. Underline the adverbial

[1] *coffee break:* the custom in American business firms of having coffee in the middle of the morning, and perhaps in the middle of the afternoon.
[2] *cotton candy:* spun sugar, which looks delicious but tastes like cotton cloth.
[3] *pagoda:* a Buddhist temple forming a tower of many stories, each with a curved roof.
[4] *Emerald Buddha:* a statue carved of green jade representing the founder of Buddhism.

in each statement you write. (Use *has,* not *have,* in making your statements.) In paragraph 1, use *for* and *since;* in paragraph 2, use *ever since;* and in paragraph 3, use adverbs of frequency with a negative implication.

How long has Marcus been in this country? How long has he attended this university? How long has he lived at his present address?

How long has Marcus been able to climb a mountain? How long has he been able to sail a boat? How long has he been interested in architecture as his major?

Has Marcus sung in opera? Has he studied sculpture? Has he taken college courses in Turkey? Has he considered working in Iceland after he gets his degree?

## E 11 / Have You?

Directions: As you change the two following paragraphs of questions into statements, review the fact that the present perfect summarizes experience, while the past tense gives a single fact.

Have you looked a mile downward to the bottom of Grand Canyon? Did you see a mere thread of river far, far below? Have you admired Gainsborough's "Blue Boy" in the Huntington Gallery in Los Angeles? Did the slender boy in his blue satin suit look both sheltered and lonely? Have you gazed far up to the tops of the pines around the public rose gardens in Portland, Oregon? Did the masses of roses surprise you?

Have you heard the great organ in the Mormon Tabernacle in Salt Lake City, Utah? Did the softness and the richness of its tone proclaim it one of the great organs of the world? Have you gone swimming in Great Salt Lake? Did you try to sink? Did you find you couldn't?[1]

## Grammar: <u>but</u> as a coordinator

but: on the other hand

The coordinator *but* joins two short sentences (main clauses), making one longer or compound sentence.

---

[1] Because this lake has no outlet, the great accumulation of salt holds up any object within it.

Examples:

No one wanted war, **but** war came. Seemingly, one side won, **but** really both sides lost.

*But* can also join single words:

little **but** mighty      difficult **but** worthwhile      tired **but** happy

*But* can also join phrases:

not with the head **but** with the heart
not in the city **but** in the country
not by one act **but** by a continued effort

### Oral Practice I

Directions: Listen to the first half of a compound sentence. Add a second half, beginning with *but.* Use *one* and *today,* also.

Examples:

Bill broke a plate yesterday, . . .
Bill broke a plate yesterday, **but** he hasn't broken **one today.**

Marie wrote a composition yesterday, . . .
Marie wrote a composition yesterday, **but** she hasn't written **one today.**

1. Pete did a lab experiment yesterday, . . .
2. Pete read a book yesterday, . . .
3. He washed his car yesterday, . . .
4. He bought a pack of cigarettes yesterday, . . .
5. He had a steak yesterday, . . .
6. Marie was late to class yesterday, . . .
7. She drank a Coke yesterday, . . .
8. She fell off a bicycle yesterday, . . .

### Oral Practice II

Directions: Listen to the first half of a compound sentence, repeat it, and add a second half beginning with *but.* This time, however, use *any* and *since.*

Examples:

I bought three paperbacks several weeks ago, . . .
I bought three paperbacks several weeks ago, **but** I haven't bought **any since.**

Aki read three biographies in English last year, . . .
Aki read three biographies in English last year, **but** he hasn't read **any since.**

1. I sent for five application blanks last week, . . .
2. I saw a movie every week last term, . . .
3. We had three tests on Saturday, . . .
4. Pete spent a lot of money last week, . . .
5. Marie had a bad cold last winter, . . .
6. Max taught classes in Hebrew two years ago, . . .
7. A pair of redbirds built a nest last week, . . .
8. Marie cooked three meals last weekend, . . .
9. The fire department answered five calls last week, . . .
10. Pete told a lie last year, . . .

## Dictation: Joining Two Sentences with *but*

Directions: Listen to a pair of sentences twice. Then immediately write the pair as one sentence, using a comma and *but*.

Example:

It looks like rain. It doesn't rain.
It looks like rain, **but** it doesn't rain.

*After the dictation:* open your textbook and correct your work. Look first for the comma before *but.* Then correct the spelling and put in any words omitted.

1. I want to go. I can't this time.
2. I have met that man. I don't remember his name.
3. I like spring. I like summer better.
4. Pete has worked hard. Bill has worked harder.
5. A car is comfortable. A jet is faster.
6. I have seen a redbird. I haven't seen a bluebird yet.
7. Ali is late. I'll wait a little longer.

## Grammar: <u>however</u> as a sentence connector[1]

*However,* similar in meaning to *but,* is often used as a "sentence connector" between two closely related sentences, especially in writing:

---

[1] Look for additional sentence connectors under "Meaning Links," p. 294.

The President's advisers have discussed the problem at length. **However,** no decision has been reached.

*However,* can also be placed last in a sentence or before the main verb:

No decision has been reached, **however.**

No decision, **however,** has been reached.

Older usage frequently formed a compound sentence with a semicolon (;). This usage, though correct, is generally reserved now for formal writing.

The problem has reached major proportions; **however,** no permanent solution is in sight.

### Dictation: *However*

Directions: Listen to the seven pairs of sentences in the previous dictation again. This time, keep each pair as two sentences. Begin the second sentence with *however,* followed by a comma.

Example:

It looks like rain. It doesn't rain.
It looks like rain. **However,** it doesn't rain.

After the dictation, when you correct your work, make sure your second sentence begins with *however.* Also, make sure of the comma after *however.*

### Listen and Write: Spring and Winter

Directions: Listen twice to the first paragraph, and then write and correct your work. Follow the same procedure with the second paragraph.

Spring has come to the Midwest. It has been cold all month, although it is April. It is still cold, but suddenly the grass is growing. Birds are singing. We have already had two good rains. When we have another, spring will come with a rush.

Winter has come to the Midwest. The leaves have fallen. The little rivers have frozen. It is December 14. Four inches of snow fell during the night. Now people are forcing their cars slowly through the snow. However, the fir trees have become things of beauty. Their broad branches are green. Their heavy load of snow is white. The combination is beautiful.

## FREE WRITING

### E 12 / A Difficulty Analyzed

Directions: First, tell the chief difficulty you have had in learning to *write* English in the past. Give one or more examples. Then say what kind of help you need now. (A difficulty analyzed is a difficulty one-third solved.) Use this outline:

Paragraph 1: The difficulty stated (topic sentence or paragraph)

Paragraph 2: The difficulty made clear by examples

Paragraph 3: What can be done
By yourself
By your instructor

## SINCE ANSWERING WHY?

So far, *since* has been used in this text only in time phrases: "since the beginning of the twentieth century", "since yesterday." *Since* has a second meaning. It can also answer *why,* as a *because*-clause does:

**Since** I am not superstitious, I am willing to be the thirteenth guest at dinner.

I will go to the football game **since** everyone else is going.

The following list provides a summary of the contrasts between *since* and *because.*

| *Since* | *Because* |
| --- | --- |
| **Since** generally begins a sentence. | **Because** generally follows a main clause, except in formal writing. |
| A **since**-clause is followed by a comma. | A **because**-clause following a main clause requires no comma. |
| **Since** answers **why** casually, without emphasis: **Since** I was tired, I lay down for half an hour. | **Because** answers **why** strongly: I was sleeping in the daytime **because** I was very tired. |

**E 13 / Using *Since* and *Because***

Directions: Change the *because*-clause at the end of the following sentences to a *since*-clause at the beginning of the sentence. Remember the comma after the *since*-clause.

Example:

The bus drivers went on strike **because** they wanted more money.

**Since** they wanted more money, the bus drivers went on strike.

1. The strike affected many people because they did not live near their work.
2. Some people stayed in town because they had friends in the city.
3. Some people went to a hotel because rooms were available.
4. A lot of bus-riders drove to work the next morning because they had cars.
5. Many drivers offered seats to neighbors because they had room in their cars.
6. People took the strike calmly because they were big-city dwellers.
7. People stayed home in the evening because getting home was hard work.
8. People did a lot of visiting over the phone because the telephones were working.
9. Strangers talked to each other freely because everyone was "in the same boat."

## Spelling: Rule 1

Instructor:   Spell **plan**
Student A:   p l a n

Instructor:   Spell **planning**
Student B:   p l a n n i n g

Instructor:   Spell **planned**
Student C:   p l a n n e d

Instructor:   Spell **planner**
Student D:   p l a n n e r

Instructor:   Why did everyone double the **n**?
Student E:   There is a rule that says, "Double the final consonant before a suffix beginning with a vowel."

Instructor:   In the words on the blackboard, what are the suffixes?
Student F:   **ing**, **ed**, and **er**.

**Dictation**[1]

Directions (instructor to class): "I am going to dictate two short paragraphs. The suffixes will be *ing, er,* or *ed.* Double the consonant just before these suffixes."[2]

After the dictation, correct your work, looking for the doubled consonant. Give yourself a *C* (correct) on your paper for every consonant correctly doubled.

Players are running on the football field. Their feet are fitted with heavy shoes. Their heads are fitted with heavy caps. They are not batting the football. They are not dropping it. One big player just stopped a runner. He stopped him with his body.

I planned my vacation early. I dropped letters to all my friends. I told them I was getting three weeks off. I stopped extra spending. I shipped my golf clubs and tennis racket ahead. I hopped on a plane on August 2. I dropped into a seat tired but happy.

**FREE WRITING**

General direction: Write on one or more of the following topics. Hand in an outline of your main points. (A reminder: Use examples.)

E 14   Television as a Force for Change
E 15   Modern Transportation as a Force for Change
E 16   Modern Methods in Agriculture as a Force for Change
E 17   (a topic of your own choice)

[1] The instructor's process for giving dictation is first mentioned on p. 27.
[2] Vowels and consonants as the terms are used in the spelling rules refer to *letters,* not *sounds.*

# Section F

## The Past Perfect Tense
## Spelling: Rule 2

**Grammar: the nature of the past perfect tense**

The past perfect tense, like the past tense, tells what happened in the past. However, the past perfect names the *earlier of two actions.* The other action is in the simple past tense, either in the same sentence or in a sentence nearby:

Lee's watch had stopped. He re-wound it. (Which is the earlier action?)

Quiet returned when the jet had passed. (Which is the earlier action?)

Mr. Smith leaped from the train. He had left his briefcase on a bench in the station. (Which is the earlier action?)

| | *With Past Perfect* |
|---|---|
| Earlier action: My tooth ached for two days. Later action: I called the dentist. | When my tooth **had ached** for two days, I called the dentist. |

**Dictation: New Experiences**

Directions: Since *had* and *have* can sound somewhat alike when spoken quickly, so as soon as you have finished, go over your work, marking each correct use of *had* and *have* with a *C* and making any necessary changes.

I **had** never **had** a meal in a cafeteria before I came to this country. I **have had** three meals a day in a cafeteria since the beginning of the term. I **had** never **studied** English five hours a day before I came to this country. I **have** attended English classes twenty-five hours a week since the beginning of the term. I **had** never **studied** until midnight before I came to this country. I **have studied** until midnight three times this week.

## F 1 / Pete's New Second-hand Car

Directions: Copy the two following paragraphs, putting the verbs in parentheses into the past perfect tense, underlined.

Example:

Pete (always want) to have his own car.

Pete **had** always **wanted** to have his own car.

Pete (always plan) to get a car when he received his first big raise. On Thursday he (receive) the raise.

On Friday after he (deposit) his paycheck, he went to Opportunity Row. Pete knew cars, and after he (visit) every show room on the street, he found a small, almost good-as-new sports car. The former owner (drive) it very little. Since Pete (already pass) his driver's test, after he (sign) three sets of papers and (make) a substantial down payment, the car was his to drive away.

Free writing: Write an additional paragraph beginning, "This is what happened next."

## Oral Practice: the past perfect with *wish*[1]

Directions: Listen to the sentence given you. Respond with "I wish," or the cue given you, and a statement in the past perfect.

Examples:

Instructor:   It rained yesterday.
Student:       I wish it **had been** sunny.

---

[1] This usage does not require an earlier action. The past perfect is used because the action is not real—because it did *not* occur in the past.

Instructor:   Only a small crowd attended the soccer game.
Student:      I wish **everybody had come.**

1. I bought a black coat. I wish . . .
2. I ordered pie for dessert. I wish . . .
3. I didn't leave the dormitory until five minutes before class time.
4. The school paper didn't print a word about our meeting.
5. Marie didn't start her term paper until yesterday evening. She wishes now (that) . . .
6. Hing took geology as his required science course. Now he wishes (that) . . .
7. Mrs. Kilroy has gained ten pounds.
8. I missed the re-run of *Gone with the Wind.*[1]
9. George bought a TV set with a very small screen. Now he wishes (that) . . .
10. We lost the game Saturday by a single point. We certainly wish (that) . . .
11. I saw a dull movie Saturday evening.
12. Sunday evening I stayed up late watching a horror movie on TV.

## Grammar: the progressive past perfect tense

The progressive form of the past perfect tense indicates that the earlier action had been going on for some time:

We **had been waiting** for over twenty minutes when suddenly five buses appeared in succession.

I understood the clerk easily, for I **had been living** in the United States for almost a year.

### F 2 / Frustrations in a Series

Directions: Complete the following paragraph of partial statements, which are in the *progressive* past perfect, with statements of your own in the simple past. (Since your completed statements will be compound sentences, put a comma before *but.)*

I had been expecting a check from home since the first of the week, but. . . . I had been looking in each mail, too, for a certain letter, but. . . . I had been waiting since the middle of the week for a

[1] *Gone with the Wind:* a movie about the American Civil War which draws large audiences whenever it is re-run.

long-distance call from my cousin in Chicago, but. . . . I had planned
to get all my weekend studying out of the way on Friday, but. . . .
I had fully intended to go to the International Club party Saturday
evening, but. . . . I had been hoping at least for good weather on Sunday,
but. . . . However, next week . . . (complete in the future tense or
with "going to").

Free writing: Add a second, more cheerful paragraph of your own,
based on the ideas in the first paragraph. Use the progressive past
perfect and the simple past perfect, as was done in the first paragraph.

Example:

The check I **had been looking for** came Monday. Nothing was wrong
at home. The mails **had** just **been** unusually slow.

## Grammar: two actions; two sentences

As you know, the past perfect tense names the earlier of two
actions. The second and later action is usually in the same sentence. However, it can be in a sentence nearby:

By five o'clock the parade **had ended.** (earlier action)
The reviewing stand **was deserted.** (later action or fact)

I **had** never **seen** an American President take the oath of office before.
(earlier action)
I **will** always **remember** this day. (later action)

Note that when the past perfect is the only tense in the sentence,
a specific time signal must be given: *by five o'clock* (first example); *before* (second example).

### Oral Practice

Directions: Respond to the sentence given with a second sentence
in the past perfect.

Example:

Instructor:   Tom swam under water easily. (Why?)
Student:      He **had learned** to hold his breath without thinking about it.

1.  My alarm clock didn't go off this morning. (Why?)

2. My wrist watch wasn't running. (Why?)
3. The smell of smoke drifted up from the dormitory kitchen. (What had the cook done?)
4. When I came to pay for my breakfast, I was embarrassed. (What had you left in your room?)
5. In class, I answered a difficult question. (Why?)
6. When it came time to hand in the homework, I was embarrassed again. (Why?)
7. What had you done with your homework?
8. Had you ever done this before?
9. On the whole, had you had a reasonably good morning?

## Grammar: <u>because</u> with the past perfect

*Because*, answering *why*, is much used with the past perfect:

A fire engine came rushing down our street because someone **had turned** in an alarm.

Women began taking plastic rain hats out of their handbags because it **had started** to sprinkle.

### Oral Practice

Directions: Repeat the sentence given and add a *because*-clause[1] in the past perfect tense.

Example:

Instructor:  Everyone poured into the lecture hall.
Student:     Everyone poured into the lecture hall **because** a well-known politician **had come** to speak.

1. The speaker was late. (Why?)
2. His voice was hoarse. (Why?)
3. The speaker's microphone worried him. (What had the committee on arrangements failed to do?)
4. The speaker stopped answering questions from the floor. (Why?)
5. The speaker left the platform. (Why?)
6. Those eager to hear him left the hall unhappy. (Why?)

[1] *To the instructor:* This exercise will be simplified if students merely respond with a *because*-clause.

**F 3 / Using *Because* in Writing**

Directions: First orally and then in writing make one sentence out of the two given you. When you change the order of the sentences, use the past perfect and *because*.

Examples:

Hing learned how to take an objective test. He made a good score.

Hing made a good score **because** he **had learned** how to take an objective test.

1. Hing ran around the athletic field six times. He took a rest.
2. The university bus failed to appear. He finally walked back to the dormitory.
3. Lee wanted a Polaroid[1] camera for six months. He bought one yesterday.
4. Haruko needed a warmer coat for the past three weeks. She bought a pure wool coat on sale.[2]
5. Haruko shopped successfully by herself. She was proud of her purchase.
6. Marie wanted all winter to see an American city with a French Quarter. She spent spring vacation in New Orleans.
7. She saw New Orleans. She came back from spring vacation happy.
8. The French Quarter reminded her a little of home. She loved it.

## Grammar: tenses with <u>just/already</u> and <u>before/after</u>

When *just* and *already* are used, the past perfect must be used:

We had **just** opened our programs when the lights went down.

The play had **already** begun when two late-comers entered our row.

Since *before* and *after* in themselves indicate which is the earlier action, the past tense is frequently used for both actions:

The bank **closed** Friday **before** I reached it.

After my roommate **investigated** his own financial state, he lent me five dollars.

Nevertheless, the past perfect tense is often used with *before*

---

[1] *Polaroid camera:* a camera which develops pictures within sixty seconds.
[2] *on sale:* at a reduction from the original price.

and *after,* especially in the precision which is one of the elements in good writing:

After Washington **had retreated** across New Jersey, his ill-clothed army went into winter quarters at Valley Forge.

## Punctuation: the comma after the introductory adverbial clause, reviewed

An introductory adverbial clause is regularly followed by a comma, whatever tense is used:

Present tense:  When you **hear** anything, be sure to let me know.

Present perfect:  Although Anne **has** not **seen** Venice yet, she intends to.

Simple past:  As the clock **struck** midnight, Cinderella fled.

### F 4 / *After*

Directions: Complete the partial statements below. Put a comma after the introductory adverbial clause.

Example:

After it had rained three days in succession . . .

After it had rained three days in succession, the fourth day dawned brilliantly clear.

1. After we had walked for an hour without reaching a village . . .
2. After we finally remembered the road map in the bottom of the knapsack . . .
3. After we had been picked up by a kindly family on its way to Kennebunk Port[1] . . .
4. After we found an inn in Kennebunk Port with a vacancy . . .
5. After we had broiled lobster and corn-on-the-cob[2] for dinner . . .
6. After Mr. Smith's taxi had been creeping through traffic toward the airport for an hour . . .

[1] *Kennebunk Port:* a center of lobster fishing on the Atlantic Ocean in the state of Maine.
[2] *corn on-the-cob:* sweet corn boiled lightly and eaten with butter and the fingers from the foot-long cob.

7. After Mr. Smith had stood in a ticket line for fifteen minutes . . .
8. After he had checked the big Arrival-Departure board to find his proper gate . . .
9. After he had walked three blocks to Gate 22-A . . .
10. After he had finally sunk into his seat on the plane . . .

## Punctuation: the comma and the adverbial clause, continued

An adverbial clause following a main clause normally does not require a comma:[1]

We had stopped **because the car was not steering properly.**

We hunted **until we located a puncture in the left rear tire.**

We walked until we found a garage **since we had to have help.**

### F 5 / *Before*

Directions: Make one sentence out of each pair given. Change the progressive past of the first sentence to the *progressive past perfect*. Change the second sentence to a *before*-clause. Use no comma.

Example:

Bill was living in an undergraduate dormitory. He decided to find something else.

Bill **had been living** in an undergraduate dormitory **before** he decided to find something else.

1. Bill was living among noisy undergraduates. He arranged to share an apartment with Pete.
2. Pete was living alone. Bill came.
3. Both students were thinking seriously about their college majors. They changed them.
4. Bill was taking accounting. He changed to computer science.
5. Pete was taking business administration. He changed to electrical engineering.
6. Pete was working without satisfaction in an office. He began to work in a garage.
7. Saturday morning Pete was hunting over an hour for a minor rattle in his new second-hand car. He located it.

[1] However, if the adverbial clause stands in strong contrast to the preceding main clause, a comma is sometimes used: "I know he interests her, because she says she hates him."

8. He was working only fifteen minutes. He eliminated it.
9. The dark color of his car was making Pete discontented. **He and** Bill painted it fire-engine red one Saturday morning.
10. Pete was finding a full-time job and evening classes exhausting. His new red car gave him energy for everything.

## Grammar: <u>when</u> with the past perfect

Since *when* does not indicate which of two past actions is the earlier, the past perfect is frequently used to make the distinction clear:

When I arrived at the box office, the tickets **had** all **been** sold.

We **had given up** expecting Hing **when** he walked in.

**When** Mrs. Smith **had placed** the roast in the oven, she sat down to read the evening paper.

### F 6 / When

Directions: Make one sentence out of each pair of sentences given. Begin the first sentence of the pair with *when* and change the tense to the past perfect. Use a comma at the close of the introductory adverbial clause.

Example:

Mrs. Smith compared her time with the TV announcer's. She set her watch forward five minutes.

**When** Mrs. Smith **had compared** her time with the TV announcer's, she set her watch forward five minutes.

1. The workman finally located the loose wire. He repaired the lamp easily.
2. Mrs. Smith thanked the repairman repeatedly. He said, "No trouble, glad to help you out."
3. Word about the new man's good work and pleasant ways reached Mrs. Jones. She called him about her vacuum cleaner.
4. Mrs. Smith tried to defrost her refrigerator and failed. She went straight to the phone.
5. The new repairman was in town two months. He had all the work he could handle.

## F 7 / The First Hour of the Flight

Directions: As you change the three following paragraphs of questions into statements, note how frequently you are using the past tense compared with the past perfect. (The past tense is the normal tense for narrative writing: the only use of the past perfect is to name the earlier of two actions.) Underline the past perfect whenever you use it.

How recently did you take a long airplane ride? From what country to what country were you flying? How long had you been planning this trip? How early did you get to the airport? How long had you been standing in line before you boarded the plane?

Had you already fastened your seat belt when the hostess made her inevitable request? Did you watch with interest as a hostess covered her pretty nose with an oxygen mask and showed everyone how easy it was to breathe normally? Had[1] it ever occurred to you that you might need such a mask on a plane trip? Did you read the card telling how to exit by a window—one leg, body, other leg? However, had you read somewhere the chances of a plane accident are now 0.15 for each million passengers?

Was it a pleasure to have coffee soon after the plane was airborne? Was it an even greater pleasure to see the hostesses approaching with a tray full of food in each hand? Had you known about pulling down a small shelf from the back of the seat in front of you? Did you dine comfortably off this shelf? At the end of an hour had you come to feel that the plane was a safe and comfortable place to be?

## *Spelling: For the Student Working Alone*

There will be one or two spelling rules in each section now until ten rules have been covered. If you are working on spelling by yourself, perhaps ahead of the class, try the following procedure:

1. Look first at the examples given under a rule, rather than at the rule.
2. Next, in the paragraph of dictation, underline the words to which the rule evidently applies.

---

[1] Americans often use *did* rather than the British *had* in questions such as this one. The question then would require the simple form of the main verb: "Did it ever *occur* . . ."

3. Now, after you have a grasp of the principle involved, read the rule.
4. Next, get a friend to dictate to you, using the instructor's method of repetition or some modification of it.
5. Finally, check your work for errors—and have your friend check, too.

## Spelling: Rule 2

When a word of two or more syllables is accentuated on the *last* syllable, follow Rule 1 (p. 167):

begin′—beginning—beginner

occur′—occurred—occurrence

transfer—transferred′—transferring

If the accent does not fall on the last syllable, the final consonant is not doubled:[1]

I **read** every day.
I **sleep** every night.

o′pened, opened      lis′tening, listening      remem′ber, remembered

The dictionary sometimes gives two ways to spell a word, the British way, in addition to the American way. In such instances, either spelling is acceptable:

| American | British |
|----------|---------|
| traveling | travelling |
| worshiped | worshipped |
| canceled | cancelled |

### Dictation: A Pleasant Occurrence

A friend referred me to this school. I had my credits transferred early. I omitted no part of my record. I was referred to the proper office. I was admitted to the college without delay.

In the beginning, everything seemed strange. However, something pleasant occurred during registration. A stranger permitted me to use and keep his list of courses. He said he had committed everything he needed to memory. This small occurrence lifted my spirits.

[1] Exceptions, or seeming exceptions, will not occur in dictation. Students can apply the rule confidently.

## Listen and Write: A Gang Fight

I was only thirteen then, but I was a full member of my cousin's gang in the inner city. We often fought with another gang because we didn't want them on our street.

One Saturday night, our gang had chased the other gang into an open parking lot. Suddenly some one was pointing a gun at me. Just before he fired, my cousin stepped in front of me. The bullet hit him in the stomach. They took him to the hospital, but in two weeks he was out and doing all right. He had stepped in front of me on purpose. He took the bullet intended for me. He was a good cousin and a good leader.

## Summary: the Past Perfect Tense contrasted with the Present Perfect

| *Past Perfect* | *Present Perfect* |
|---|---|
| The past perfect involves two actions: | The present perfect involves one action: |
| The parade had passed before we arrived. | The new term has begun. |
| Both actions were completed in the past: | The action began in the past, generally comes up to the present, and often implies connection with the future: |
| I had dropped the letter in the mailbox before I realized my mistake. | I have been here for three months. (I expect to stay longer.) |
| | The present perfect can imply habitual or repeated action: |
| | I have learned to like coffee. (The liking is habitual.) |
| | I have used the coffee machine in our building again and again. (The action is a repeated one.) |
| The past perfect can involve only one action when an expression of time implies a previous action: | Action in the present perfect can be completed at an unnamed time in the past. |

By five o'clock the parade
had ended.

I have seen that play.

## F 8 / A Review of *Had* and *Have*

Directions: Review the difference between *had* and *have* by putting the proper form, underlined, into each sentence. (Remember to use *has* after the third person singular.)

Hing (had/have) never seen a building forty stories tall before he came to this country. He (had/have) now seen "skyscrapers" in both New York and Chicago. He (had/have) seldom ridden in an elevator before he came to this country. He (had/have) now ridden in an elevator every school day for the past six months.

Hing (had/have) never put a coin into a vending machine before he came to this country. Now he (had/have) acquired the habit of putting a dime into the coffee machine in his building in the middle of every morning. When he (had/have) pressed the proper knobs, the obliging machine pours him a paper cup of coffee, with cream and sugar added. Hing (had/have) never had quite this type of service in his own country.

## FREE WRITING

General directions: Write on one or more of the following topics. Begin with the sentence given and then tell your story with no further thought of tenses. Hand in a brief outline indicating your main points.

## F 9 / Something Exciting

Directions: Begin, "I had never taken part in anything so exciting until I came to the United States."

## F 10 / Something Learned

Directions: Begin, "I had never understood the feeling of Americans for their country until I came to the United States."

## F 11 / The Fashions on This Campus

Directions: Begin, "The fashions on this campus are not those of the world outside."

**F 12 / The Young and the Old**

Directions: Begin, "I had never seen such an interesting instance of friendly contact between the young and the old before."

**F 13 / (a topic of your own choice)**

# Section G

---

## The Modals
## Spelling: Rule 3

### Grammar: the nature of the modals

The following words, called modals, add shades of meaning to English. They represent not facts, but possibilities, obligations, uncertainties, habitual action in the past, etc.

| Present Form | Past Form |
|---|---|
| can | could |
| may | might |
| shall | should |
| will | would |
| must | had to |
| ought (to) | _____ |

It **may** rain tomorrow. (possibility)

We **should** be prompt. (obligation)

We **could** try, at least. (uncertainty)

In elementary school, we **would** sing on Friday afternoons. (habitual past action)

Note that the modal is followed by the simple form of the verb:

| | Modal | Simple Form | |
|---|---|---|---|
| It | may | rain | tomorrow. |
| We | should | be | prompt. |

## List: With Examples of Use

ABILITY

can: present ability, to be able to:
Pete **can** take a car apart.
**Can** you understand English over the telephone?
The doctor **can** see you tomorrow at 9:30.

could: past ability
I **could** swim under water when I was five.
Mona **could** read in the family library when she was nine.

Jon **could have** gone to West Point on a scholarship, but he didn't. He went to Columbia instead.

could: lack of ability
I wish I **could** add without paper and pencil.
I wish I **could** take notes in shorthand.

OBLIGATION OR DUTY

Everyone eligible to vote **ought to/should** vote.
I **ought to/should** write half a dozen letters this weekend.
Even near factories, the air **ought to/should** be reasonably free of pollution.

We **should not (shouldn't)** be afraid to face a new idea.

**Ought to** and **should** are interchangeable in affirmative statements. **Should not (shouldn't)** is generally used in negative statements and questions.

NECESSITY

One **must** drive on the left in England.
I am out of stamps. I **must** get some more. I **mustn't** forget to.
We **have to**[1] take our mid-term tests on Friday.
By the fourth grade, we **had to** know the multiplication tables perfectly.

---

[1] *Have to/had to* are not modals but are used because *must* has no past form.

## POSSIBILITY

Jean has lived in Paris for ten years. He **must** speak French very well.
You **must** find New York exciting, even if it is tiring.

Everything **may** turn out very well. I certainly hope so.
I **might** get to Washington in time for the cherry blossoms, but I doubt it. (**Might** is less positive than **may**).

I **would** take a long walk every afternoon if I had time. I don't, unfortunately.

I **would** like[1] to cross the United States with you by bus on the way home. I **would** promise now if I were sure I **could.**

## FUTURE TIME

The meeting **will** start promptly at 8:00.
The first item of business **will** be the election of officers.
I **will** (**I'll**) be ready by six. (promise)
I **will** (**I'll**) solve this problem if it takes half the night. (determination)

## PERMISSION

You **may** use your dictionaries.

## HABITUAL PAST ACTION

When we were children in Korea, the first thing on New Year's morning, we **would** bow to our parents. We **would** thank them for the gift of life.

We **used to**[2] look forward to New Year's. Our parents **used to** make sure that we had delightful new clothes and new toys.

## REQUESTS

**May** I help you?
**Might** I help you? (less direct, possibly more courteous than **may**)

**May** we leave when we have finished the test?
(**May** is preferable to **can**, which means "to be able to.")

**Shall** I put these papers in your office?
**Shall** we leave the party in a few more minutes?
**Shouldn't** we wait a little before passing judgment on the new orchestra?

[1] *Should like,* formerly the preferred form, is correct but now in limited use.

[2] *Used to,* not a modal, can take the place of *would* when both terms indicate habitual past action.

**Shall** and **shouldn't** are now generally limited to first-person questions asking agreement. **Will** is far more widely used.

**Would** you close the door? (less of a command than "Will you close the door?")

**Would** you tell me what this word means?

My watch has stopped. **Would** you give me the time? (Never, "What time is it?")

**Would** you **like to** go to the concert Saturday evening? Or **would** you **rather** go to a movie? (forms of invitation)

## THE NONREAL PRESENT[1]

### Grammar: the nature of the nonreal present

When a course of action is still possible, however unlikely, it is said to be in the "nonreal present."

| | *Modal* | *Simple Form* | |
|---|---|---|---|
| We | can | fly | to Los Angeles for Christmas. |
| We | could | get | a reservation tomorrow. |
| We | would | be | there in seven hours. |
| We | will | have | good service on the plane, I know. |

The action named is not fact, but it could become so. The action points toward the future.

### Oral Practice I: *can*

Directions: Use the phrase given you and *can* to say how quickly you are able to perform certain daily acts if you have to.

Example:

Instructor:   dress in eight minutes.
Student:      I **can** dress in eight minutes if I have to.

---

[1] The useful term "nonreal present" refers to the *form* of the modal. It does not cover the meaning of the modal in every instance.

1. get up at 5:30
2. eat breakfast in seven minutes
3. go without breakfast
4. write neatly
5. speak English all day
6. study in a noisy lounge
7. study with my neighbor's radio on
8. study all night
9. study all weekend
10. hurry on a hot day

## Oral Practice II: *could*

Directions: Use the phrase given you and *could* to say what you were able to do before you went to school.

Example:

Instructor: climb a tree
Student:   I **could** climb a tree before I went to school.

1. swim under water
2. fight with my brothers
3. ask my mother for money
4. count to a hundred
5. read about the three little bears
6. ride a small bicycle
7. make clothes for my doll
8. recite a long poem in Spanish
9. sing a song in three languages
10. go skating with my mother and my little brother

## Oral Practice III: *can* in contrast with *could*

Directions: Student A will mention something he *could* do at home which he cannot do here. Student B will respond with something which students *can* do here but *cannot* do at home.

Example:

Student A:  In Tokyo I **could** relax with my friends in a tea house after classes.
Student B:  But here you **can** talk with university graduates from all over the world.

## FREE WRITING

### G 1 / Contrasted Advantages

Directions: Write a paragraph beginning, "No one environment can give you every advantage, but every environment can give you some advantages. For example, . . ." Contrast what you could do at home with what you can do here.

### Oral Practice I: *should* and *will*

Directions: Form sentences using first *should* and then *will.*

Example:

Instructor:   get up earlier
Student:       I **should** get up earlier, and in the future I **will.**

1. do more reading in English
2. speak English in the halls between classes
3. talk with more Americans
4. clean my room every week
5. save more money
6. listen to the news every evening
7. begin to study early for exams
8. arrive for all exams ten minutes early
9. bring two pens to every exam
10. read all examination directions carefully
11. read my own answers carefully
12. have some special fun at the end of exam week

### Oral Practice II: *should* and *ought to*

Directions: Student A will put the phrase given him into a sentence using *should.* Student B will agree with Student A, using *ought to* and *now.* (*My* will change to *your* in Student B's reply.)

Example:

Instructor:   decide on the subject of my term paper
Student A:   I **should** decide on the subject for my term paper.
Student B:   I agree with you. You **ought to** decide on the subject of your term paper now.

1. go to the library
2. go on a diet

3. stop smoking
4. wash my hair
5. mend my jacket
6. get my hair cut
7. pay my library fine[1]
8. do more pronunciation exercises
9. write a "thank you" note to my hostess

## Oral Practice III: *would* and *could*

Directions: Listen to the statement given you. Say "I wish" and make a statement with either *would* or *could.*

Example:

Instructor:   Pete isn't coming to the party.
Student A:   I wish he **would.**
Instructor:   He'd like to come.
Student B:   I wish he **could.** Does he have to work?

1. I can't play any musical instrument.
2. The committee isn't putting any dancers on the program.
3. Perhaps the sun will shine for the next thirty days.
4. I can't write my exercises in ten minutes.
5. My friends from Chicago haven't appeared yet.
6. The cafeteria never serves Oriental food.
7. I can't understand American slang.
8. My American friends never talk politics when I'm around.
9. I can't get out of town on weekends.
10. I'm sorry I can't join you for dinner tonight.

## Oral Practice IV: *must* as necessity

Directions: Listen to the phrase given. Use it to form a sentence saying what a student *must* do (what it is necessary to do). Tell why in a second sentence.

Example:

Instructor:   have a checking account
Student:   A student **must** have a checking account. If he doesn't, he **must** carry all his money with him.

---

[1] *library fine:* the sum of money charged by a library when a book is kept beyond the agreed time.

1. get some sleep every night
2. comb his hair every morning
3. meat, fresh fruit, and vegetables every day
4. a quiet place to study
5. memorize his schedule of classes
6. stay calm during tests

**Further directions: Now form negative statements using *must not* (mustn't). Add *why*.**

Example:

Instructor:  leave his room unlocked
Student:     A student **must not (mustn't)** leave his room unlocked. If he does, he may find something missing.

7. carry a lot of cash
8. walk down the middle of the road
9. worry about his girlfriend at home
10. stay away from class parties

### Oral Practice V: *must* as reasonable supposition

Directions: Listen to the statement. Two or three students will respond with a reasonable supposition using *must.*

Example:

Instructor:  The bus is late.
Student A:   Traffic **must** be unusually heavy.
Student B:   The regular driver **must** not be on duty.
Student C:   One or two buses **must** be in the repair shop.

1. Ali is sitting with his eyes closed.
2. Marie is putting on her coat.
3. Lee is consulting his dictionary.
4. The instructor is gathering up his books and papers.
5. Everyone in the cafeteria is looking happy.
6. Those seven boys eat together every night.
7. Occasionally our instructor joins us for dinner.
8. Everyone is moving toward the TV set now.

### Oral Practice VI: *could, wouldn't,* and *would*

Directions: Listen to the question. Answer, using *could, wouldn't,* and *would.* (Write the three modals on the blackboard first).

Example:

Instructor: What would you do if the bell rang for a fire drill?
Student: I **could** be lazy and stay in my seat, but I probably **wouldn't**. I **would** leave the building with everyone else.

**With *wouldn't* use either *probably*, which leaves a little room for doubt, or *certainly* (surely).**

1. What would you do if a cashier gave you too much change?
2. What would you do if you saw two men fighting in the street?
3. What would you do if the director asked to see you?
4. What would you do if you had a seat on a bus and noticed a very old woman standing?
5. What would you do if you were given a ticket to that puzzling game, American football?
6. What would you do if your hostess offered you a strange dessert?
7. What would you do if you had to run a block to catch a bus?
8. What would you do if you thought an assignment unreasonably long?
9. What would you do if the teachers went on strike?

### G 2 / The Anxious Passenger

Directions: Copy the following questions asked by an anxious wife as a couple ride by taxi toward an airport. Make up answers by the husband, who remains irritatingly calm. Increase the effect of some of his answers with *certainly, naturally,* and *of course.*

Example:

Q: Do you think we may miss the plane?
A: We **certainly** may. We should have started earlier.

Q: If we miss this plane, can we get a later plane today?
A:

Q: Could we ask the driver to go around that big truck?
A:

Q: Do you think he would like it if we did?
A:

Q: Would it be better to relax?
A:

Q: Might we get into a traffic jam near the airport?
A:

Q:   On the other hand, could we arrive at the airport in another twenty minutes, find a porter waiting, and board our plane with five minutes to spare?

A:


## G 3 / An American in (name your own city)

Directions: Make statements based on the four following paragraphs of questions, underlining the modals. Take particular care to place objects directly after the verb forms, as shown here:

|     | *Verb Forms* | *Object* |     |
| --- | --- | --- | --- |
| He  | ought to try | tacos and enchiladas | by all means. |
| He  | should see | Mexico City | without fail. |

When an American is visiting (name your own city) for the first time, what **ought** he to see first? Then what **should** he see without fail? What **might** he enjoy seeing almost as much?

What drink **might** he find refreshing late in the afternoon? What national dishes **ought** he to try, by all means? What dessert **should** follow these dishes?

Where **could** a visitor see five thousand (or seventy-five thousand) of your fellow countrymen enjoying themselves? What sport **should** he observe at least once? If he is lucky, what yearly sports event might he see?

If an American wants to enjoy himself in your country, what national customs **should** he be sure to follow? What about money?


## G 4 / A Tourist in (name any city)

Directions: Write much more freely than you did in *G* 3, completing a partial statement and then adding further information of your own. After you have finished, underline the modals you find you have used.

Example:

Those who love beauty . . .

Those who love beauty **might** visit the Chicago Art Institute, or they **might** prefer to take a taxi and ride along the breathtaking Lake Shore Drive, next to Lake Michigan.

Every tourist visiting (name of city) for the first time. . . . promptly. Then, having seen what every tourist must see, . . . Those who like to place a few small bets. . . . Those whose great love is beauty. . . . Those who prefer to go shopping. . . . Those who want an excellent meal away from other tourists. . . . In short, every tourist can enjoy himself in (name of city), whatever his interests are.

## FREE WRITING

### G 5 / The Unique[1] Attraction of (name a city)

Directions: Write on the unique attraction of some city you know well. Follow the organization of the example below, which is embodied in this outline:

I. Introduction (one paragraph)
II. The unique attraction (one or more paragraphs)
III. Conclusion (one paragraph, possibly a single sentence)

#### Unique Attraction of New Orleans

Every tourist visiting New Orleans for the first time promptly has lunch at Antoine's; takes his first stroll through the French Quarter;[2] considers what he may buy, eat, and drink before he leaves; and then, in all probability, attends one of the hour-long sessions of traditional jazz in Preservation Hall.

Preservation Hall is a huge former stable, ugly but serviceable, where elderly black men play traditional Dixieland jazz. There is no food or liquor sold on the premises. There is no admission charge, either. Everyone simply drops a dollar bill in the basket on a chair by the door.

It is strange in this day to feel a crowd moved by music so unfashionable. Toward the end of the hour the leader sings the first verse of "The Old Rugged Cross" and then asks the audience to help him out by singing the verse with him the second time. The crowd, probably surprised that it can produce the words, sings more and more strongly to the end.

Every session at Preservation Hall ends with the rousing song, "When the Saints Go Marching In." This is the great favorite of the marching bands, which still act as escort at many black funerals.

[1] unique: the only one of its kind.
[2] The French Quarter (Vieux Carré) dates from the eighteenth century, when France ruled Louisiana.

On the way to the cemetery, the band plays suitably solemn hymns, but on the way back the band and the mourners break into rejoicing that their brother has gone marching into Paradise.

A number of the pleasures of New Orleans are memorable, but an hour in Preservation Hall is unique.

## Oral Practice I: the modals

Directions: Listen to the sentence given you. Change it to a sentence with the same meaning using a modal.

Examples:

Pete is able to drive any make of car.
Pete **can** drive any make of car.

As a teen-ager, it was my custom to lie on the floor to read.
As a teen-ager, I **would** lie on the floor to read.

1. I am always able to relax over a good detective story.
2. Lee was able to stand on his head when he was five.
3. We have permission to bring a dictionary to the test.
4. I am going to go home by way of Paris.
5. I am out of cash; I have to get to the bank.
6. Everyone is here but Hing. The doorbell is ringing. (must be)
7. It is a car-owner's duty to drive carefully near a school.
8. It is a citizen's duty to write to his congressman.
9. At home, my friends always met at a certain tea house after classes.
10. I am going to see my adviser tomorrow.
11. In Hong Kong, I named my price and walked away, looking back.
12. In India, I said, "Too much."

## Oral Practice II: situations in the nonreal present

Directions: Consider the situation presented to you. Make one or more statements about it, using the modals or *had better.*

Example:

Instructor:   A warning bell is ringing at a railroad crossing, but a car still has time to cross the tracks.

Student A:   The car **should** wait. It **had better** wait.
Student B:   According to law, it **must** wait.
Student C:   Accidents **can** happen when a car still "has time."

1. A stranger is completely lost in a foreign city.
2. Miss Liu leaves a package on a bus.

3. Mr. X buys an alarm clock. It runs too fast.
4. Marie wants to pay her tuition fee in three installments.
5. She wants to take out books from the library.
6. Pete finds his library books are six days overdue.
7. A life guard is on duty, but Jack is afraid to dive.
8. Three students in the lounge want the musical on TV. The fourth wants the world news.
9. Smoke is pouring out of the roof of a house.
10. You wake up one morning with a fever.
11. You can see *Gone with the Wind* for a dollar in the university movie series.
12. You are thinking of buying a second-hand car.

**Listen and Write: Sights for a Visitor**

Directions: Listen to the following paragraph twice. Then write down what you remember. Correct the errors you consider important. Mark with a *C* each modal used.

A visitor to our university **ought to** see our new stadium first. Then he **should** see our fine library. He **ought to** stay long enough to see the newspapers from his own country in the library. Then he **might** like to see life along our little river. Ducks **would** be swimming. Students **would** be sitting on the grass in pairs, talking. No one **would** be hurrying.

## Punctuation: the comma with **and**

A comma is used before *and* to connect two complete statements (independent clauses) within one sentence. (Such a sentence is called compound.) (For Reference, p. 307 II)

| First Statement | | Second Statement |
| --- | --- | --- |
| The newscast began, | and | everyone settled down to listen. |
| The news was not good, | and | everyone stirred uneasily. |

A comma is not used between pairs of words, especially between verbs:

The comedian **joked** and **sang**.

The bluejay **scolded** and **scattered** the smaller birds.

## Dictation: Punctuating the Compound Sentence

Directions: In the following paragraph of dictation, place a comma only in the compound sentences. (The conjunctions in this dictation will be *and* and *but*.)

Pete is sharing his apartment now. Bill pays half the rent, and Pete pays the other half. The boys share the work, but they make it very easy. Bill cooks something simple, and Pete cleans up the kitchen. He always washes the dishes, but he never dries them. He seldom dusts. Pete does not really believe in dusting, and Bill doesn't either. Bill's girlfriend sometimes drops in. She looks around the apartment and smiles a little, but she doesn't say a single word about the housekeeping.

## Spelling: Rule 3

Drop the final *e* from a verb before adding *ing:*

write—writing     lose—losing     shine—shining     come—coming

## Dictation I

We are having a fine vacation. We are taking long walks. We are dancing every evening. We are dining well. The sun is shining every day. We are not writing any letters, but we are writing postcards. We are coming home on Sunday. Friends are coming to the airport to meet us.

## Dictation II

Miss Jones was having a bad morning. She was typing an important report. She knew that trouble was coming. Her typing had to be perfect, and Miss Jones was not a shining success at typing.

## FREE WRITING

### G 6 / A Letter to Rachanee

The Situation

Rachanee is from Indonesia. She is twenty-two. Somehow she persuaded her conservative, well-to-do[1] parents to allow

[1] *well-to-do:* having enough money for comfortable living.

her to come to the United States to study English for a single term.
Then her visa expired, and she had to go home.

Although Rachanee does not type very well, her father easily
found a position for her in a highly respected company. Now she
copies memorandums all day and files papers alphabetically.
The work depresses her. She hates it.

What is Rachanee to do? She would like to be a bilingual
secretary in Washington, D.C., and without much doubt she has the
ability to get out into the world and struggle for what she wants.
But she does not wish to hurt her parents.

For Class Discussion

1. Might Rachanee be able to persuade her parents that the easy,
   pleasant life of home was not right for her?
2. Her parents let her leave home once for a limited time. Why might
   they be willing to do so again?
3. Rachanee has no contacts at present with other young people with
   a special interest in the West. What might she do about this situation
   without leaving her own large, metropolitan city?
4. If Rachanee wants a more interesting job in any country, what
   preparation must she make?
5. If her parents say **No** to everything, what should Rachanee do?

**Directions for G 6: Write a letter giving Rachanee your best thinking
on her problem. Use the opening suggested below or one of your own.**

Dear Rachanee,                                            Date

Since I do not know you and this letter is not going to be
mailed, I can speak freely.

I am a man/woman, _____ years old, married/unmarried,
from _____. It seems to me . . .

## G 7 / A Different Letter

**Directions: Use the same beginning as in G 6, *but* substitute a mas-
culine name for "Rachanee." Now what will you say?**


## THE NONREAL PAST

### Grammar: the nature of the nonreal past

When a course of action is no longer even a possibility, it is said
to belong to the nonreal past. The action points to the past:

We might have won, but we didn't.

Hing could have sung, but he wouldn't.

The modal phrase expressing the nonreal past is formed with three verbs: a past-form modal, *have* (never *has*), and the past participle of the main verb:

|  | Past Form Modal |  | Past Participle |
|---|---|---|---|
| We | might | have | won. |
| Hing | could | have | sung. |

### Oral Practice I: *should have*

Directions: Consider the various situations presented. Respond by saying what the person *should have* done.

Example:

Instructor:   Marie did not understand the assignment. She said nothing.
Student A:   She **should have asked** a question.
Student B:   In fact, she **should have asked** several questions until she was sure she understood.
Student C:   She **should** not **have left** the class until everything was clear.

1. Marie felt ashamed because she did not understand the assignment.
2. Anne put her handbag on the seat beside her in the bus. When she got up to leave, the handbag was gone.
3. Lee likes to walk alone on the campus at midnight.
4. One night he met a robber. He resisted handing over his money.
5. He did not tell the campus police about the incident.
6. Marie stayed out of speech lab because she hated her machine.
7. Aki went to class without breakfast because he didn't want to get up before the dining room closed.
8. Aki wrote his composition in pencil because he wanted to do a lot of erasing.
9. Aki did not go to the dance because he did not know any girls.

### Oral Practice II: *must have*

Directions: Consider the situation presented. Respond by saying what *must have* happened.

Examples:

Instructor:   The sidewalks are wet.
Student A:    It **must have rained** last night.
Student B:    It **must** not **have thundered**. I didn't wake up.

1. This toast is almost black.
2. What is that crash in the kitchen?
3. You say it is time for lunch? It is only 10:00 o'clock by my watch.
4. Lee is smiling.
5. It is 8:30 Monday morning, and Aki is rubbing his eyes.
6. A traffic policeman is signaling to Pete.
7. Before long, the policeman goes back to his station smiling.
8. Now Pete is driving on, more slowly than before.

## Oral Practice III: modals to fit the situation

Directions: Use more than one modal in commenting on the situation presented.

Examples:

Instructor:   Hing wanted to see one of the most popular musicals on Broadway.
Student A:    He could have gone to the box office and asked how many months he would have to wait for a ticket.
Student B:    He could have gone back to the box office around 7:00 P.M. and told the ticket seller that he would wait near his window until curtain time. (Some one might turn in a ticket.)
Student C:    He might have gone to a legitimate ticket broker, paid for an orchestra seat, and paid the broker's moderate fee.
Student D:    He could have gone to a "scalper" and paid as much as seventy-five dollars on the black market.

1. When Aki got off the plane at Kennedy Airport, he did not know how to reach the exit.
2. He took a taxi into the city. He did not observe that buses were running from the airport to the center of New York.
3. The cab driver complained about the size of his tip.
4. At the hotel, Aki merely said, "I'd like a nice room."
5. When he ordered his first meal, he put his finger down on an item and said, "I'll have that."
6. When he telephoned from his room and no one answered, he failed to inform the operator. (These calls, therefore, appeared on his bill.)
7. He did not think of looking under **Foreign Restaurants** in the Yellow Pages of the telephone book.

8. He did not get any information from the Convention and Visitors Bureau across the street from Grand Central station.
9. He did not buy a subway map.
10. When a friend in the suburbs invited him to dinner, he merely memorized the directions. He did not write them down.

## FREE WRITING

### G 8 / A Bad Day for Aki

Directions: Begin, "Aki has had a bad day." Tell what Aki did not do. Say what he could have done, should have done, or might have done at the university or elsewhere. Write one paragraph.

Example:

Aki stayed in bed until the cafeteria had closed. He should have gotten up at 7:30. Then he would have had time for a good breakfast. (He had paid for it.)

## STATEMENTS WITH IF

### Grammar: if with the real present

Notice how real the situations are in the following:

| Condition | Result |
|---|---|
| If it rains, | people grumble. |
| If the weather is fine, | people smile. |

The result clause can stand first in the sentence, making a comma unnecessary:

| Result | Condition |
|---|---|
| People are apt to smile | if the weather is fine. |

### Oral Practice

Directions: Complete the following *if*-clauses with statements in the real present.

Example:

If an exam looks hard, . . .

If an exam looks hard, I count to ten before I write anything.

1. If I finish an exam a few minutes early, . . .
2. If everyone in the hall afterward calls the exam hard, . . .
3. If I want something to eat between meals, . . .
4. If I want a candy bar, . . .
5. If I have to make an important purchase, such as a suit, . . .
6. If my roommate approves of my purchase, . . .
7. If I have to take notes on a lecture, . . .
8. If I can't read my notes afterward, . . .
9. If I have to sign a legal paper, . . .

## Grammar: <u>if</u> with the nonreal present

When a course of action is not fact but is possible, however unlikely, it is said to be in the "nonreal present." The action, though not fact, could become so. Such action points toward the future:

| Condition | Result |
|---|---|
| If someone gave me $10,000, | I would go around the world. |
| If I went around the world, | I would take a thousand pictures. |

The useful term "the nonreal present" does not cover every meaning of every modal in the present form.

Examples:

A motorist **may** not pass another car on a hill.

All drivers **must** stay within the speed limit.

### G 9 / A Few Daydreams[1]

Directions: Copy the topic sentence. Then complete the partial statements in the three following paragraphs, using *would, could,* and *might.* Underline as in the example.

[1] *daydreams:* fancies indulged in while awake.

Example:

If I had my way about the weather, . . .

If I had my way about the weather, it **would be** spring all year.

There is no harm in a few daydreams. If a friend with a car suggested, . . . If transocean telephone calls only cost two dollars for three minutes, . . . If the rules allowed pets in the dormitories, . . .

I might give a talk about my country if . . . . I might even speak on the university television station if. . . . Certainly I would be willing to talk about my country for five minutes in class if. . . .

If this country contained only half as many cars as it does, . . . If heads of state were frank with each other, . . . If everyone in the world had as good an opportunity as everyone else, . . .

*Free writing:* Add an additional paragraph giving a few daydreams of your own.

## Grammar: <u>if</u> with the subjunctive <u>were</u>

The subjunctive *were* represents a condition contrary to fact (the opposite of fact):

If I **were** in China (I'm not), I would try to see everything.

I would accept the invitation if I **were** you. (But I am not you, of course.)

If the students **were** deeply interested in Alaska (they are not), they would go to the lecture.

Note: The subjunctive *were* is used after singular subjects as well as plural subjects.

### G 10 / Not Facts

Directions: First orally and then in writing, complete the two following paragraphs of partial statements, using the subjunctive *were*.

If I were in Paris now, . . . If I were in Rome, . . . If I were on the eighty-sixth floor of the Empire State Building, . . .

I would visit the Louvre if . . . I would climb the ruins of the Forum if . . . I would locate the Statue of Liberty if . . . In short, I would see the great sights of the world if . . .

Free writing: Add a paragraph of your own, using *if* and *were*.

## Grammar: <u>if</u> with the nonreal past

When a course of action is no longer even a possibility, it is said to belong to the nonreal past. The action points to the past:

If we had made one more touchdown (we didn't), we **would have won** the game.

If the instructor had dismissed the class early (he didn't), we **could have had** a coke between classes.

When an *if*-clause is used with the nonreal past, its verb is in the past perfect tense:

| Contrary-to-Fact Clause | Main Clause (Unreal Past) |
|---|---|
| If Pete **had been** a good sailor, | he would have entered the race. |
| If he **had been** a good sailor, | he might have been on the crew. |
| If he **had been** a good sailor, | he could have managed the jib.[1] |

The contrary-to-fact clause can also be placed last in the sentence:

| Main Clause | Contrary-to-Fact Clause |
|---|---|
| Pete could have managed the jib | if he had been a good sailor. |

Note that the nonreal past can occur without an *if* clause:

Definite past time given:
1. We **could have seen** the ballet last night.

Compound sentence pattern:
2. I **should have worked** in the library this morning, but I didn't.

Progressive form:
3. Where was Jim yesterday? He **may have been** fishing.

It is possible to use the past perfect tense with the nonreal present:

If Mr. Z **had received** fifty more votes, he **would be** mayor now.

If we **had elected** Mr. Z, we **might be** sorry now.

[1] *jib*: a triangular sail in the front of a sailboat.

**Oral Practice**

Directions: Complete the partial statement given you with the three-verb modal form of the nonreal past.

Example:

Instructor:   If Pete's alarm clock had gone off at 4:00 A.M., . . .
Student:      He **would have thrown** a pillow at it.

1. If Pete's alarm had not gone off at all this morning, . . .
2. If the shower had produced only cold water, . . .
3. If Bill had dropped a fried egg on the floor, . . .
4. If the toast had burned, . . .
5. If the coffee had boiled over, . . .
6. If Pete had failed to put his homework into his briefcase, . . .
7. If Bill had left all his small change on the living room table, . . .
8. If he had offered the bus driver a five-dollar bill, . . .
9. If he had arrived at work a half hour late, . . .
10. If he had made a serious error on his first work sheet, . . .

**G 11 / Past Possibilities**

Directions: Complete the partial statements in the following paragraph with an *if*-clause in the past perfect tense, underlining the verb.

Example:

I would have begun graduate study sooner . . .

I would have begun graduate study sooner, if I **had known** the difficulty of the work of my present department.

   I would have come to this country five years ago. . . . I would have taken more English in my own country. . . . I might have received my visa with less delay. . . . In the United States, I could have worked part-time. . . . I might have rented an apartment. . . . I would have added one more course to my schedule. . . .

## Grammar: <u>had had</u>

The past perfect tense of the verb *have* is *had had.* The auxiliary is *had;* the main verb (past participle) also is *had*:

I would have seen the new exhibition in the university museum if I *had had* more time yesterday afternoon.

## G 12 / Using *Had Had* in Writing

Directions: First, insert *if I had had more time* into each partial statement orally.

Example:

I would have finished this paragraph with more examples . . . on Monday.

I would have finished this paragraph with more examples **if I had had more time** on Monday.

When writing, copy the topic sentence, insert the *if*-clause, and underline *had had*.

All I needed this past week was a few more hours in each day. I would have studied seven hours . . . on Monday. I would have lingered after lunch talking . . . on Tuesday. I would have gone to the concert . . . Wednesday. I would have listened to the candidates debate on TV . . . on Thursday. Surely I would have cleared out my desk . . . Friday. Best of all, I would have gone into the city . . . over the weekend.

## G 13 / If Betty Only Had

Directions: Complete the following paragraph of *if*-clauses in the past perfect tense with three-word verb forms, underlined, in the main clauses.

Example:

If Betty had understood some of the uses of trigonometry, . . .

If Betty had understood some of the uses of trigonometry, she **would have studied** it more willingly.

If Betty had felt less helpless about trigonometry, . . . If she had depended less on her friends, . . . If she had persisted when she got the wrong answer the first time, . . . In short, if she had made a stronger general effort to pass, . . .

## G 14 / Who Was the Ghost?

Directions: First, listen while your instructor reads "The Situation" below. Then tell what was said in your own words. Then write the four paragraphs, changing the first two paragraphs of questions into statements and dealing with the last two paragraphs as indicated.

The Situation

One afternoon early in January a few years ago, three school girls and their teacher went to visit the beautiful Jumel Mansion far up on Manhattan Island in New York City.

The Jumel Mansion is a very old house by American standards. George Washington held military trials in its elegant drawing room during the American Revolution. Now it is a museum, open to the public.

No attendant appeared as the four approached the house. No one at all appeared except an old woman who spoke to the visitors briefly from a second-story balcony. The visitors spoke briefly to her.

Then the curator[1] of the museum appeared. She said there could not possibly have been anyone on the balcony. The door leading onto the balcony had been padlocked[2] for years.

Note: The use of *was* instead of *were* in the first paragraph below indicates that the situations are being presented as not definitely contrary to fact.

If there was a figure on the balcony of the Jumel Mansion, would some persons call it a ghost? If it was a ghost, could it have been Madame Jumel herself? In her old age, years after she had first married and then dismissed the reputed traitor, Aaron Burr, might she have been unhappy?

On the other hand, might the figure have been Mary Philipse, who had lived in the house before Madame Jumel? After Mistress Philipse had declined the proposal of the obscure young George Washington and married a more prominent man, might she, too, have been unhappy?

If I had seen the figure on the balcony, . . . . If the old woman had called, "I'll be down in a minute," . . .

I am satisfied/not satisfied to have science say firmly that there could not possibly have been a figure on the balcony outside the padlocked door. (Say **why** or **why not**.)

## FREE WRITING

### G 15 / My Ghost Story

Directions: If you know a good ghost story, tell it, without definitely stating that it could not be fact.

[1] *curator:* a person in charge of a museum.
[2] *padlock:* a special lock, sometimes added to a door as a second lock.

**The Peacock Room, designed by James McNeill Whistler.**
[Courtesy of the Smithsonian Institution,
Freer Gallery of Art, Washington, D.C.]

## G 16 / A Tangle[1] of Problems

The Situation

In Washington, D.C. there is a small, important museum called
the Freer Gallery of Art. It has an interesting collection of
Eastern art and one unique feature, the Peacock[2] Room.

The Peacock Room was designed over a hundred years
ago by the highly talented, highly self-centered painter, James
McNeill Whistler.[3] This account tells of the ruthless drive by which
Whistler secured the setting he wished for his notable painting
"Princess from the Land of Porcelain."[4]

[1] *tangle:* a twisted, confused mass.
[2] *peacock:* a large bird with beautiful green, blue, and gold-colored
feathers. The tail feathers can be spread and held upright, like a large fan.
[3] *James McNeill Whistler,* 1834–1903: American painter; lived in England.
[4] *porcelain:* fine china, often blue and white flowered jars, made in China
more than a thousand years ago.

The painting had been purchased by a wealthy ship owner, Frederick Leyland, to emphasize the beauty of the collection of porcelain which decorated the dining room of his new house. Young Henry Jeckyll had decorated the room with both the porcelain and the picture in mind.

When Whistler was invited to see the result, he was pleased with the prominent place given his picture, high on the wall at one end of the room. However, he asked the owner's permission to subdue the other decorations just a little in order to bring out the silver and rose of the princess's delicate robes. Mr. Leyland gave his permission and went out of town.

Whistler began by painting out the small red flowers of the leather hangings covering the walls. Next, he cut off the red border of the rug. From this point he went on, sometimes with the owner's permission and sometimes without it. In the end, the leather hangings, brought to England by Catherine of Aragon at the time of her marriage to Henry VIII, were completely covered with blue paint.

Now the peacock motif began to appear. Huge peacocks were painted around the room, their blue-green tails spreading against a gold background. Two angry peacocks high at one end of the room confronted one another opposite the Princess. The finished room was strange, beautiful, and costly. One cost was a final, undignified quarrel.

No contract had ever been drawn up, but seemingly the original understanding was that Whistler was to receive five hundred guineas for his work. When he presented a bill for two thousand guineas, Mr. Leyland refused to pay it. Eventually, he paid a thousand pounds, which Whistler regarded as an insult.

The insult lay, not in the reduction from the amount asked, but in the fact that the payment was in pounds, not guineas. A guinea was only worth a shilling more than a pound, approximately fourteen cents in American money. The point, however, was that professional men were paid in guineas; tradesmen were paid in pounds. In revenge, Whistler painted the two angry peacocks, one clutching a pile of shillings to represent Mr. Leyland, the second with its tail proudly spread to represent Whistler himself.

A second cost of the room was the fate of young Henry Jekyll, the original decorator. He was cut to the heart by what had been done to his work. Eventually he was found talking wildly of flowers and peacocks while he covered the floor of his bedroom with gold paint. He died without regaining his sanity.

As for Frederick Leyland, who had had the discernment to buy "The Princess," he put away his collection of porcelain and let the room have its way. He had had a masterpiece forced upon him, and he accepted the fact.

**Directions:** Begin, "Here is my comment on the part played by each of the three men who had a part in creating the Freer "Peacock Room." Give your writing a clear outline by using the last name, underlined, of the three men as subtitles. Use the sentences in the examples as you find convenient.

Examples:

*Jeckyll*
   This young man, with talent of his own, was destroyed by his collision with a greater talent. He **might have, could** not **have** . . .

*Leyland*
   The owner paid well for a room which contained a permanent insult to his dignity. Yet . . . .

*Whistler*
   The artist destroyed irreplaceable beauty in order to create his own beauty. He **should have, should** not **have, might have, could have** . . .

## Listen and Write: *The Lady or the Tiger*[1]

**Directions:** Write down the first sentence of a paragraph; then listen to the paragraph twice. Then write down what you remember.[2]

   In the old days, a barbaric[3] king lived in a far-off country. He had great power, and he loved to laugh. Also, he liked to play barbaric jokes with the law. When a man broke the law, the king did not always send him to prison. Sometimes he ordered the man to come to the king's arena[4] and then invited all the people to come and watch.
   After the people were in their seats, the king would sit down on his high throne, and the prisoner would step into the center of the arena. Opposite him were two doors exactly alike. Behind one door was a hungry tiger. Behind the other door was a

[1] Author, Frank R. Stockton, American, 1832–1900.
[2] *To the instructor:* It is probably best not to work on more than two paragraphs a day.
[3] *barbaric:* not civilized, often cruel.
[4] *arena:* a big building or open space with seats all around, used for sports.

beautiful lady. The prisoner could open either door. His freedom
was complete. But he had to open a door. If the tiger came out,
it ate the man. Then the people were sad because the man was
guilty. If the beautiful lady came out, a priest married the two
immediately. Then the people were glad because the man was
innocent. Either way, the king was pleased with himself.

A day came when the king was not pleased. He discovered
that his beautiful daughter, the princess, had been in love
with the wrong man for many months. The young man was handsome
and brave, but he was not the son of a king. His position in
life was low. The king was very angry. He did not send the young
man to prison. He named a day for him to appear in the arena.

Now the princess loved the young man with all her heart.
With the help of gold, she discovered the secret of the two
doors. Then she faced a dreadful question. Which did she want
for her lover—the lady or the tiger? The lady was beautiful,
and she had smiled at the lover more than once. The princess hated
her. And yet the tiger! The blood! The princess was barbaric,
like her father. Was the lady to have the lover when the princess
could not? After many days and nights, she made up her mind.

On the dreadful day, all the people gathered in the arena.
The king sat down on his high throne. His daughter, white and
silent, sat beside him. The young man walked to the center of the
arena and looked up at the princess. His eyes asked, "Which
door?" She lifted her hand and made a slight, quick movement
to the right. No one but her lover saw her. He turned and
walked with a firm and rapid step across the empty space.
He went to the door on the right and opened it.

Which came out, the lady or the tiger?[1]


## FREE WRITING

### G 17 / The Lady or the Tiger: My Solution

Directions: Cover three main points in your composition:

1. Which door do you think the princess pointed to? What makes you
   think so?
2. What do you think the princess should have done?
3. The author was unfair to his readers. Do you mind?

---

[1] To the end of his long life, Stockton maintained that he did not know
which came out of the right-hand door. It all depended upon what the
reader thought of the princess.

Sample solutions:

If the princess had been civilized, she would have married her lover in secret months before.

The princess should have indicated the door with the tiger and died with her lover.

She should have indicated the door with the lady and then negotiated with the lady and the lover not to marry. She was a princess. She should have been able to get her man.

# Section H

---

## The Passive Voice
## With and Without a By-phrase
## Spelling: Rules 4 and 5

**Grammar: the passive voice with a by-phrase**

In the active voice, the subject acts. In the passive voice the subject is acted upon:

|  | Subject | Verb | Object | By-Phrase |
|---|---|---|---|---|
| Active voice | The tiger | ate | the goat. | — |
| Passive voice | The goat | was eaten | — | by the tiger. |
| | | | | |
| Active voice | The chairman | read | the report. | — |
| Passive voice | The report | was read | — | by the chairman. |

When a sentence is changed from the active to the passive voice, the original subject, the performer, then appears after the verb as a by-phrase.[1] (The verb itself is some form of *be* plus the past participle. Note *was eaten* and *was read* above.)

**Oral Practice**

Directions: Change the following sentences in the active voice into the passive voice with a by-phrase.

Example:

Active voice: Betty arranged the picnic.

[1] For the passive forms without a by-phrase, see this section, p. 215.

Passive voice: The picnic was arranged **by Betty.**

1. Anne made the sandwiches.
2. Marie made the salad.
3. Mrs. Smith furnished the fried chicken and rolls.
4. José produced fine Colombian coffee.
5. Hing brought fine black tea.
6. Pete and Bill provided the transportation.
7. Everyone had a good time.

8. Henry Ford made the first inexpensive automobile.
9. The Wright brothers made the first inexpensive "flying machine."
10. Leonardo da Vinci had drawn plans for a flying machine four hundred years earlier.

11. A Frenchman drew the plans for Washington, D.C.[1]
12. A Frenchman designed the Statue of Liberty.[2]
13. An American proposed the League of Nations.[3]

## THE PASSIVE FORMS

In the passive voice, the main verb is the past participle. Tense is expressed by various forms of *be* and *have*:

| Tense | | Be/Have | Past Participle |
|---|---|---|---|
| Present | I | am | seen. |
| | He | is | seen. |
| | They | are | seen. |
| Past | I | was | introduced. |
| | They | were | introduced. |
| Future | I | will be | examined. |
| | They | will be | examined. |
| Present perfect | I | have been | notified. |
| | He | has been | notified. |
| | They | have been | notified. |
| Past Perfect | I | had been | admitted. |
| | They | had been | admitted. |

[1] Pierre Charles L'Enfant, 1754–1825.
[2] Frederic Auguste Bartholdi, 1834–1904.
[3] the *League of Nations*: the unsuccessful forerunner of the *United Nations*, proposed by President Woodrow Wilson in 1919.

The future perfect passive tense, although seldom used in speech, is occasionally used in writing:

Many new sources of energy **will have been developed** by 1980, we hope.

## The Progressive Passive Forms

There are only two tenses in the progressive passive, the present and the past. Both have some form of *be,* the present participle *being,* and the past participle as the main verb:

| Tense | | Be | Being | Past Participle |
|---|---|---|---|---|
| Present | I | am | being | helped. |
| | He | is | being | helped. |
| | They | are | being | helped. |
| Past | I | was | being | helped. |
| | They | were | being | helped. |

## H 1 / Congress

Directions: Turn the two following paragraphs of statements into the passive voice. Underline the verbs.

Examples:

Active voice: The Senate will debate a bill of great importance tomorrow.

Passive voice: A bill of great importance **will be debated** by the Senate tomorrow.

Progressive active: The committee is completing certain details tonight.

Progressive passive: Certain details are **being completed** by the committee tonight.

The Senate passed a bill of major importance today. Its provisions will affect the lives of millions. The senators debated the bill at great length. Now the President will sign it.

A congressional subcommittee is holding important hearings. The committee has asked experts to testify. The major networks are not going to televise the proceedings. However, their newscasters will summarize the findings of the committee.

## H 2 / A New Job for Ahmad

Directions: Change each statement in the following paragraph into the passive voice with a *by*-phrase. Underline as in the example.

Active voice: Ahmad has just received an interesting offer.

Passive voice: An interesting offer **has** just **been received** by Ahmad.

The Allied Chemical Company (just employ) Ahmad. The personnel manager hired him yesterday. The general manager (assign) him to the plastics division. His new boss (introduce) him to his fellow workers this morning. His new associates (welcome) him immediately and heartily. All his friends are (now congratulate) him. Ahmad (just take) a big step forward.

## H 3 / To the Age of Six

Directions: Write two paragraphs, crowding in a variety of facts about the first six years of your life. Use some of the following passive verb phrases and others that occur to you.

Paragraph 1
  was **born** (where, when)
  was early **taught** by my mother to
  was later **taught** by my father to
  was **taken** by my grandfather
  was **told** stories about _____ by my grandmother

Paragraph 2
  was **sent** to school (where, when)
  was promptly **told** to
  was soon **taught** to
  was sometimes **scolded** for
  was more often **praised** for

## Grammar: the passive voice without a <u>by</u>-phrase

Sentences in the passive voice frequently do not have a *by*-phrase; no performer of the action is named after the verb. There are at least three such situations:

1. The performer is unknown:
   The jewels **were stolen** some time Tuesday night.
   Corn **is grown** extensively in the state of Illinois.

2. An impersonal approach is wise:
   "Seemingly, an error has been made." (better than "You have made a mistake on my order.")
   "The matter will be rectified within a few days." (No one is blamed, but the matter will be taken care of promptly.)

3. The subject in the active voice is an impersonal **someone, we** or **they,** eliminated in the passive voice:

   Active voice:    **Someone** left the classroom windows open last night.
   Passive voice:   The classroom windows **were left** open last night.

   Active voice:    **We** must do more about air pollution.
   Passive voice:   More **must be done** about air pollution.

   Active voice:    **They** have removed the wrecked car.
   Passive voice:   The wrecked car **has been** removed.

## Oral Practice

Directions: Change the statement given you into the passive voice without a *by*-phrase.

1. Someone sweeps the classrooms every night.
2. Someone straightens up the chairs afterward.
3. Someone washes the blackboards every night.
4. Someone puts out more chalk afterward.

5. They cut a road through the jungle.
6. They brought modern ways to a primitive people.
7. They did both good and harm to the people.

8. We must find jobs for all who want them.
9. We must conquer the problem of drug addiction.
10. We must find a way to end modern warfare.
11. We should preserve our finest old buildings.
12. In general, we should preserve our artistic heritage.

13. They have painted the whole dormitory.
14. They have put new furniture in the first-floor lounge.
15. They have installed an automatic coffee machine in the snack bar.

## Listen and Write: How to Make Tortillas[1]

Directions: Listen to the reading twice. Write down this beginning statement now: "Tortillas are Mexican bread."

[1] To *the instructor:* The words *tortillas* and *tacos* should be placed on the blackboard before the two dictations, so that the students need not hesitate over the spelling.

Part I

Tortillas are Mexican bread. Here is how they are made.
Cornmeal and water are mixed until they are thick. Then the mixture
is patted between the hands into thin, flat cakes. Next, the cakes
are placed on a very hot iron sheet. When one side is browned, the
cook turns the tortilla over and browns the other side.

**Directions: Write down this partial statement now: "Tortillas are
eaten with . . ."**

Part II

Tortillas are eaten with the fingers, with butter, with salt, or
with nothing. A hungry boy may eat six or seven tortillas, along
with everything else in his meal.

Very often tortillas are filled with meat, chicken, cheese, or
beans. Then they become a new dish called **tacos**.

## H 4 / Returning a Purchase

**Directions: Copy the following incomplete letter, supplying the in-
formation the blanks require.**

Your address
Date

Address,
out-of-town store                        Attention: Customer Service

Gentlemen:

On (month, day) I ordered a plastic raincoat (small/medium/large)
in size, and _____ in color, as advertised in (newspaper) of
(month, date.) A money order for _____ was enclosed with
the order.

Somehow, an error was made in filling the order.[1] The coat
I received . . . (say what was wrong.)

I am returning the raincoat by parcel post, insured. May I ask
you to fill the order as given on (month, day.)

Very truly yours,
(your name)

[1] Formal business letters often use the passive voice when an impersonal
approach is wise.

## Spelling: Rule 4

Keep the final e before a suffix beginning with a consonant (*ful*, *ly*, *ment*, *less*, etc.). Such words will not be verbs.

| Adverbs | Nouns | Adjectives |
|---|---|---|
| surely | amusement | hopeful |
| sincerely | excitement | hopeless |
| separately | engagement | useful |
| fortunately | encouragement | useless |
| nicely | amazement | careful |
| freely | announcement | woeful |
| strangely | advancement | gleeful |
| savagely | inducement | |
| wisely | | |
| cutely | | |

### Dictation I

The candidate was actively asking for votes. Surely he spoke sincerely. Some voters said he did not speak wisely. Others said they liked his speaking frankly. Secretly, the majority intended to vote for the other man.

### Dictation II

Surely we all need amusement. We came to the party hopeful of a little excitement. An engagement was announced. This was encouragement to great excitement. However, the party ended quietly.

## Spelling: Rule 5, Part I

If *ly* is added to a word already ending in *l*, a doubled *l* results in the new word:

natural—naturally     usual—usually     real—really

### Dictation

Marcel had only a year to spend in the United States. Naturally he wanted to talk to as many Americans as he could. Usually Americans also wanted to talk to him. Really he had very little trouble when he spoke English. He spoke carefully, and the

Americans spoke carefully. Financially they had many interests in common.

## Spelling: Rule 5, Part II

The suffix *ful* has only one *l*. However, if *ly* is added to a word already ending in *ful*, a double *l* results.

careful—carefully     thoughtful—thoughtfully     hopeful—hopefully

### Dictation
The class prepared for the mid-term composition thoughtfully. During the test everyone wrote carefully. At the end of the hour, everyone left hopefully. Results would not be known for two days.

### FREE WRITING

#### H 5 / Progress in (name of country)

Directions: Write about what progress has been made in your country during your lifetime. Write on three subtopics only in order to keep your composition fairly short. Turn in a brief outline with your composition.

#### H 6 / Changes in Education

Directions: Write about what changes should be made in order to improve the educational system in your country. Write on three subtopics only. Turn in a brief outline with your composition.

#### H 7 / The Exercise of Civil Rights

Directions: Begin, "Great progress has been made in the last few years in the exercise of their civil rights by _____." Name a minority group in the United States or in your own country. Write of gains in three fields, perhaps job opportunities, educational opportunities, and participation in professional sports. (Keep in mind the difference between having the legal right to do something and having a practical opportunity to do it). Turn in a brief outline with your composition.

## H 8 / Space Travel

Directions: Begin, "Great progress has been made in the last few years in the field of space travel." Write on three subtopics and turn in a brief outline with your composition. In your concluding paragraph, begin some sentence, "It is my hope that . . ."

## H 9 / International Cooperation

Directions: Begin, "Some progress has been made in the last few years in increased cooperation among nations." Hold this vast subject to three well-selected examples.

In your concluding paragraph, bring in the idea that greater progress in cooperation must be achieved if the human race is to survive, if this is your conviction. Turn in a brief outline with your paper.

## H 10 / (a topic of your own choice)

# Section 9

---

**That-Clauses**
**Included <u>Wh</u>-Questions**
**Say, Tell, Ask, Explain**
**Spelling: Rule 6**
**The One-Sentence Quotation**
**Writing Conversation**

## THAT-CLAUSES

### Grammar: <u>that-clauses</u>

A statement can be included in another statement as a *that-*clause:

| Statement: | | That-*clause* |
|---|---|---|
| It is raining again. | I wish | (that) it wouldn't rain so much. |
| The ground is very wet. | I hear | (that) the ground is too wet to plant crops. |

As the parentheses indicate, *that* can be used or omitted in an included statement.

### List

A great variety of verbs can be followed by a *that*-clause, among them the following:

| | | |
|---|---|---|
| agree | discover | predict |
| announce | doubt | realize |

221

| | | |
|---|---|---|
| answer | feel | say |
| assert | forget | state |
| assume | hope | think |
| believe | know | understand |
| decide | maintain | wish |

## Oral Practice I

**Directions: Complete the following partial statements in the simple present tense.**

1. It is easy to **assume** (that) carelessly dressed teenagers . . .
2. Yet I **feel** (that) these boys and girls . . .
3. Some older people may **decide** (that) . . .
4. It is easy to **doubt** (that) . . .
5. However, I **believe** (that) . . .
6. Certainly I **hope** (that) . . .

**Further directions: Complete the following partial statements in the future tense.**

7. Once again, the weather man **has predicted** (that) . . .
8. Our instructor **has** just **announced** (that) . . .
9. A prominent politician **has stated** (that) . . .
10. I **have decided** (that) . . .

## Oral Practice II

**Directions: Complete the partial statements with the past-form modal supplied.**

1. Saturday morning was fair and warm, just as the weather man had predicted. Our club suddenly **decided** (that) . . . **(would)**
2. Our president liked our plan. He **announced** (that) . . . **(would)**
3. Our refreshment committee is equal to anything. They **said** (that) . . . **(could)**
4. We walked for two hours, enjoying the clear air and the autumn colors of the trees. We **forgot** (that) . . . **(might)**
5. The sky grew dark. It began to rain hard. We **hoped** (that) . . . **(might)**
6. The rain did not stop. We **decided** (that) . . . **(had better)**
7. Luckily, the rain was warm. We **knew** (that) . . . **(would not)**
8. We arrived at the dorm soaking wet but not chilled.[1] We **agreed** (that) the weather man . . . **(had better)**

[1] *chilled:* unpleasantly cold.

**I 1 / My Family Speaks about English**

Directions: Copy the completed statements. Complete the partial statements with a verb from the list on pp. 221–222 and a *that*-clause.

Example:

I . . .

I **knew** that my family had all studied English. I **believed** they had all found it a little hard.

I decided one day to ask the members of my family whether English was hard or easy to learn.

I started with my grandfather, who was sitting in his arm chair. He. . . . My grandmother had a different opinion. She. . . . My father came in at that moment. He. . . . My mother answered with a proverb. She. . . . Then I turned to my little brother, who was flying a toy airplane. He. . . . My family did not let me escape giving my opinion. I. . . .

**FREE WRITING**

**I 2 / An Opinion of Mine**

Directions: Make use of a few of the partial statements in the example below, or express your opinion on an entirely different subject. Write one paragraph.

Example:

I **feel** strongly (that) this school could get along very well without examinations. I **realize** that. . . . I **agree** that. . . . However, in my own experience I have **discovered** that. . . . In short, I **believe** that. . . .

## INCLUDED <u>WH</u>-QUESTIONS

### Grammar: included <u>wh</u>-questions

A *wh*-question can be asked by itself, or it can be included in a statement:

Question:   Where's Pete?
Statement:   (**wh**-question included): I don't know **where Pete is.**

An included question takes statement form after the question word:

| I don't know | why | Subject | Verb |
|---|---|---|---|
| I don't know | why | Pete | went to town. |
| I don't know | when | he | will be back. |
| I don't know | what | he | will say. |

## List: <u>wh-words</u> used in included questions

| | | |
|---|---|---|
| who | whether | what time |
| (whom) | (or not) | whose book |
| what | how[1] | which room |
| when | how often | etc. |
| where | how many | |
| which | how soon | |
| why | how much, | |
| | etc. | |

## Oral Practice I: I don't know

Directions: When you are asked a question or given a command say, "I don't know," and complete the statement. Perhaps add a second statement of your own.

Example:

Question:   What do you think of daytime TV?
Statement:   I don't know **what I think of daytime TV.** I never watch it.

1. Who tells the best jokes on TV?
2. Which TV or radio station carries the most music?
3. Name a TV series that contains violence in every program.
4. Name a TV program that deals with the trials (and joys) of family life.
5. Name a TV program that you feel gives biased coverage of the news.[2]
6. What program puts the most people in a good humor at the end of the day?
7. What old-fashioned Western is still on the air?
8. Who watches TV at two in the morning?
9. What important newscasts come on the air just after dinner?

[1] As a matter of convenience, the *how* question words are placed with the *wh*-words.
[2] *biased coverage:* favoring one side of a public question over another.

## Oral Practice II: I'm sorry

Directions: Pretend it is your first day on the campus. When you ask for information, you encounter only other newcomers, who reply with one of two courteous negatives (placed on the blackboard):

I'm sorry, I can't tell you . . . I'm new here myself.

I'm sorry, I can't explain . . . (complete the statement).

1. How do I get a college catalog?
2. Where is the registrar's office?
3. When do we have to pay our bills?
4. Please explain how to use this catalog.
5. Please explain what a snack bar is.
6. Please tell me how often it rains here.
7. Where can I get some stamps?
8. Please explain to me what an adviser does.
9. Where does the college bus stop?
10. How soon will the term end?

## Oral Practice III: A Great-Artists Series

Directions: Include an indirect question in answering the question asked. Follow this statement with a sentence of explanation.

Example:

Instructor:  Do you know **what a "Great-Artists Series" is?**
Student:  I know **what a "Great-Artists Series" is.** (included question)
The university brings singers, orchestras, and dancers to the campus. (explanation)

1. Do you know what a season ticket is?[1]
2. Do you know why most students buy a season ticket?
3. Do you know where to buy one?
4. Have you decided where you want to sit?
5. Do you remember where you sat last year?
6. Do you remember whom[2] you enjoyed most last year?
7. Can you tell me what well-known orchestras are coming this year?
8. Have you heard what great soprano will appear?

---

[1] If a student buys a season ticket, he can see every performance from the same good seat at a very low price, compared to single admissions.
[2] *Who* is acceptable instead of *whom* in conversation.

9. Do you know how many dance companies are coming?
10. Can you tell me what night the series begins?

## I 3 / I Can Tell You

Directions: Complete the two following paragraphs of partial statements with included *wh*-questions. Underline the question word.

Example:

I can tell you <u>how much</u> fine beef is exported from Argentina.
I can tell you <u>who</u> our greatest sports hero is.

Just let me tell you about (name of country.) I can tell you **how far**. . . . I can tell you **how many**. . . . I can tell you **what** crops. . . . I can tell you. . . . In addition, I can tell you. . . .

If you are interested in art, I can tell you **where**. . . . And I can tell you **what**. . . . If you are interested in a business position, I can tell you **what** company. . . . Moreover, I can tell you **whom**. . . . In short, I can tell you **how** to take advantage of. . . .

## FREE WRITING

## I 4 / Progress

Directions: Write a paragraph beginning, "How ignorant I was my first two weeks on the campus!"

Example:

I didn't know where the college auditorium was.[1] I wondered why the instructor took attendance.

## Grammar: <u>whether</u>

If an included *wh*-question can be answered by *yes* or *no*, *whether* is often used:

Student A:   Is it going to rain?
Student B:   I can't say **whether** it is going to rain (or not).
Student C:   Are you planning to take Dr. Simpson's psychology course next term?

[1] The present tense may also be used. (See *Attracted Tenses*, p. 232.)

Student D:   I hear it is a very good course, but I haven't decided
             **whether** I am going to take it (or not).

The use of *whether* is standard in writing. *If* is often used in
speech:

I can't decide if it is going to rain or not.

**Oral Practice**

Directions: Listen to the question and the words which follow. Form a
new sentence using *whether*.

Example:

Student A:   Do you think this store sells unpainted furniture?[1] (Let's
             find out . . .)
Student B:   Let's find out whether they sell unpainted furniture or not.

1. Do I want to go or don't I? (I can't decide . . .)
2. Are we going in the right direction? (I'll ask . . .)
3. Did I lock my door? (I'm not sure . . .)
4. Do we have homework for tomorrow? (I'm not sure . . .)
5. Is that building City Hall? (Can you tell me . . .)
6. Does this bus stop at 120th Street? (I'd better ask . . .)
7. Will Mr. X or Mr. Y be elected next Tuesday? (No one can say . . .)
8. Is there an electrical repair shop near the campus? (I don't
   know . . .)
9. May students park their cars on the campus? (I'd certainly like to
   know . . .)
10. Will the dorm have banana splits[2] for dessert Friday evening? (I'm
    having a guest. I'd certainly like to know . . .)

## Grammar: <u>ask</u>, <u>explain</u>, <u>say</u>, <u>tell</u>

|               *Ask*               |             *Explain*             |
| --------------------------------- | --------------------------------- |
| A person is often mentioned with  | A person is often mentioned with  |
| ask:                              | explain:                          |

---

[1] *unpainted furniture*: simple, inexpensive furniture, often bought by students and painted by them.
[2] *banana splits*: a favorite student dessert, made with a banana, split lengthwise. On this, students pile mounds of ice cream, a sweet sauce, nuts, and candied cherries.

Bill **asked the instructor** a question.

A person does not need to be mentioned with **ask:**

Bill **asked** a question.

**Ask** is often used with a direct quotation:

Chu **asked,** "What does this word mean?"

**Ask** is often used with included *wh*-clauses:

Chu **asked** what the word meant.

*Say*

**Say** often introduces a direct quotation:

Pete said, **"The horse show is in town."**

**Say** can introduce a **that**-clause:

Pete said **(that) the horse show was in town.**

**Say** may or may not name the person addressed:

Pete said **to Bill,** "The horse show is in town."

Bill said, "Let's go."

**Say** can introduce a directly quoted question:

Bill said, "Will it be hard to get tickets?"

Please **explain** this problem **to me.**

I'll **explain** it **to you** if I can. ("Explain me" is ungrammatical.)

A person does not need to be mentioned with **explain:**

Please **explain** this problem.

**Explain** is not used with a direct quotation.

**Explain** is often used with included *wh*-clauses:

Hing **explained** what the word meant.

*Tell*

**Tell** cannot introduce a direct quotation. Quotation marks are never used after **tell.**

**Tell** can introduce a **that**-clause:

Pete told Bill **(that) the horse show was in town.**

**Tell** must name the person addressed ("told that" is ungrammatical).

Pete told **Bill** (that) this show was better than last year's.

**Tell** can introduce an included *wh*-question:

Pete **told** Bill **where** to get tickets.

**Tell** can mean "to give the facts":

Pete **told** the officer the truth.

A **to**-phrase can be added at the end of the sentence:

Pete **told** the truth **to the officer.**

## I 5 / On Old-Timer to a Newcomer

Directions: Chu has been in the United States less than twenty-four hours; Hing has been here for six months. Copy the paragraph below, filling the blanks from the following list:

asked Hing     explained . . . to Chu

told Chu       explained

Underline the words you insert.

    Chu _____ _____ why the people on the streets were in such a hurry. Hing _____ _____ that Americans hurried from habit, whether they had to or not. Chu _____ _____ why Americans talked so fast. Hing _____ _____ that Americans only seemed to talk fast. Chu _____ _____ whether it was safe to cross a street filled with cars. Hing _____ the system of traffic lights _____ _____. He _____ its safety features clearly.

## I 6 / A Stranger Whom I Helped

Directions: Complete the partial statements in the three following paragraphs with included *wh*-questions or *that*-clauses.

    I saw a man the other day hesitating just inside the entrance to a large, crowded cafeteria. I knew immediately. . . . Although the stranger might have refused curtly,[1] I asked him whether. . . . He replied with relief that. . . . I learned without surprise. . . .

    I guided the stranger to a pile of trays. I explained. . . . I showed him the silverware and napkins. I told him. . . . We moved together along the food counter. I pointed out where (meats). . . . Next, I pointed out where (vegetables). . . . The stranger's eyes brightened when (desserts) . . . . When we reached the coffee urn, I showed him how to. . . . When we reached the cashier, I explained that. . . . before eating.

    The stranger was grateful. He told me. . . .

[1] *curtly:* almost rudely.

**Listen and Write: The Traffic Accident**

When Pete got back to his apartment one evening, he told Bill that he had been in a traffic accident. He said that he had thought he had time to make a certain turn, but he hadn't. Another car smashed into the side of his car.

Both young men had to go to the police station. Pete told the officer the truth. The officer said that Pete's fine would be twenty-five dollars. Whether the other young man was driving too fast or not, he had the right of way. Bill said to Pete, "I think you were both lucky."

## Spelling: Rule 6

If a word ends in y preceded by a consonant, y is changed to i before any suffix except *ing*:[1]

| *Verbs* | *Nouns* | *Adverbs* |
|---|---|---|
| study—studies | lady—ladies | noisy—noisily |
| studying | party—parties | easy—easily |
| try—tries | duty—duties | steady—steadily |
| trying | city—cities | weary—wearily |
| copy—copies | | |
| copying | | |
| worry—worries | | |
| worrying | | |

If a word ends in y preceded by a *vowel*, the rule usually does not apply:

enjoy—enjoyed     play—played     toy—toys

Common exceptions:

day—daily     pay—paid     say—said

**Dictation I**[2]

We cheered our team noisily. We bet on it heavily. Naturally we had a betting limit of a quarter. We thought our team would win easily. It lost. We went home sadly.

[1] *Exception:* Final y does not change to i when the suffix is *ing* under any circumstances. For example, hurry—hurrying, carry—carrying, party—partying.

[2] *To the instructor:* It is suggested that you choose among the first five dictations and then use VI and VII.

## Dictation II

Ladies like parties. They plan for them happily. They give them easily. Ladies consider parties one of their duties.

## Dictation III

Bill goes to school in one of our largest cities. He studies hard. He studied five hours yesterday. He carries a heavy briefcase to the university every day. He copies nothing from other students. He relies on his own efforts. He tries his best.

## Dictation IV

Betty has many duties. She goes to class every day. She copies all her assignments from the blackboard. She hurries home when classes are over. Then she studies. She seldom worries. Over the weekend, she goes to parties happily.

## Dictation V

Many countries now have at least a few modern factories. The citizens of such countries tell many stories about the high salaries paid in such factories. These stories may or may not be true.

## Dictation VI

Everyone in this course is trying his best. Everyone is studying hard. Almost everyone is carrying at least eight hours of work. No one is playing. Everyone is praying for lighter work next quarter. Yet most students are applying for permission to take more hours.

## Dictation VII

Marie is trying to live within her salary. She is not buying anything on credit. She is not worrying. She is enjoying what she has. She will be applying for a more demanding position soon.

## ATTRACTED TENSES

*Past/Past*

### Grammar: the convention of attracted tenses

Until recently, a convention[1] in English said that when the verb in the introductory clause was in the past tense, the verb in the *that*-clause *had to* be in the past tense; it was "attracted" into the past tense by the introductory verb.

Examples:

The candidate said (that) he **needed** our votes next Tuesday.

The teacher told the children (that) the earth **was** round.

Such sentences are grammatical and still often written, but one may now use a tense that expresses the facts:

The candidate said (that) he **needs** our votes next Tuesday.

The teacher told the children (that) the earth **is** round.

In the above examples, the reality or *force of the facts* is so strong as to break through the normal attraction to the past of the main verb.

### Oral Practice: told his cousin that

Directions: When you are given a direct quotation, give the same information through a *that*-clause, an indirect quotation.

Instructor: Eugene said, "I am learning something about transportation in the United States." (direct quotation)

Student: Eugene **told his cousin**/roommate/girlfriend that he was learning something about transportation in the United States. (indirect quotation)

1. Eugene said, "Superhighways cross the continent."
2. Eugene said, "Traffic moves endlessly on these highways."
3. Eugene said, "A four-lane highway is something to see."
4. He said, "Huge trucks travel on these highways."
5. He said, "These trucks carry tons of freight."
6. He said, "The trucks travel all night."

---

[1] *a convention*: a customary way of doing things.

7. Eugene said, "On long trips, one man drives and one man sleeps."
8. He said, "In the morning both men stop for a big breakfast."

## I 7 / Some Proverbs of Benjamin Franklin's

The following short, wise sayings, or proverbs, are a few of the many with which Benjamin Franklin enriched the almanac which he published yearly for twenty-five years before the American Revolution. The predictions about the weather were guesses, but the proverbs, gathered from many sources and polished by Franklin, are a pleasure still.

Directions: First, read the proverbs aloud with your instructor, making sure of the meaning. Then give the information in the direct quotation orally, using *told* and a *that*-clause. Finally, write the sentences using *told* and *that*.

Example:

Benjamin Franklin said to his skeptical readers, "Hunger is the best pickle."[1]

Benjamin Franklin **told his skeptical readers that** hunger is the best pickle.

1. Benjamin Franklin said to his colonial readers, "Genius without education is like silver in the mine."
2. Franklin said to the self-reliant backwoodsmen of Pennsylvania, "God helps those that help themselves."
3. Franklin said to the farmers among his readers, "Men and melons are hard to know."
4. Franklin said to his readers, "A little neglect can breed great mischief."
5. Franklin said to the taciturn[2] Yankees who bought his almanac, "The worst wheel of the cart makes the most noise."
6. Franklin, an extremely successful diplomat, said to his plain-speaking countrymen, "A spoonful of honey will catch more flies than a gallon of vinegar."

Further directions: In the following sentences practice the use of the past tense or the past form of the modal after a *that*-clause.

[1] *pickle:* a vegetable preserved in vinegar and spices and eaten as a relish.
[2] *taciturn:* inclined to silence.

Example:

Franklin said, "A child and a fool imagine that twenty shillings and twenty years can never be spent."

Franklin said that a child and a fool **imagined that** twenty shillings and twenty years **could** never be spent.

7. Franklin said, "A penny saved is a penny earned."
8. Franklin, writing in his almanac, said, "Three can keep a secret if two of them are dead."
9. Franklin declared, "Nothing but money is sweeter than honey."
10. Franklin, a printer, said truly, "He that has a trade has an estate."[1]
11. Franklin, who finally knew the great of two continents, said, "None but the well-bred man knows how to confess himself in a fault or to acknowledge himself in an error."
12. Franklin, an extremely hard worker, said, "All things are easy to industry."

## FREE WRITING

### I 8 / Franklin versus (name of country)

Directions: Compare a few of Franklin's proverbs with similar proverbs in your country. List them in this convenient form:

1. Franklin:


2. Your country (named):

If there is a certain difference in meaning, even though the proverbs are similar, point it out.

Fill out your list, up to ten items, with proverbs well-known in your country whether or not they remind you of Franklin's. Add a few words of explanation as seems wise.

*Past/Past Perfect*

### Grammar

When the verb in the quoted statement is in the past tense, the verb in the indirect statement is in the past perfect tense, particularly in writing:

---

[1] *an estate:* a piece of land, especially a large piece.

---

Example:

Franklin **said** in his autobiography, "In 1732 I first published my almanac." (past tense/past tense)

Franklin **said** in his autobiography that in 1732 he **had** first **published** his almanac. (indirect statement/past perfect tense)

Orally, both verbs are often left in the past tense. However, in writing, the greater precision of the past perfect is preferred.

### I 9 / Josiah Franklin

Directions: First read the sentences orally in class, using the past perfect in the indirect statement, the *that*-clause. (Note the change from *I* to *he*.)

Example:

Franklin said, "I proceeded in my electrical experiments with great alacrity."[1]

Franklin said (that) he **had proceeded** in his electrical experiments with great alacrity.

1. Franklin said in his *Autobiography*, "*Josiah*, my father, married young and carried his wife with three children to New England about 1682."
2. Speaking of his father's health, Franklin said, "He had an excellent constitution."
3. Franklin also said, "He was ingenious,[2] could draw prettily, was skilled a little in music." (Write **had been skilled**.)
4. Franklin, who appraised his father's character discerningly, said, "His great excellence was a sound understanding and a solid judgment."
5. Franklin then remarked, "He was also consulted by private persons about their affairs when any difficulty occurred." (Write **had been consulted**.)
6. Speaking of his mother, Franklin said, "My mother likewise had an excellent constitution."
7. Franklin stated with satisfaction, "I never knew either my father or mother to have any sickness but that of which they died, he at eighty-nine and she at eighty-five years of age."

[1] *alacrity*: eager action.
[2] *ingenious*: good at inventing.

## THE ONE-SENTENCE QUOTATION

The one-sentence quotation, with an appropriate footnote, gives authority and life to expository writing such as a term paper. Words such as *said* and *stated* may introduce a one-sentence quotation, interrupt it, or follow it. Note the use of commas in the following example.

introducing
    Robert Southey has **said,** "Men are never so likely to settle a question rightly as when they discuss it freely."[1]

interrupting
    "Men are never so likely to settle a question rightly," Robert Southey has **stated,** "as when they discuss it freely."

following
    "Men are never so likely to settle a question rightly as when they discuss it freely," Robert Southey **said** over a century and a half ago.

### I 10 / Writing the One-Sentence Quotation

Directions: Take a single statement from the preface of this book or a statement from any other book you choose, and practice introducing, interrupting, and following the quotation with guide words such as *said* and *stated,* as has been done in the example above.

Place a numbered footnote at the bottom of your page, as has been done in the sample paper, pp. 209-303. (See also *Footnotes for books,* Section M, p. 296.)

## WRITING CONVERSATION[2]

Example:

    "Would you like to get out of town for the weekend?" Hing asked.
    "You know I would," Lee replied.
    "My car's back from the garage," Hing said, "so let's drive up into Connecticut."

[1] Robert Southey (British poet and writer, 1774–1843), *Colloquies on the Progress and Prospects of Society.*
[2] *To the instructor:* Writing Conversation is chiefly meant for students preparing to take freshman English. Extra time on Section M, *The First Term Paper,* is likely to prove more profitable to other students.

"What's Connecticut?"

"It's a state, and it's beautiful country. Bring your camera."

"My camera—where is it?" Lee asked.

Hing said softly, "Where did you leave it?"

"I don't know," Lee answered unhappily. "Why can't I remember?"

The following conventions in regard to writing conversation, except for quotations several paragraphs in length (13) below, are illustrated in the foregoing example.

1. Use double (not single) quotation marks.
2. Begin a new paragraph every time the speaker changes.
3. Introduce a quoted speech with a comma, not a colon.
4. Use a comma, not a period, when the "dialog guides," **asked, said, answered, replied,** etc., follow a quoted sentence: "Let's go for a long ride," Hing said.
5. However, use a question mark, not a comma, after a quoted question: "What's Connecticut?" Lee asked.
6. **Said** may be used with a quoted question, as well as with a quoted statement.
7. **Asked** may be used with a quoted question only.
8. **Said,** and other dialog guides, may interrupt a quoted sentence.
9. When a dialog guide interrupts a quoted sentence, place commas before and after the interruption and resume the quotation with a small letter.
10. When a dialog guide comes after one quoted sentence and before a second, be sure to begin the second sentence with a capital.
11. Use **one** pair of quotation marks for a succession of sentences in a paragraph, so long as the quoted matter is not interrupted.
12. Omit **said** and its equivalents when the reader can easily identify the speakers without such help.
13. When a quotation extends for several paragraphs, place quotation marks before each paragraph and both before and after the last paragraph.

## FREE WRITING

### I 11 / This Weather

Directions: Write a short conversation between yourself and a fellow countryman who cannot become reconciled to the weather he is experiencing.

Begin, "The school isn't so bad, "began (name of friend), "but the weather is impossible." Proceed to agree or disagree with your fellow countryman, but be sure to begin a new paragraph every time the speaker changes.

Since this is your first composition requiring the punctuation of conversation, use the familiar "dialog guides," *said, replied, asked,* and perhaps *answered.*

## I 12 / No Peace

Directions: Begin,

"Where to?" said the cab driver.
"To _____," I replied and leaned back for an uneventful ride.

Since this is your second composition requiring the punctuation of conversation, experiment with a few of these dialog guides:

Cab driver (bad mood): **muttered, growled, snarled.**

Cab driver (talkative mood): **began, continued, confided, stated firmly.**

Yourself: **sighed, groaned, said between my teeth, explained again that.**

## I 13 / A Patient Policeman

Directions: Tell of a time when you asked a policeman for information and received a patient, detailed reply. Be sure to mention where and when the incident took place.

## I 14 / When I Knew Less English

Directions: Recount some incident from the days when your English was not yet adequate. How did you get into difficulty? How did you get out? What use did you make of English? Be sure to mention place and time near the beginning of your account.

## I 15 / A Story Often Told in My Family

Directions: Tell a story often told by some member of your family. Perhaps you have heard the story almost too often, but it is a good story, only needing a fresh listener. Be sure to mention the narrator when you mention place and time.

## I 16 / The Quarrel

Directions: What started the quarrel? How did it develop—who said what? How did the conflict end? Or did it end? Was there a deep, unmentioned reason for the quarrel?

## I 17 / (a topic of your own choice)

**Portrait of Benjamin Franklin by the Scottish artist David Martin.**
[Photo by National Geographic, courtesy of
White House Historical Association.]

# Section 7

## Gerunds and Infinitives
## Spelling: Rules 7 and 8

### GERUNDS

#### Grammar: the nature of gerunds

A gerund is a verb form ending in *ing* and functioning as a noun:

We appreciate your **coming**. (direct object)

I am fond of **swimming**. (object of a preposition)

**Swimming** exercises the whole body. (subject)

Long-established custom says that certain verbs are followed by the gerund, not the infinitive. Among such verbs are the following:

#### List I: verbs followed by the gerund

| | |
|---|---|
| appreciate | mind (object to) |
| avoid | miss |
| consider | postpone |
| delay | practice |
| deny | prevent |
| enjoy | recall |
| finish | resist |
| imagine | stop |
| | suggest |

Do not attempt to memorize the four lists which will appear in this section. If the verb you are looking for does not appear on one of the lists, use the gerund; the gerund is used more frequently than the infinitive. Besides, many verbs can be followed by either the gerund or the infinitive.

Examples:

I don't like **cooking**.
I do like **to eat**.

I remember **meeting** you before.
Did I remember (take care not to forget) **to lock** the door?

Haruko prefers **walking** to **riding** the bus.
She prefers **to walk** rather than **to ride** the bus.


## Oral Practice

Directions: Complete the partial statement given you, using a gerund. Then repeat the complete sentence.

Examples:

Instructor:   The youngsters admitted . . .
Student:      . . . admitted **breaking** the window. The youngsters admitted **breaking** the window.

Instructor:   Pete dislikes . . .
Student:      . . . dislikes **doing** exercises. Pete dislikes **doing** exercises.[1]

1. The gunman **admitted** . . .
2. This is very kind of you. I **appreciate** . . .
3. The candidate on TV was not frank.[2] He **avoided** . . .
4. If you are going to leave the country, don't **delay** . . .
5. Stopped by a policeman, the motorist **denied** . . .
6. I **enjoy** . . .
7. In the speech lab, I **keep** . . .
8. Pete needs new license plates, yet he **postpones** . . .
9. Flu shots will **prevent** your . . .
10. I don't **remember** . . .

[1] Note: Gerunds, like verbs, can take noun objects: Pete dislikes doing exercises.
[2] *frank*: not afraid to say what one thinks.

## J 1 / Getting and Answering Letters

Directions: Change the two following paragraphs of questions into statements, putting a word from the list below, underlined,[1] into each blank. Use every word, but don't use any word more than twice:

| | | |
|---|---|---|
| enjoy | finish | dislike |
| consider | postpone | stop |
| appreciate | | |

Do you _____ getting letters from your friends at home? Do you _____ receiving such letters one of the brightest spots of your day? Do you _____ reading these letters more than once? Do you _____ hearing about the smallest details of your friends' activities?

Do you ever _____ answering letters you have thoroughly enjoyed receiving?[2] Do you sometimes _____ settling down at your desk when you should? Do you sometimes _____ writing at the slightest excuse? Do you ever _____ writing with a sigh of relief? Do you _____ answering letters a pleasure or hard work?

## J 2 / Robin Hood

Directions: Copy the three following paragraphs, putting a verb from the list below,[3] underlined, into each blank. Use every word, but don't use any word more than twice:

| | | |
|---|---|---|
| enjoy | practice | resist |
| avoid | admit | keep |
| consider | dislike | deny |

I hope you will _____ hearing the old story of Robin Hood again.

Robin Hood _____ to robbing the rich long ago in Merrie England, but he _____ robbing the poor. He _____ taking from the rich and giving to the poor a good deed. He _____ being a criminal, although he was an outlaw.

Robin Hood and his men _____ living in towns. They _____ living in Sherwood Forest. They _____ paying taxes. They _____ shooting their long bows for hours at a time. They _____ going back to live in town. They _____ on living in the forest for years.

[1] These verbs are taken from the longer list on p. 240.
[2] You may wish to use some negatives in this paragraph.
[3] These verbs are taken from the longer list on p. 240.

## Grammar: gerunds after prepositions

If a verb form follows a preposition, it will probably be a gerund (unless the preposition is *to*, the sign of the infinitive):

**by** asking    **on** arriving    **after** registering

### Oral Practice I

Directions: Answer the following *how*-questions with a phrase beginning with *by*. (A gerund will follow.)

Examples:

Instructor:   How do you keep up with the news?

Student A:  **By watching** a national newscast on TV.

Student B:  **By getting** a daily paper.

Student C:  **By reading** the Associated Press releases in the student paper.

1. How do **you** keep up with the news?
2. How do you keep from spending too much money?
3. How do you find out what a strange word means?
4. How do you find your way in a strange city?
5. How do you order a meal when you cannot read the menu?
6. How do you decide what to tip?
7. How do you locate some one who speaks your language?
8. How do you find your hotel when you have lost the address?

### Oral Practice II

Directions: Make a full statement using the phrase suggested.

The Learning Process

Example:

I **believe in preparing** the hardest lesson first.

1. believe in preparing
2. object to memorizing
3. depend upon remembering
4. proud of learning
5. now succeed in pronouncing
6. never worry about passing
7. depend upon reviewing

8. plan on taking
9. proud of being

A Little Pleasure

10. plan on going
11. excited about seeing
12. also interested in seeing
13. count on finding

Friends

14. sorry about missing
15. talk about their visiting
16. plan on their spending

## Grammar: idioms

Frequently a preposition unites with the word before it to form an idiom—an expression difficult to understand through analyzing the meaning of each word separately:

fond of[1]      used to[2]      tired of[3]

### Oral Practice: *fond of, used to, tired of*

Directions: Add a gerund to the idiom *fond of,* making a complete statement.

Examples:

Instructor:   What is Lee **fond of** doing in the summer?
Student:      He is **fond of** sailing in the summer.

Instructor:   What is he **fond of** doing in the winter?
Student:      He is **fond of** skating on the frozen river in the winter.

1. From references to Pete in various exercises, what do you think he is **fond of** doing?

---

[1] *fond of:* to like, to enjoy doing.
[2] *used to:* to be accustomed to, liking not necessarily implied. (A second meaning of *used to* implies habitual action in the past: I *used to* read a lot for pleasure.) In this sense, "used to" is followed by the simple form of the verb.
[3] *tired of:* to be weary of, to wish no more of.

2. What isn't he **fond of** doing?
3. From various references to Betty, the school girl, what would you say she is **fond of** doing?
4. As you know small boys, what are they **fond of** doing?
5. As you know businessmen, what are they **fond of** doing?
6. When you were a teen-ager in your own country, what were you **fond of** doing?

Directions: Add a gerund to the idiom *used to,* making a complete statement.

Examples:

Instructor: What are you **used to** doing after breakfast?
Student: I am **used to** making my bed, although I do not enjoy the process.

Instructor: What are you **used to** doing about 7:45 A.M.?
Student: I am **used to** waiting on the corner for the school bus. In the summer I don't really mind.

7. What are you **used to** doing as soon as you enter this classroom?
8. Where are you **used to** sitting?
9. What are you **used to** saying to your neighbors, "Good morning" or "Hi!"?
10. What is the instructor **used to** doing as soon as he enters the room?
11. What are you **used to** doing with your corrected papers?

Directions: Add a gerund to the idiom *tired of,* making a complete statement.

Examples:

I am seldom **tired of** talking; I am sometimes **tired of** listening.

12. Just now I am **tired of** . . .
13. Sometimes I am **tired of** . . .
14. I am never **tired of** . . .
15. The same subject is in the news too often. I am **tired of** . . .
16. Wouldn't you like to go dancing tonight? Are you ever . . .

## J 3 / The Modern Housewife

Directions: Copy the two following paragraphs, filling the blanks with appropriate gerunds, underlined, from this list. Use each word once.

using          pulling
making         sweeping
completing     running
doing

    The modern housewife is accustomed to _____ her own housework. She is used to _____ a vacuum cleaner. She is opposed to _____ heavy rugs with a broom. On the other hand, she is used to _____ her groceries home from the supermarket in a shopping cart.
    She depends on _____ labor-saving devices daily. She plans on _____ her household tasks quickly and efficiently. She succeeds in _____ her home an attractive one.

## J 4 / Talking to Americans

**Directions: Complete the partial statements in the paragraph below with the following phrases, underlined.**

**Informal:** talking to, chatting with
**Formal:** holding conversations with, speaking with, conversing with

    I consider . . . Americans as valuable as my classes in English. I never miss . . . my American classmates on the campus. I seize every opportunity to practice . . . my instructors. The difficulties of speaking English never prevent my . . . the elderly, who have leisure to talk. I enjoy . . . friendly American children, too. As long as Americans are willing, I will keep on . . . them.

## Spelling: Rule 7

When the sound is like $\overline{\text{ee}}$ /i/, put *i* before *e* except after *c*:

receive     deceive     ceiling     receipt     conceit

Otherwise:

piece     believe     brief     chief     niece     relief

Common exceptions:

leisure     either     neither     seize

### Dictation I

Once I met a thief. At that moment I heard the chief of police was coming. This brief piece of news gave me great relief. It made me believe in the chief. It made me believe in my own luck, too.

### Dictation II

Mr. Smith received the news gladly. He had not been deceived. The ceiling had been painted. The receipt covered all repairs. He perceived that no deceit had been practiced.

### Dictation III

Betty is not conceited. She receives compliments with pleasure, but she is not deceived. She never calls a big compliment deceit, however. She perceives that the compliment was meant to give pleasure.

## Spelling: Rule 8

When the sound is not like $\overline{ee}$ /i/, the spelling is generally *ei*:

neighbor    weigh    height    their    foreign

Common exception: friend.

### Dictation I

Our neighbors have eight children. The littlest weighs forty pounds. The height of the tallest is less than five feet. When friends of the children come over to play, the neighbors sigh. The neighbors put their hands over their ears.

### Dictation II

The candidates had no leisure. At the height of the campaign they weighed every word they said. The newspapers found their sayings freighted with meaning. Foreign students watched the campaign in amazement and amusement.

## INFINITIVES

## Grammar: verbs followed immediately by <u>to</u> and the infinitive[1]

The same long-established custom which says that certain verbs are followed by the gerund says that certain other verbs are followed by the infinitive:

|  | *Verb* | *Infinitive* |  |
|---|---|---|---|
| The hostess | tried | to make | her guest comfortable. |
| The guest | offered | to help | with the dishes. |

## List II: verbs followed immediately by <u>to</u> and the infinitive

| | | |
|---|---|---|
| agree | intend | promise |
| decide | learn | refuse |
| expect | like | seem |
| fail | need | try |
| forget | offer | want |
| hope | plan | |

### Oral Practice

Directions: Put each of the verbs in the preceding list into this one statement, placed on the blackboard:

Everyone _____ to try very hard.

Note the difference in meaning resulting from a change of verbs:

Examples:

Everyone **agreed** to try very hard.

Everyone **promised** to try very hard.

Everyone **refused** to try very hard.

### J 5 / The Wrong Way

Directions: Complete the partial statements in the two following paragraphs with *to* and an infinitive. Underline as follows:

[1] The infinitive: the simple form of the verb, generally preceded by *to*: *to make, to help, to work.*

Example:

Aki pretended . . .

Aki **pretended to understand** when he did not.

 Since Aki was not fond of speaking English, he **failed**. . . . In fact, sometimes he actually **refused**. . . . When the dorm had a party, he seldom **agreed**. . . . With his fellow countrymen, he spoke the language he was used to; he never tried. . . . In class, tired of the effort required to learn a new language, when he did not understand an explanation, he **pretended**. . . .

 If Aki had acted differently, he could have **learned**. . . . He might reasonably have **expected**. . . . Suddenly English would have **seemed** . . . . In fact, all day long Aki might have wanted. . . .


## J 6 / Abdu's Plans

Directions: Complete the statements in the following paragraph with verbs from the list[1] below, plus an infinitive. Use each verb only once. (All the verbs will **not** be needed.)

Example:

Abdu likes to . . .

Abdu **likes to work** in a laboratory.


## List III: selected verbs from List II

| decide | intend | plan |
|--------|--------|------|
| expect | learn  | try  |
| hope   | like   | want |
|        | need   |      |

 Since Abdu is an American citizen, he . . . do his undergraduate work in the United States. He . . . earn a Bachelor of Science degree (B.S.) in four years. Once he has his B.S., he . . . study abroad. After earning a second degree, he . . . return to the United States. Then he . . . find a responsible position in his field.

---

[1] These verbs are taken from the longer list on p. 248.

# Grammar: verbs followed first by a noun or pronoun[1] and then by to and the infinitive

|  | Verb | Noun or Pronoun | Infinitive |
|---|---|---|---|
| The speaker | urged | his audience | to vote. |
| He | told | us | to vote. |

Note that the object of the verb acts as subject of the infinitive.

## List IV: verbs followed first by a noun or pronoun

Among the verbs followed first by a noun or pronoun and then by *to* and an infinitive are the following:

| | | |
|---|---|---|
| advise | *help | *prepare |
| allow | hire | *promise |
| *ask[2] | instruct | remind |
| encourage | invite | tell |
| *beg | order | urge |
| force | permit | *want |
| get | persuade | |

### Oral Practice

Directions: Put each of the verbs in the preceding list into this one statement, placed on the blackboard:

The instructor _____ Pete/him to take more math.

Note the difference in meaning resulting from a change of verbs:

Examples:

The instructor **advised** Pete to take more math.

The instructor **persuaded** Pete to take more math.

The instructor **urged** Pete to take more math.

---

[1] Linguists use the term "noun phrase" to cover "noun or pronoun."
[2] Verbs with an asterisk (*) can also be followed directly by the infinitive: I promised *to come.*

## J 7 / Advice to Haruko

Directions: Copy the three following paragraphs, expanding the words in parentheses in one of two ways:

Her mother encouraged (her __ go).
Her mother encouraged **her to go.**

She urged her grandmother not (__ worry).
She urged her grandmother not **to worry.**

**Underline as in the examples.**

Everyone had something to say as soon as Haruko's parents announced that they would allow (her __ come) to the United States to study.

Her high school principal advised (her __ take) some review lessons in English before she left Japan. The principal encouraged (her __ think) about advanced work in her own field. He did not try (__ force) (her __ do) anything. He did instruct (her __ take) advantage of the fine library in her new college.

Her father permitted (her __ open) a bank account in her own name. Her littlest brother reminded (her __ send) him a toy spaceship. Friends of the family in the United States wrote and invited Haruko (__ visit them. Her best friend reminded (her __ write). She told her grandmother not (__ worry). She persuaded (her not __ worry).

## FREE WRITING

## J 8 / Advice to Me

Directions: Write of the advice given to you when your relatives and friends first learned that you were going to study abroad. How did the wisdom, the interests, and the anxieties of these persons show in their advice? What, of all the advice given you, has proved most practical?

# Grammar: the "short infinitive"

Some verbs, especially those of the senses and of action, are followed by the infinitive without *to*, often called the "short infinitive" or the simple form of the verb.

Examples:

Senses: We **heard** the dog **bark.** (not "to bark")
Action: We **helped** the father **rescue** the child. (not "to rescue")

| | Subject | Verb | Object | Infinitive without *to* | |
|---|---|---|---|---|---|
| Senses | We | heard | a dog | bark. | |
| Action | We | helped | the father | rescue | the child. |

## List V: verbs followed by the short infinitive

Verbs of the senses

feel:  We **felt** excitement **rise** in the crowd.
hear:  We **heard** a roar **come** from 70,000 throats.
notice:  We **noticed** a little old lady shouting.
see:  We **saw** the line man **drop** back for the field goal.
watch:  We **watched** the ball **sail** directly between the goal posts.

Verbs of action

help:  We **helped** my uncle **paint** his barn.
let:  He **let** us **climb** the longest ladder.
make:  We **made** the barn **look** fine.
notice:  However, we **noticed** the sky **growing** darker and darker.
watch:  We **watched** rain **fall** on our fresh paint.

**Oral Practice**

Directions: Change the two sentences given you into one sentence. Use an infinitive without *to*.

Examples:

I watched the fire. It blazed higher and higher.
I watched the fire **blaze** higher and higher.

I heard the freight train. It roared through the night.
I heard the freight train **roar** through the night.

1. I saw a black cat. It waved its tail angrily.
2. I watched the cat. It spit at a small dog furiously.
3. I watched a lifeguard help a young swimmer. He reached the shore safely.
4. I let young Billy play my favorite record. He played it for hours.
5. I heard a redbird. It sang sweetly.
6. I heard a blackbird. It sang harshly.[1]

---

[1] *harshly:* the opposite of sweetly.

7. I noticed a cook in a restaurant window. He tossed a pancake[1] into the air.
8. We felt the wind. It blew strongly.
9. We helped the blind man. He crossed the street safely.
10. Hing helped a small boy. They flew his kite.
11. We watched the team. They practiced until dark.
12. We watched the election returns. They came in rapidly.

## Listen and Write: The Beautiful Nights of Ramadan

Directions: Write down the first sentence of a paragraph before you begin to listen to that paragraph. Listen to each paragraph twice before writing.

During Ramadan, the ninth month of the Islamic calendar, Mohammedans are permitted to eat and drink only at night. During the day we eat nothing. We drink nothing. We do not allow ourselves even a stick of chewing gum to modify our thirst. We suffer, but we are happy to suffer for our religion.

The nights of Ramadan are beautiful. A cannon at sunset signals the permission to eat and drink. We have delicious dishes of beef, lamb, and chicken with steamed rice. We have a big, green salad, too. However much we eat, we are still able to enjoy baklava, a rich dessert made with honey.

After dinner, we are no longer hungry, of course. But it is still a pleasure to drink Turkish coffee and to enjoy all sorts of sweets and little cakes with our friends.

How much sleep are we able to get? Sleep is a problem. We do our last eating at 3:00 or 4:00 A.M. Everyone is supposed to appear in his office by 9:30. To be strictly truthful, we are sometimes a little late. However, it is equally true that the nights of Ramadan are beautiful.

## FREE WRITING

### J 9 / A Great Festival

Directions: Write of a yearly period in your own country which combines religion, feasting, and general good will. Turn in an outline with your composition.

---

[1] *pancake*: a thin, flat cake fried in a pan. A skilled cook can turn a pancake over by a twist of his wrist, which tosses the pancake high into the air.

## J 10 / (a topic of your own choice)

Directions: Choose a topic which has not been touched on in these assignments: some limited section of your professional knowledge, your opinion on a major controversy in the news. Or what?

# Section K

## Relative Clauses
## Spelling: Rule 9

**Grammar: the nature of relative clauses[1]**

Examine the following sentences:

The man <u>who came to dinner</u> stayed three weeks.
The boy <u>whom the agency sent</u> stayed three years.
The job <u>that the boy came to fill</u> was in the shipping department.
The young woman <u>to whom he handed his papers</u> filed them.
The agency <u>which sent the boy</u> collected its fee the first week.

In the foregoing examples, note how the underlined clause restricts or defines the meaning of the noun just before it:

"The man."
"Which man?"
"The man **who came to dinner**."

"The job."
"What job?"
"The job **which the boy came to fill**."

---

[1] Some linguists use *that* as well as *which* for things. The distinction is not of major importance.

The restricting or defining relative clause,[1] specifies a particular one, or ones, so that the speaker and hearer, or writer and reader, agree easily and completely as to who or what is meant. (Compare this statement with that made about *the*, p. 84.)

Later (p. 268) a second type of relative clause will be introduced, one used more often in writing than speaking.

## List:

**who:** refers only to persons
   This is the man **who** (subject) interviews applicants.

**whom:** object form of **who**
   There is the man **whom** (direct object) you should see.
   He is the man **to whom** (object of preposition) you must speak.

**which:** refers to things, to animals,[2] and to groups of people
   the building **which**      the dog **which**      the committee **which**

**that:** may be substituted for **who, whom,** and **which**
   the building **that**      the dog **that**      the committee **that**      the friend **that**

**whose:** indicates possession by persons, animals, things and groups of persons
   the man **whose** plane left without him
   the cat **whose** pink tongue appeared briefly between his teeth
   the building **whose** doorway was hand-carved
   the committee **whose** long labor was ended

## RESTRICTIVE (defining) CLAUSES

### Oral Practice: *who* and *which* as subject

Directions: Listen to the pair of sentences given you. Put the second sentence into the first.

Examples:

The girl is absent today. The girl sits in front of me.
The girl **who sits in front of me** is absent today.

---

[1] *To the instructor:* Since the terms *restrictive* and *nonrestrictive* communicate almost nothing to many students, the terms *defining* and *commenting* are offered as alternatives (Francis Christensen, *Notes Toward a New Rhetoric*, New York, Harper & Row, 1967, p. 95).

[2] Unless an animal is treated as a human being.

The exercises are likely to be[1] helpful. The teacher assigns them.
The exercises **which the teacher assigns** are likely to be helpful.

1. The bus driver knows me. He drives the 4:50 bus.
2. The young man knows me. He checks our meal tickets.
3. The women don't know me. They serve the hot food in the cafeteria.
4. My aunt lives in New York. She writes to me regularly.
5. Another aunt lives in Los Angeles. She writes to me occasionally.
6. The letters are in English. My twelve-year-old cousin writes them.
7. TV commercials are very clever. Some men write them.
8. Crime stories use violence regularly. Highly paid men write them.
9. The men are always well prepared. The men give the nightly newscasts.
10. The men speak distinctly. The men give the broadcasts.

## K 1 / The Committee Meeting

**Directions:** Write each pair of sentences as one sentence. Put the second sentence into the first. Underline the defining clauses (restrictive clauses).

Examples:

The man called the meeting to order. The man was a little late.

The man **who called the meeting to order**[2] was a little late.

The table was large and polished. The committee sat around it.

The table **around which the committee sat** was large and polished.

1. The problem was important. The problem was under consideration.
2. The committee could not reach a decision. The committee met all afternoon.
3. The member received no inspiration from it. The member had a view of the park through the picture window.
4. The dog slept. The dog lay at the chairman's feet.
5. The rug was Turkish. The rug lay on the polished floor.
6. The secretary was happy. The secretary had had very few notes to take.
7. The committee was not happy. The committee had not been able to reach a decision.

[1] *likely to be:* (idiom) probably will be.
[2] Restrictive (defining) clauses, the type you will be writing until p. 268, are not set off by commas.

8. The chairman was very unhappy. The chairman called a meeting for the following afternoon.

*The problem of* whom    Until recently, the object form *whom* had to be used both for the direct object and the object of the preposition under all circumstances. The form *whom* is still preferable in writing, but American custom has accepted two ways of eliminating the problem of *whom* in speech, one for the direct object (this page) and one for the object of the preposition (p. 263). Watch for these two ways as you work.

## Grammar: eliminating direct object <u>whom</u>

|  | Relative Clause | | |  |
|---|---|---|---|---|
|  | *Object* | *Subject* | *Verb* |  |
| A man | whom | everyone | trusted | was Washington. |
| A man | — | everyone | trusted | was Washington. |
| A building | which | I | admire | is the old Town Hall. |
| A building | — | I | admire | is the old Town Hall. |
| The last song | that | the chorus | sang | was "Til We Meet Again." |
| The last song | — | the chorus | sang | was "Til We Meet Again." |

## Oral Practice

Directions: **Listen to the sentence given you. Repeat it, omitting** *whom* **or** *which.*

Examples:

There goes the instructor **whom** I want you to meet.
There goes the instructor I want you to meet.

This is the letter to the editor **which** I want you to read.
This is the letter to the editor I want you to read.

1. The first book **which** Lee read in English was **Gulliver's Travels.**
2. The first student **whom** he met in class was Miss Liu.
3. The department **which** he has decided to enter is electrical engineering.
4. An American in politics **whom** I can name easily is _____.
5. A sports figure **whom** everyone knows in my country is _____.
6. The newscaster **whom** I find most satisfactory is _____.

7. The present-day style **which** I like least is _____.
8. The student **whom** the director called into the office was Pete.
9. The advice **which** the director gave Pete was to study harder.
10. The promise **which** Pete slowly gave was to try harder.

## Grammar: retaining <u>whom</u> as direct object in writing

In writing, *whom* is still considered preferable to *who* as the direct object form.

Examples:

The French painter **whom** I especially enjoy is Cézanne.[1]

The man **whom** the British called the Iron Duke was Wellington.

### K 2 / *Whom* and *Which* as Direct Objects

Directions: Copy the following sentences, putting *whom* or *which*, underlined, into the blanks. In particular, accustom yourself to writing *whom*.

1. A painter _____ I admire is van Gogh.[2]
2. A humorist _____ I have discovered recently is James Thurber.[3]
3. An African lioness _____ Joy Adamson[4] treated as a member of the family was the humanized Elsa.
4. An American newspaper _____ I sometimes read is _____ (name, underlined).
5. A policeman _____ people trust knows his neighborhood.
6. Some of the buildings _____ we saw in Philadelphia made early American history come to life.
7. Three of the patriots _____ we recalled in Independence Hall were Jefferson, Franklin, and John Adams.
8. A present-day political leader _____ I watch with interest is. . . .
9. An American novelist _____ I eventually expect to know better is. . . .
10. The composer, classical or modern _____ I find most enjoyable is. . . .

---

[1] *Paul Cézanne,* 1839–1906: French painter of the outdoors.
[2] *Vincent van Gogh,* 1853–1890: Dutch painter.
[3] *James Thurber,* 1894–1961: American humorist and playwright.
[4] Joy Adamson, *Born Free,* New York, Pantheon, 1960.

## Grammar: retaining relatives as subjects

*Who,* which, and *that* cannot be omitted when they are subjects of relative clauses.

Examples:

This is Dr. Goto, **who** teaches the violin. (not "This Dr. Goto teaches the violin.")

George has a camera **which** develops pictures instantly. (not "George has a camera develops pictures instantly.")

I have a clock **that** keeps almost perfect time. (not "I have a clock keeps almost perfect time.")

### K 3 / Retaining and Omitting *Who, Whom,* and *Which*

Directions: Copy the following sentences, filling the blanks, underlined, with relative pronouns only when the relative is a subject. *Omit any relatives which would be objects.*

Examples:

People _____ live in glass houses should not throw stones.

People **who** live in glass houses should not throw stones. (subject expressed)

T. S. Eliot is a poet I intend to read some day. (**whom** is not to be expressed, so the sentence is copied as it stands).

1. The pet _____ is easily first in popularity in the city is the dog.
2. Gabrielle introduced us to a drama critic _____ she knows well.
3. I know someone _____ knows someone _____ can get us tickets to the most popular play on Broadway.
4. Martin Luther King was a man _____ millions loved.
5. We have a man in our office _____ can speak five languages.
6. The rights of minorities is a subject _____ is occupying the country.
7. Pollution is another subject _____ will not disappear.
8. A writer _____ is especially honored in my own country is _____.
9. A man _____ the Russians honor is _____.
10. A man _____ is honored by the Chinese is _____.
11. A man (or woman) _____ I honor is _____.

## Grammar: omitting <u>who is/are</u>

Although subject *who* cannot be omitted from a relative clause, *who is/are* can be omitted.

Examples:

A man (or woman) **who is** angry should watch out.
An **angry** man or woman should watch out. (adjective only retained)

The men **who are** waiting to see the Mayor can come in now.
The men waiting to see the Mayor can come in now. (present participle retained)[1]

The lake, **which is** polluted, cannot be used for swimming.
The **polluted** lake cannot be used for swimming. (past participle retained)

### Oral Practice

Directions: Omit *who, which, that,* and any form of *be* directly following. Retain the adjective or participle.

Examples:

The child who is busy learns from his play.
The **busy** child[2] learns from his play.

The boy who is whistling is from the drugstore.
The boy **whistling** is from the drugstore.

We found the robin's nest which was hidden in our apple tree.
We found the robin's nest **hidden** in our apple tree.

1. A woman who is silent is rather unusual.
2. A woman who is talkative is often amusing.
3. A man who is cautious is sometimes wise.
4. Men who are bold are frequently wise.
5. A person who is tense works at a disadvantage.
6. Students who are systematic work with confidence.
7. A test that is fair covers important class work.
8. Students who are taking a test should work confidently.
9. A test that is marked thoughtfully acts as a teacher.

---

[1] Linguists usually call the present participle the *ing*-form and the past participle the *en*-form.
[2] Note that the adjective has moved to its normal position before the noun.

10. The bird that is singing out of sight is a redbird.
11. The bus which is standing with its motor running is wasting gasoline.
12. The roses which were picked yesterday morning are still fresh.
13. The traffic sign that was knocked over said "Dangerous Curve."
14. A dog which is barking is noisy but not dangerous.

## K 4 / Without *Who, Which,* and *That*

Directions: Omit *who, which, that,* and any form of *be* directly following. Underline the adjective or participle you retain.

Examples:

Drivers who are speeding in traffic are dangerous.
Drivers **speeding** in traffic are dangerous.

A typist who is efficient finds work easily.
An **efficient** typist finds work easily.

1. The salesman who is waiting in the outer office will soon go inside.
2. The man who is inviting the salesman inside is the buyer.
3. The samples which are packed in the salesman's case are printed forms.
4. The forms which are printed in red are sales slips.
5. The forms which are printed in black are invoices.
6. The other supplies which are running low are not discussed.
7. Another salesman who is selling these supplies will be in the next day.
8. A newspaper which is thick contains a lot of advertising.
9. Advertisements which are humorous are often effective.
10. Advertisements which are beautiful are often effective, too.
11. Editorials which are wordy[1] are not read to the end.
12. Editorials which are well written may be read to the end.

## Spelling: Rule 9

When the simple form of a word ends in *o* preceded by a consonant, add *es:*

go—goes    do—does    hero—hero**es**    potato—potato**es**
tomato—tomato**es**    veto—veto**es**

---

[1] *wordy:* using too many words for the number of ideas expressed.

Common exceptions:

piano—pianos     radio—radios

## Dictation

Heroes do not fight with potatoes and tomatoes. They sometimes play pianos and radios. However, what heroes do with their leisure time depends upon the heroes.

## Grammar: prepositions in restrictive (defining) relative clauses

*Whom,* not *who,* must be used directly after a preposition:

The person **to whom** Eugene appealed was a truck driver.

However, especially in speech, there is a simple way to eliminate the use of *whom:* omit the relative and keep only the preposition:

The person Eugene appealed **to** was a truck driver.

### Oral Practice: retaining the preposition only

Directions: Repeat the sentence given you, eliminating *whom* but keeping the preposition.

Example:

The person **from whom** Eugene received help was a truck driver.

The person Eugene received help **from** was a truck driver.

1. The number of businessmen to whom I write is small.
2. No one to whom I write lives in Alaska.
3. No one to whom I write lives in New Zealand.
4. Several persons to whom I write live in (name of country).
5. Chaucer is a poet about whom I know little.[1]
6. Shakespeare is a poet about whom I know something.
7. Thorndike and Barnhart are two editors[2] in whom I have confidence.
8. They are editors on whom a student can depend for simple, clear definitions.

[1] *Geoffrey Chaucer,* 1340?–1400: the first great English poet.
[2] E. L. Thorndike and Clarence L. Barnhart, *Junior Dictionary, Seventh Edition,* Scott, Foresman, Glenview, Ill., 1968.

## Grammar: <u>whom</u> and <u>which</u> after prepositions

The form *whom* must follow immediately after a preposition—and this structure occurs fairly frequently in writing:

Henry VIII is a king **for whom** the English have a genuine liking.

*Which* often follows a preposition, but there is no change in form:

The building **in which** English royalty are crowned and married is Westminster Abbey.

### K 5 / *Whom* and *Which* after Prepositions

Directions: Copy the following sentences, inserting *whom* or *which,* underlined.

1. A TV performer in _____ I take an interest is (name).
2. One man to _____ the Nobel Peace Prize has been given is (name).
3. A public park in _____ I take pleasure is (name).
4. A subject to _____ the newspapers are now devoting much space is (name).
5. A public figure about _____ there is much discussion is (name).
6. The school in _____ I am now studying is (name).
7. The person to _____ one can go concerning a personal problem is (adviser).
8. The alert woman from _____ one receives help with the **Reader's Guide** is (reference librarian).
9. The field of study in _____ I feel the greatest interest is (name).
10. The university to _____ I might transfer for graduate study is (name).

## Grammar: <u>what</u>

*What* is no longer considered a relative pronoun, since it does not refer to a noun earlier in the sentence.[1] Instead, it is grouped with the *wh*-questions, which are followed by a statement form.

[1] At one time *what* was considered to imply the two words *that which.*

Examples:

I don't know **what he will say.**

We didn't know **what we should do.**

Finally a stranger told us **what we had better do.**

*What* is mentioned here because certain languages push students toward using *what* when they should use *who* or *which:*

Wrong: A city **what I am fond of** is Boston.

Right:    A city **which I am fond of** is Boston.

## K 6 / *Which* versus *What* in Boston

Directions: Fill in the blanks in the following four paragraphs with either *which* or *what,* underlined.

Boston is a city _____ takes one back to pre-Revolutionary America. Here and there, in this modern city, one can sense _____ the spirit of the Revolutionary patriots was.

For example, the orders _____ came to the civilian army outside Boston on June 17, 1775, were to defend Bunker Hill. However, the officers consulting together decided that _____ they had better do was to defend Breed's Hill. They did. The battle _____ has gone down in history as the Battle of Bunker Hill was fought on Breed's Hill. That is _____ they say in Boston, and that is _____ the monument _____ stands on Breed's Hill says.

If you ask directions of a stranger on one of the narrow streets _____ crisscross old Boston, you are almost sure to receive an answer _____ is both courteous and lengthy. If you forget some part of _____ you have been told and check with a second stranger, he is likely to say, "I can't see _____ made someone tell you **that.** Now _____ you will find much simpler . . ."

Individualists knew _____ they thought in 1775; they know _____ they think today. It is the self-esteem of the inhabitants for the past three centuries _____ gives charm to a visit to Boston.

## Grammar: <u>whose</u>

*Whose* indicates possession. The most frequent possessors are persons:

The senator **whose** picture is on the first page is our senator.
The workers **whose** strike is over are almost satisfied.

*Whose*, like *that*, is also used for animals, things, and groups of persons:

The dog **whose** attitude was watchful was guarding a four-year-old boy.

A newspaper **whose** editorials are often quoted is *The New York Times.*

The group **whose** purpose was to see the Mayor had a program ready.

**The Oberlin (Ohio) College Conservatory of Music, designed by Minoru Yamasaki and Associates.**
[Oberlin College; photo by Epstein and Szilagyi]

## Oral Practice I

Directions: Read the two following paragraphs aloud in class, noting how varied the meaning can be of nouns preceding *whose*.

An architect _____ work is much sought after in the United States is Minoru Yamasaki. He designs buildings _____ modern lines free the imagination.

College students _____ classes take them daily into one of Mr. Yamasaki's new buildings count themselves fortunate. Professors in the college, _____ judgment in architecture is discerning, speak warmly of "contrasts in spatial relationships." Only a black cat, whose tail is firmly wrapped around its feet, sits on the top step of the new building unimpressed. _____ cat is it?

## Oral Practice II

Directions: Complete the following partial statements. Use "I admire," as in the example or vary the pattern with "I like," "I don't like," or "I respect." For example,

Example:

A painter whose . . .

A painter whose portraits I admire is John Singleton Copley.[1]

1. An artist whose . . .
2. A composer whose symphonies . . .
3. A writer whose books . . .
4. A newscaster whose clear pronunciation . . .
5. A sports figure whose record . . .
6. A fountain whose beauty . . .
7. An automobile whose performance . . .
8. A newspaper whose editorials . . .
9. A dog whose bark . . .
10. A cat whose long fur . . .

## Grammar: wh-questions: whoever, whichever, whatever, wherever, whenever

*Ever* added to a relative pronoun produces a new word, a *wh*-question word, meaning *any person, any time, any thing*, etc.:

[1] *John Singleton Copley*, 1738–1815: early American portrait painter.

Bring **whoever wants to come.** Invite **whoever/whomever** you wish.
Julius talks to students in his own field **whenever he can.**
Do **whatever you think best.**

## K 7 / Traveling Lightly.

Directions: Copy the following paragraph, using once each of the
*wh*-question words listed. Underline the words inserted: *wherever,
whoever/whomever, whenever, whatever, whichever.*

     The best advice to give any traveler is "Leave behind
_____ you can." Take only one coat. Take _____ will keep
out the wind, resist rain, and provide enough warmth. _____
you arrive at a strange airport, find the chief exit easily by
following the crowd. Stay _____ you can locate a convenient
hotel, clean and moderate in price. Be sure to write ahead
to _____ you know in the city.

# NONRESTRICTIVE (commenting) CLAUSES

## Grammar: the nature of nonrestrictive (commenting) clauses

When a relative clause merely comments on a specimen already
identified, it is called *nonrestrictive* and is set off by commas.
Such clauses appear very commonly after proper nouns:

Mrs. Kilroy, **who loves cream in her coffee,** is worrying about her
weight.

The *Manchester Guardian,* **which is outstanding among British newspapers,** is frequently quoted in the United States.

Relative *that* cannot be used in nonrestrictive clauses. "Mrs.
Kilroy, *that* loves cream in her coffee," is ungrammatical.

## Oral Practice: Coffee Hour

Directions: Take turns reading "Coffee Hour" aloud in class. Eliminate *whom* and *which* whenever possible. Keep *which* in the two
clauses set off by commas. These clauses are nonrestrictive, commenting in nature.

The student who is standing with his coffee near the door of the lounge is from Port-au-Prince. The student to whom he is talking is from Bogotá. The instructor who is pouring coffee is from Salt Lake City. The event which is taking place is Coffee Hour for foreign students in an American university.

The group which sponsors Coffee Hour is the foreign-student faculty. The faculty members who are present are talking to the students who know the least English. The girl with whom the pronunciation teacher is talking is very shy. The subject which they are discussing is the weather.

The cookies which Hing intends to sample next are chocolate. The napkins which he is ignoring are paper. The spoons, which have grown old in the service of foreign students, are not silver.

Coffee Hour, which comes daily between 11:00 and 11:30, forms a pleasant break in the morning's classes.


## K 8 / The Adams Family

Directions: Copy the four following paragraphs, each sentence of which contains a relative clause. Set off the nonrestrictive clauses with commas.

The family which has been the most consistently distinguished in American history is the quiet Adams family.

John Adams who was the first of his family to come into national prominence was the second President of the United States. John Quincy Adams who was the son of John Adams was the sixth President of the United States. The man who held the difficult post of American Minister to England during the Civil War was Charles Francis Adams, son of John Quincy Adams.

The Adams who holds the greatest reputation as a writer among all the Adamses is Henry, of the fourth generation. His ironic[1] book, *The Education of Henry Adams*, which challenged American thinking in 1912 does so today.

In Franklin D. Roosevelt's Cabinet the man who held the post of Secretary of the Navy was Charles Francis Adams III who was a member of the fifth successive generation of the Adams family to serve its country well.

[1] ironic: one thing is said and another is meant.

## K 9 / The Second President

Directions: First orally and then in writing make one sentence out of each of the following pairs of sentences. Insert the second sentence into the first as a commenting clause (a nonrestrictive clause), or add the second sentence to the first. Either way, commas will be required.

### Clause inserted

During the eight years Washington was President, John Adams presided over the Senate. John Adams was Vice-President.

During the eight years Washington was President, John Adams, who was Vice-President, presided over the Senate.

### Clause added

John Adams married Abigail Smith. Abigail Smith came from a keen-minded, cultivated family.

John Adams married Abigail Smith, who came from a keen-minded, cultivated family.

1. John Adams did his duty all his life long. He was a New England Puritan.
2. Young John Adams stood among the first three in his graduating class. He had showed marked ability at Harvard.
3. After graduating at nineteen, Adams had no choice but to become a lawyer. He would not become a clergyman.
4. He married Abigail Smith. Abigail Smith became an unusual wife.
5. She had many duties. The duties were varied and often difficult.
6. She practiced patience in the new White House. The White House was unfinished, under-furnished, and damp.
7. Adams led in founding the United States Navy. The navy, from that time to this, has always had a ship called **The John Adams**.
8. Adams managed to keep the country out of war. Adams had continuous trouble with France.
9. Nevertheless Adams was unpopular. Adams did not know how to explain his policies to the people.
10. After a single term in office, Adams returned to a quiet life on his farm near Quincy, Massachusetts. Adams had been a strong, honest, but unpopular President.

**FREE WRITING**

### K 10 / The Partner in My Past

Directions: Begin, "I had a variety of friends when I was a child, but the friend with whom I had the most fun and got into the most trouble was _____."

### K 11 / A Friend in This Country

Directions: Begin, "Life is easier for me in this country because I have a friend who/whom . . ."

### K 12 / (a topic of your own choice)

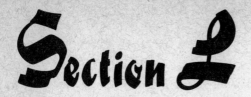

# Section L

---

## Comparisons
## Spelling: Rule 10

**Grammar: the nature of comparisons**

There are three degrees of comparison:

1. Comparisons implying some sort of equality between two items:

My course is **similar to** yours.

I hope it will be **as interesting as** yours.

2. Comparisons implying difference between two items:

I hope my course isn't **harder than** yours.

I don't want to work **harder than** you do.[1]

3. Comparisons made among three or more items:

The hard**est** course I have ever taken was a course in my senior year in high school.

The hard**est** (adverb) I have ever worked was on that course.

---

[1] Most comparisons in this section will be made with adjectives. Note, however, that the second *harder* in 2 above is an adverb answering *how*.

272

## Grammar: comparisons using <u>similar to</u> and <u>different from</u>

Sameness: My ambitions for the future are **similar to**[1] yours.

Difference: My work will be **different from**[2] yours, however.

### Oral Practice

Directions: When a question is asked, *Student A* will respond with a statement using *similar to* (or *like*). *Student B* will follow with a statement using *different from*.

Examples:

Instructor:    Is a watch similar to a clock?

Student A:    You might say a watch is **similar to** a clock. They both tell time.

Student B:    On the other hand, a watch is very **different from** a clock. You generally wear a watch on your wrist. You put a clock on a wall or a shelf or desk.

1. Is a pen similar to a pencil?
2. Is a tiger similar to a cat?
3. Is a horse similar to a car?
4. Is a snack similar to a meal?
5. Is a cake like a loaf of bread?
6. Is an electric light like a candle?
7. Is a bus similar to a bicycle?
8. Is an instructor similar to an adviser?
9. Is a president similar to a king?
10. Is an editorial similar to a letter to the editor?
11. Is an argument similar to a quarrel?
12. Is a discussion similar to a decision?
13. Is a policeman similar to a soldier?
14. Is an apartment similar to a house?

## Grammar: comparisons using <u>as</u> . . . <u>as</u>

Comparisons with *as . . . as* imply equality:

Lee is **as** tall **as** Lou (is).

---

[1] *Similar to* is generally used in formal writing. *Like* is generally used orally.

[2] "Different *than*" is sometimes heard, but "different *from*" is generally preferred.

He works **as** hard **as** Lou (works).

He is **as** hard a worker **as** Lou (is).

His courses are **as** hard **as** Lou's (are).

## Oral Practice

Directions: Take the two words given you and make an *as . . . as* comparison:

Example:

Instructor:   textbook . . . large
Student:       This textbook is **as** large **as** that one.

1. chair . . . old
2. chair . . . hard
3. chair . . . soft
4. window . . . wide
5. window . . . narrow
6. piece of chalk . . . long
7. bus route . . . long
8. pair of shoes . . . comfortable
9. old sweater . . . comfortable
10. dress . . . short

## L 1 / Introducing Citizen Benjamin Franklin[1]

Directions: Complete the *"as . . . as"* comparisons called for by the words in parentheses. When writing underline as in the examples.

Examples:

Benjamin Franklin was (level-headed) any man who helped to write the Constitution.

Benjamin Franklin was **as level-headed as** any man who helped to write the Constitution.

His self-control was (similar) Washington's.

His self-control was **similar to** Washington's.

His ability to joke was (far different) Washington's.

His ability to joke was **far different from**[2] Washington's.

---

[1] *Benjamin Franklin*, 1706–1790: American patriot, diplomat, inventor.

[2] For example, it was Benjamin Franklin who wrote, "Three can keep a secret if two of them are dead."

Benjamin Franklin was (valuable) any citizen in colonial America. He was (many-sided) Jefferson. He was (public-spirited) Washington. He worked (hard) John Adams. Moreover, he was (skillful a mediator)[1] this country ever had.

Franklin's schooling was (similar) that of other poor boys in colonial Boston. A total of three years' schooling was not (different) what other workingmen's sons received. However, Franklin's efforts to educate himself were far (different) the efforts of most men. Near the beginning of his *Autobiography,* see how he worked to make his writing (similar) that of the *Spectator.*

## Grammar: comparisons

1. Comparisons using one-syllable words, plus *er than:*

Lee is taller than Lou (is).

He is a harder worker than Lou (is).

His courses are harder than Lou's (are).

2. Comparisons using a few two-syllable words, generally ending in *y,* plus *er than:*

| | |
|---|---|
| busy—busier than | healthy—healthier than |
| early—earlier than | lazy—lazier than |
| easy—easier than | lovely—lovelier than |
| funny—funnier than | pretty—prettier than |
| happy—happier than | steady—steadier than |
| clever—cleverer than | noble—nobler than |
| narrow—narrower than | wealthy—wealthier than |

3. Comparisons using words of two or more syllables, plus *more than:*

Lee is **more** efficient **than** Lou (is).

He works **more** steadily **than** Lou (works).

His solutions to problems are generally **more** intelligent **than** Lou's (are).

Christopher Marlowe said almost four hundred years ago, "Comparisons are odious."[2] Test the truth of this statement by means of the foregoing examples.

[1] *mediator:* one who tries to make two persons or nations friendly by helping to settle their differences.
[2] *odious:* hateful, offensive.

## Oral Practice I

Directions: When you are given a question, answer with a full statement. Note that the verb in a *who/which* question is singular, even though the answer is likely to be plural.

Examples:

Instructor:   Which is taller, trees or grass?
Student:       Trees are taller than grass.
Instructor:   Who is taller, men or women?
Student:       Men are taller than women, usually.

1. Who is **taller,** children or adults?
2. Who is **happier,** children or adults?
3. Who is **busier** than you are?
4. Who comes to class **earlier** than you do?
5. Who flies an airplane more **easily** than you fly one?
6. Which is **funnier** a comedy or a Western?
7. Which is **narrower,** a street or a sidewalk?
8. Which is **lovelier,** a rose or a weed?
9. Who ought to be **healthier,** the student who walks to class or the student who rides to class?
10. Who is **cleverer,** Bill or Pete?

## Oral Practice II

Directions: Listen to a sentence with *but.* Change it into a comparison using *er than* or *more . . . than.*

Examples:

Instructor:   Anne is tall, but Marie isn't.
Student:       Anne is taller than Marie.
Instructor:   Marie is very musical, but Anne is not.[1]
Student:       Marie is more musical than Anne.

1. Bill is studious, but Pete isn't.
2. Bill is quiet, but Pete isn't.
3. Bill is tall, but Pete isn't.
4. Pete is a careful driver, but some of his friends aren't.
5. Bill is a hard worker, but the man at the next desk isn't.
6. This textbook is expensive, but that one isn't.

[1] Both girls are musical, but one is more musical than the other.

7. This building is old, but the chemistry building isn't.
8. Oral practice is easy, but free writing isn't.
9. The speech lab is modern, but the Administration Building isn't.
10. The 4:50 bus driver is friendly, but the 5:10 driver isn't.

## L 2 / Benjamin Franklin and His Parents

Directions: Read orally in class or copy the three following paragraphs, making comparisons between pairs of items by adding *er* to
the words in parentheses. Underline such words if writing.

Of the seventeen children in the family of Josiah Franklin,
fourteen were (old) than Benjamin and two were (young). Benjamin
was born on January 17, 1706, sixty-nine years (early) than
the American Revolution.

Josiah Franklin, who had thirteen children sitting at his table
at one time, was (busy) than many fathers. He was (wise), too.
He worked far (hard) to find the right trade[1] for his fifteenth child
than a (lazy) father would have done. When he finally apprenticed[2]
twelve-year-old Benjamin to his (old) son James, a printer,
there proved not to be a (clever) printer's apprentice in the colonies.

Abiah Franklin, Josiah's second wife and Benjamin's mother,
may not have been (pretty) than other mothers in early Boston;
we do not know. We do know that her ten children were
(healthy) than many children of that day. Her life was not (limited)
than that of other Puritan women; it probably was (happy).
She had no sickness except that of which she died at eighty-five.

## Grammar: irregular comparisons[3]

| Simple | Comparative | Superlative |
|---|---|---|
| much, many | more | the most |
| little | less | the least |
| few | fewer | fewest |
| good | better | the best |
| bad | worse | the worst |

[1] *trade:* a skill by which to make a living.
[2] *apprenticed:* to put under the care of an employer for instruction in a trade.
[3] *much, many, little,* and *few* are noncounts. (Review p. 92).

Examples:

There are **more** people in Tokyo than in London.
Some summer days are **less** humid than others.
My cold is **worse** today. How is yours—**better**?

### L 3 / Franklin in Contrast with Keimer[1]

When Franklin was twenty-one, a man named Keimer offered him high wages to take over the management of his printing house and to train his five unskilled workers, called "hands." Soon after he began to work, Franklin saw that Keimer intended first to use him to train the "hands" and then to discharge him. "I went on, however, very cheefully," Franklin says in his *Autobiography*, "and brought his hands by degrees to mind their business and to do it better."

Directions: Read orally in class or copy the four following paragraphs, basing your comparisons on what you know about Franklin and what you guess about Keimer. Underline your choice of the words in parentheses if writing.

Franklin could read Keimer's motives (more/less) easily than Keimer could Franklin's. Franklin managed his own business life (more/less) wisely than Keimer did his.

Franklin was a far (more/less) competent printer than Keimer was. Yet, as the five hands became (better/worse) at their work, Franklin was (more/less) necessary to Keimer. As a result, Keimer became (more/less) civil[2] to Franklin.

Finally, when Keimer was rude to Franklin in public, Franklin became as . . . as (angry) Keimer. After (more/fewer) angry words, Franklin took his hat and walked out.

One man was as . . . as (far from level-headed) the other that day. However, as time passed, Franklin's situation in the world grew (better/worse). Keimer's grew (better/worse).

### Grammar: comparisons among at least three items

1. Comparisons using one-syllable words, plus *est*:

---

[1] This note is condensed from Franklin's *Autobiography*, written in 1771. Note the formality of the style.
[2] *civil*: ordinarily polite.

December is **the shortest** day of the year.

January is often **the coldest** month of the year.

Three A.M. is one of **the darkest** hours of the night.

## 2. Comparisons using a few two-syllable words, plus *est*:

busy—busiest

early—earliest

easy—easiest

funny—funniest

happy—happiest

clever—cleverest

narrow—narrowest

healthy—healthiest

lazy—laziest

lovely—loveliest

pretty—prettiest

steady—steadiest

noble—noblest

wealthy—wealthiest

## 3. Comparisons using words of two or more syllables plus *the most*:

**The most** beautiful scenery in my country . . .

**The most** respected officeholder in my city . . .

**The most** widely read daily newspaper in this country . . .

## 4. Irregular superlatives:

**The worst** wheel of the cart makes **the most** noise.—Benjamin Franklin

One of **the best** conditions for writing is solitude.

**The least** favorable condition for writing is a talkative roommate.

## Note that "one of" may be followed by a comparison:

One of **the coolest** fabrics for summer clothing is linen. (superlative degree)

Air conditioning is **a better** way to cool a room than most electric fans. (comparative degree)

## 5. Special uses of *best*

To put one's **best** foot forward (to do all one is capable of doing)

All for the **best** (for the ultimate good)

To be at one's **best** (to be at the height of one's powers)

**Oral Practice**

Directions: When you are given a question, answer with a full statement in the superlative degree.

Examples:

Instructor:  What is the quickest way to get to town?
Student:    **The quickest** way to get to town is by car.
Instructor:  What is the most important river in Africa?
Student:    **The most important** river in Africa is the Nile.

1. What is **the busiest** street in this city?
2. What is **the busiest** street in your home city?
3. What is **the earliest** sign of spring in your country?
4. What is **the earliest** sign of fall (autumn) in your country?
5. What subject do you like best?
6. Who is the funniest comedian on TV just now?
7. What colors make small girls look **prettiest?**
8. Are **the wealthiest** always **the happiest?**
9. What kind of recreation makes you **happiest?**
10. Where is **the most beautiful** scenery in Europe?
11. Where are **the most spectacular** mountains in Asia?
12. Who is one of **the most powerful** heads of state in Europe?
13. Who is one of **the most powerful** heads of state in Asia?
14. Who is one of **the most powerful** heads of state in Africa?
15. What is **the most widely read** newspaper in this part of the country?

## L 4 / The Superlative Franklin, Part I

Directions: Read orally in class or copy the four following paragraphs. If writing, underline the entire phrase expressing the superlative degree, as in the examples.

Examples:

Franklin was (best) printer Keimer had. He was by far (most skillful) man in the shop.

Franklin was <u>the best printer</u> Keimer had. He was by far <u>the most skillful man</u> in the shop.

Benjamin Franklin's life was full of superlatives. By the time he was twenty-five, he was (best) printer in the American colonies. Before he was thirty, his *Poor Richard's Almanac* had become (popular) of all colonial publications.

In his thirties he became (helpful) man in Pennsylvania for all sorts of occasions. He invented (practical) stove ever used in the colonies. He advised an army chaplain on (effective) way

to get soldiers to attend prayers.[1] By (persistent) effort he
gradually persuaded his fellow citizens to open and support the
academy which is now the University of Pennsylvania.

At forty-two Franklin drew up plans for one of (generously
arranged) retirements from business on record.[2] In his ensuing
leisure, after establishnig the fact that lightning is electricity,
Franklin became (celebrated) scientific discoverer of his
time, not only in his own country but in Europe.


## L 5 / The Superlative Franklin, Part II

Directions: Read orally in class or copy the four following paragraphs. If writing, underline the entire phrase expressing the superlative degree, as in the example.

Example:

Franklin solved (difficult) question before the Constitutional Convention.

Franklin solved **the most difficult question** before the Constitutional
Convention.

In his sixties and seventies, Franklin was (best-known)
American in Europe. Since he represented the colonies at the
court of King George III in the years just before the Revolution, he
was often (least) popular American in England. On the other
hand, when he acted as ambassador to our ally, France, during
the Revolution, he was (popular) and (highly esteemed)[3]
American in Paris.

At eighty-two, (old) member of the Constitutional Convention,
Franklin solved the one question about which the (able)
and (best) could do nothing, the question of whether (small)
and (large) states should have equal representation in the legislature.[4]

Franklin was a man of (generous) public spirit. All during
his long life his fellow citizens turned with (great) confidence
to the good sense and good humor which met in him
in (happy) combination.

[1] To give out the daily allowance of liquor just after prayers.
[2] The details are in Franklin's *Autobiography*.
[3] One superlative form can cover more than one adjective.
[4] Franklin proposed having two houses, one with proportional representation (the present House of Representatives) and the other with equal representation (the present United States Senate).

## Spelling: Rule 10

Add *es* when the simple form of a word ends in a hissing sound, a sibilant such as s [s]; sh [ʃ]; ch [tʃ]; x [ks]; or z [z].

miss—misses     dish—dishes     church—churches     box—boxes
buzz—buzzes

### Dictation I

Since Betty is going to boarding school now, she misses the dishes her mother made. However, her mother sends boxes of food to the school. Betty's roommate buzzes with excitement when the boxes come. The girls take out their few dishes and have a feast.

### Dictation II

Churches in small towns often have church suppers. Young misses bring dishes and boxes. The room buzzes with talk. Someone dashes out for matches. Everyone watches as the coffee boils. Who wishes to go to a church supper?

## FREE WRITING

### L 6 / Two Newspapers Compared

Directions: Show how a certain newspaper in your country is both similar to and different from a certain newspaper in the United States.

What types of news do both papers carry? What departments, carried by one paper, are completely omitted by the other? What departments appearing in both papers (sports or editorials, perhaps) are not similar in emphasis? In summary, what would you say each paper hopes to do for its readers?

### L 7 / A Man Larger than Life

Directions: Do for one of your own great men what an unnamed editor of *The New York Times* has done for George Washington.[1] Give briefly both the human and the heroic sides of a man "larger than life."

---

[1] Condensed from an editorial in *The New York Times*, February 22, 1965.

"If George Washington were alive today, he would thoroughly enjoy our affluent society. He had a relish for fine clothes; for scarlet cloth, gold lace, ruffled shirts, silver buckles; and he possessed a discriminating palate for fine wines. He appreciated the qualities of fine race horses and the contests in which they took part.

"On a wet, uninviting day he could spend the entire time at cards, noting his winnings and losses, neither of which was great enough to make or mar[1] his fortune. He loved the theatre. Behind the marble-like figure which we so often picture was a man of very human impulses. For too many people the monument has supplanted the man.

"Yet Washington was larger than life. He was a man exceedingly rare in history—one not corrupted by power. The high position he occupied during the Revolutionary War was returned to Congress without thought of personal ambition.[2]

"And he fought a war for eight weary years, in which the forces arrayed against him were almost as numerous on his own side as on the other: an army that evaporated in his hand, a Congress that wanted to win the war but was fearful of supplying the means to do so, a cabal of officers that combined in secret against their own chief. In the beginning for every victory there were two defeats. The miracle is not that he won, but that he endured."

---

[1] *mar:* injure.

[2] Washington went back to his large farm on the Potomac River for four satisfying years. Then, when the first President was to be chosen, "In no state was any other name [than Washington's] considered."—*Encyclopaedia Britannica,* 1967, p. 243.

# Section M

## The First Term Paper

A term paper, also called a research paper, is a long composition which requires the use of the library. Since your future instructors, if they assign term papers, will assume that you know how to write them, it is well to go through the process here, in this course.

### BEGINNING THE TERM PAPER

*Finding a subject*   If you are taking courses other than English and the instructor requires a term paper, by all means consult him about a subject suitable for his course. If you are taking English only, choose a subject within the broad field of your interests, probably your professional interests.

*Narrowing the subject*   A good term paper covers one small section of a broad subject thoroughly. One way to narrow your subject is to work until you can state what you plan to do in your paper in a single sentence.

Examples:

"The purpose of this paper is to discuss the agricultural tax in Argentina and its effect on the level of production of farm units devoted to livestock breeding."

"In this paper I am going to discuss the market structure of Japan, comparing it with the market structure of the United States, using the distribution of ethical drugs as a convenient example."

"In this paper, I am going to introduce a process which will modernize the manufacture of furniture in Taiwan."

A formal topic sentence, such as the three above, states the purpose of your paper. In the same paragraph, add briefly why the study you have chosen is needed, or why it is of special interest to you.

Example:

Taiwan must learn to make its unique furniture faster if it is to compete in the world market.

Stating the purpose of the paper and your reason for writing it within the first paragraph will assure your reader and yourself that you have something definite to say. Wide reading in your field and frequent rewriting are likely to precede a good first paragraph. Even when you are almost satisfied, it is not a bad idea to ask for a quick review of the paragraph by your instructor, your academic adviser, and your roommate. Be sure, though, that the idea finally decided upon is yours. It is your paper.

*Fundamental reference aids for using books*   Whether you made your first trip to the university library with your class or by yourself ("An Hour in the University Library," p. 68), locate the following indispensable reference aids promptly. (Aids for using magazines will follow.)

1. The author-title catalog files (and the separate subject file, if the library has one)
2. The *Encyclopaedia Britannica* and the *Encyclopedia Americana*

If your field is specialized—science, art, or public affairs, for example—the library is likely to have a special encyclopedia on that field. Ask one of the reference librarians about this possible resource. Also, look under the word *Index* in the card catalog.

The above items are only the beginning of the resources of a modern library. As you get into your research, you may find yourself consulting additional resources as different as old maps, government pamphlets, and a volume called a "bibliography of bibliographies,"[1] which the reference librarian keeps behind her own desk.

*Obtaining the books you want*   When you find a title in the author/title files which you would like to see, how do you get the book? In a library of any size, great numbers of books are not on the "open shelves," where any interested reader is free to take them down and examine them. Instead, they are in "the stacks," row after row of shelves in back rooms, to which only librarians and their assistants, called "pages," have access.

You obtain such books by making out a "paging slip" or "call slip," which asks for a limited amount of information about the author and the book. Such slips are on every table near the author/title files.

Fill out every item asked for on each book and take the slips where other students are taking their slips. In the most elaborate system of producing books from the stacks, the attendant puts the slips into a cylinder, which promptly drops out of sight. The attendant hands you a number, and you then wait on a bench with other students, watching a big board filled with numbers, which hangs above the librarians' heads. When your number lights up, some of your books have arrived.

Since the process takes as much time as it does, it is well to hand in six or seven call slips at a time. A book or two may be out; one may be lost; at least two more are likely not to prove useful to you.

*Obtaining magazines*   The back numbers of some magazines, a number of which have been bound together into a book, will be obtained from the stacks precisely as a book is obtained. Other bound magazines will be on open shelves for students to examine freely. Still other magazines, not yet bound, will have to be obtained from a librarian in charge of a "stack" for magazines only. As suggested before, ask the reference librarian whether there is a special index covering magazine articles in your field only.

Current magazines are usually on open shelves, with com-

[1] *Bibliography:* a list of books, articles, etc., about one subject.

## SAMPLE PAGING SLIP  FOR A BOOK[1]

Paging Slip

PRINT CALL NUMBERS  ON
LINES BELOW:

E

185.61

969

_____

_____

Volume_____

(Give volume only if book is from a set)

If periodical state:

Month_____

Year_____

Author  GRIFFIN

Title  BLACK LIKE ME

_____

fortable couches for reading nearby. Comparatively few magazines will require a paging slip. However, some of the older and
less-called for bound magazines may have been put into the
stacks or onto microfilm.[2]

[1] The detailed report which the page must make if he cannot locate the
book is located on p. 291.
[2] Important newspapers are converted to microfilm, also. Recall your
introduction to microfilm through *The New York Times*, p. 68.

## SAMPLE PAGING SLIP FOR A BOUND MAGAZINE

Paging Slip

PRINT CALL NUMBERS ON
LINES BELOW:

*Sci*
_____

*Am*
_____

_____

_____

_____

Volume *196 #2*
_____

If periodical state:

Month *F*
_____

Year *'57*
_____

_____

Author *RENSCH*
_____

Title *INTELLIGENCE*
_____

*OF ELEPHANTS*
_____

*Becoming acquainted with the* Reader's Guide to Periodical
Literature   The *Reader's Guide* now lists alphabetically ("in-
dexes") articles that have appeared in approximately 150 magazines of general interest and wide circulation. Indexing is done
three ways: under subject, title, and author. The first step in using
the *Reader's Guide* efficiently is to note the style in which the

items are presented. Here is an example of the style of the *Guide.*

---

PETROLEUM
> Pipe lines
Unsafe at any width: the trans-
Alaska pipe-line. R. Sherrill in
Nation: 216:74-75 Je 11'73
> Middle East
Oil and arms: battle over the
Persian Gulf. T. Szuic. New Repub
168: 21-3 Je 23'73

---

As you can see, large general subjects are printed entirely in capitals at the left-hand margin. (Note PETROLEUM in the example.) Subtitles are printed in much smaller letters in the center of the line; only the first letter is capitalized, except for proper names. The first number after the name of the magazine is the volume number. The number of pages in the article come next.

In order to save space, the titles of articles are set only *one letter* to the right of the left-hand margin. The second line of the same title is set one letter to the right of the line above it. The next title then goes back to one space from the left-hand margin. These shallow indentations are good space-savers, but they make it imperative to keep the basic system of the *Guide* in mind.

If you should find yourself temporarily lost among a mass of subtitles and articles, go back until you find a large, general title, all in capitals, printed at the left-hand margin. Then everything will fall into place.

As additional help, in the front of every volume of the *Reader's Guide,* you will find these useful lists:

1. Titles of all magazines (periodicals) indexed in the *Guide.*

Examples:

*Harper's* Magazine

*National Geographic* Magazine

*Science News*

## 2. Abbreviations of periodicals indexed

Example:

Sat R Sci—*Saturday Review of the Sciences*

## 3. Abbreviations of words in titles

Example:

il: illustrated, illustration, illustrations, illustrator

### M 1 / Practice with the *Reader's Guide*

Directions: Take any volume of the *Reader's Guide,* recent or not recent, and turn to the name of your country (all capitals, left-hand margin). Read the entire list of subtitles. Then copy one magazine article title under each of five subtitles on a 3x5 inch card, called a "note card.[1] Use the *Guide's* lack of capitals and mysterious abbreviations (explained in the front of each volume of the *Guide).*

---

HAITI

Jean-Claude's new black magic. F. Halliday. Ramparts 11: 16-20 Ja '73

Description and travel
Haiti. S. Wilkinson. il Flying 91: 67-71 Jl '72

Economic conditions
Haiti: new stirrings of hope H. Bims. il Ebony 28:70-72 Ja '73

Politics and government
Progress in Haiti: leopards and sneakers instead of Tonton Macoutes. H. Gold. il NY Times Mag p34-35 Mr 12 '72

---

### M 2 / Locating One Magazine Article

Directions: Select a magazine title from the *Reader's Guide,* one far from your usual interests, locate it, and make out a note card for it.

1. If the magazine containing your article is recent in date and widely read, look first among the magazines on the open magazine shelves.
2. If you do not find the magazine there, next try the bound magazines on the open shelves.

---

[1] For more about note cards, see p. 292.

3. If you still do not locate the magazine, make out a paging slip.

Do two things on the note card that you hand in as the assignment:

1. Write out your title with standard capitals and few abbreviations to show you understand the style of the *Reader's Guide*.
2. Say in brackets where you found or did not find the article.

---

The Intelligence of Elephants. Rensch illus-

trated Scientific American vol. 196 no. 2

pages 44–50 Feb. 1957

[ *Reported by page as not on shelf* ]

---

If your first search proved to be really no search at all, take another *Reader's Guide* and hunt for a second title. The library begins to be truly yours when you can pursue a reference until you find it.

## WORKING WITH YOUR MATERIAL

*Note cards*

Before you begin to work on your paper, see that you have three conditions favorable to work: (1) a pile of books and magazines which may prove useful (2) a quiet corner of the library where you can spread out your material (3) and a package of 3 x 5 inch index cards (note cards).

Why use note cards? Why not copy possibly useful ideas into the notebook you use every day? Note cards give you mobility. If you put one idea only on each card, it is easy to add new ideas, drop others, and rearrange the rest as often as you find necessary. Eventually you will sort your best references into a few large piles corresponding to the main points you have decided to make in your paper.

Here is a sample note card for a book:

```
E                    Why a white man decided
185.61               to pass as black
G 69


         Griffin, John Howard

         Black Like Me

         Boston, Houghton, Mifflin, 1961


     "Neither [race] really knew what went
      on with those of the other race."
                                        p. 7
   (under grad ¹
    open shelves)
```

*Writing note cards*   The following points are illustrated in the
two sample note cards:

1. Leave an inch of space blank at the top of the card. This space is
   for your own subtitle, which you will write in in pencil and probably
   change more than once. (A large, soft eraser, for pencils only, is a
   great convenience in working with note cards.)
2. Copy all the printed types of information suggested in the samples.
   Do not put yourself in the position of having to go back later for a
   footnote, for example, or a biographical entry. (Turn the title page

Here is a sample magazine card:

---

Atlan
v. 7
Je, 1871

*The mood of the North as the Civil War began*

### NEW YORK SEVENTH REGIMENT
#### Our March on Washington
##### April 19, 1861

"Only one who passed, as we did, through that
tempest of cheers, two miles long, can know the
terrible enthusiasm of the occasion. . . our
great city was with us as one man, . . ."

–Anonymous soldier
p.745

*(under grad [1]
ref rm )*

---

over to find the publication date of a book.)
3. As you read (see "Skimming," p. 294), write down just enough of
   a striking idea on your note card to let you locate it when you do your
   detailed reading later. **Put down the page.** Perhaps leave the card
   in the book or magazine for the time being.
4. Put down a possible subtitle at the top of the card.[1]

---

[1] Put down where you located the reference, so that you can find it
quickly if you wish it again.

Even if you think your notation is not useful, keep the card. You may change your mind for a reason you cannot see at the moment.

If you get a second good idea from the same book or magazine, *make out a second card.* However, this time you need to write only the last name of the author in the upper left-hand of the card before you make your note. *Put down the page.*

## "SKIMMING"

To skim is "to separate the cream from the milk." In reading, "to skim" is to locate quickly the ideas of value to you in a mass of material. The following are suggestions for skimming a book, either for your term paper or for reading in your major courses.

1. Turn first to the Table of Contents in the front of the book. Read chapter headings until you come to one you want to investigate.
2. When you find such a chapter, look at the end first. The author may have been kind enough to write a summary.
3. Then go back to the beginning of the chapter and see how much you can get by reading the first sentence only of each paragraph. Writers of formal English are likely to begin a paragraph with a general statement (a topic sentence), which they then develop by example, by contrast, by listing points, etc.
4. If you find you are going to make extensive use of a book, skim through the Preface, which comes even before the Table of Contents.[1] Here, the author says what he has tried to do in his book.

*"Meaning Links"* As soon as you find a chapter or an article likely to be of value to you, begin to look sharply for "meaning links," or transitional expressions, as you skim. When an author has presented one idea and is preparing to introduce his next, he signals his change in thought by expressions such as the following:

enumeration
   first, second, third,

---

[1] The Index, in the back of the book, lists names, places, and topics alphabetically, with their page locations. If the Table of Contents is detailed, the Index is sometimes omitted.

first, second, next, then, finally
in the first place, in the second place, in the third place,
**additional information**
moreover, furthermore (formal)
in addition, also, in fact, besides (less formal)
**contrasting information**
on the one hand; on the other hand (formal)
however; nevertheless (formal)
but, yet, or, although (in wide use)
**result**
therefore, consequently, for this reason (formal)
as a result (not formal)
**concrete detail**
for example, for instance (in wide use)
**pairs of coordinates** (all formal)
neither . . . nor
either . . . or
not only . . . but also
both . . . and


## PUTTING THE PAPER TOGETHER

### *The Preliminary Outline*[1]

As soon as you have a useful pile of note cards, or possibly just
after you have stated your purpose firmly, make a preliminary
outline, a mere skeleton which you will fill out and change as
you read and write.

Example:

    I. Introduction
       A. Purpose of the paper
       B. Your interest in the subject
   II. First main point
  III. Second main point
  IV. Third main point
   V. Conclusion or summary

[1] For the final outline of the sample term paper, see p. 298.

You may find yourself finally making five or six main points; you may find the points decidedly different from what you thought they were going to be. Nevertheless, three are enough to start with.

*Handling Points Not in the Preliminary Outline*  Here is a troublesome fact: some of the best ideas you find in your reading will not fall neatly under the points of your skeleton outline. Ideally, the subtitle you write in pencil across the top of a card corresponds to one of the points in your outline. What are you to do with these valuable, unforeseen ideas which keep cropping up? Make out cards with what seem like suitable subtitles at the moment. Then, if you find a new main idea developing under several slightly different subtitles, you can decide on which subtitle you want to keep.

*The Form of the Paper*

The following forms are not the only ones which can be used in writing a good term paper. Almost any set of forms can produce a workmanlike paper if they are used consistently.

*Subtitles*  It is recommended that subtitles be centered, capitalized as in a composition, and underlined. The subtitles then will make an informal, helpful outline of your paper. (See the sample term paper, pp. 299–305.)

*Footnotes for Books*  A simple method of making a footnote for a book is to use commas after each item and a period after the last: author (first name first), title (underlined), city, publisher, year, volume (if more than one), page or pages. A short line at the left separates the footnotes from the body of the text. Note that the number used to indicate a footnote is slightly raised, both in the text and in the footnote itself. (See the sample term paper.)

*Footnotes for Magazine Articles (periodicals)*  A footnote for a magazine article, like a footnote for a book, may use a comma after every item and a period after the last: author (first name first), "Article Title" (quotation marks), Periodical Title (underlined), date, page or pages. Note the use of quotation marks and underlining in the following examples:

1. A popular magazine:
   Arlene Croce, "Dancing," the *New Yorker*, July 16, 1973, p. 48.
2. A scholarly journal or quarterly:[1]
   Yasmeen M. Kukman, "Motivation to Learn and Language Proficiency," *Language Learning,* vol. 22, December, 1972, p. 261.

*"Blocking" quotations*   When a direct quotation is longer than three lines,[2] it should be set approximately seven spaces to the right of the rest of the text and single-spaced or "blocked." (Quotation marks are not used.)

Example:

> According to Samuel Eliot Morison, one of the most remarkable things about the American Revolution was that the young men who started it in 1774-1776 were not killed off by a rival group but were on hand to write the Constitution in 1787:

> > All modern history proves that it is easy enough for a determined minority to pull down a government, but exceedingly difficult to reconstruct, to re-establish law and order on new foundations. And in no other great revolution have the initial agitators long survived liquidation by their successors.[3]

*The Bibliography*   A research paper lists at its close the books and periodicals the writer has used in his project. The list is alphabetized, the last name first now, so that anyone wishing to make use of the resources named can find what he wishes quickly. Again, commas can be used to separate items, with a period after the last item. In an extensive bibliography, books and periodicals are placed in separate lists; in a first term paper, one list is enough. See the bibliography of the sample term paper, p. 305.

## FREE WRITING

### M 3 / The Practice Paper

Directions: Make use of perhaps three magazine articles or books in order to write a brief paper practicing the elements essential to a full-length term paper: statement of purpose, subtitles, footnotes,

[1] *quarterly:* a scholarly magazine published only four times a year.
[2] For the one-sentence quotation, review p. 236.
[3] Samuel Eliot Morison, the *Oxford History of the American People,* a Mentor Book, New American Library, 1972, vol. 1, p. 354.

bibliography, and an outline that agrees with what you have written. (Make your bibliography the six or seven magazine articles or books you skimmed before deciding on those you would use.)

## M 4 / The Term Paper (use your own title)

Directions: Keep your note cards under control. Put down the page for every note you make. Just before you hand in your final copy, read your paper over, looking sharply for the little errors which you knew better than to make. Check your footnotes and bibliography for punctuation and spelling. See that the wording of your outline, probably changed more than once, still agrees with the wording of your subtitles. Good luck.

## OUTLINE

    I. Introduction
       A. The purpose of the paper
       B. The author's interest in writing it
   II. The first Europeans
       A. Who they were
       B. Why they came
  III. How discoveries were made
       A. By birch bark canoe
       B. Along lakes and rivers
  IV. Certain French place names
   V. The Discoveries of Brule and Nicolet
       A. Brule—the vicinity of Sault Ste. Marie
       B. Nicolet
          1. The St. Mary's River
          2. The Straits of Mackinac
          3. Sault Ste. Marie
          4. Lake Huron
          5. Lake Superior
  VI. The founding of the Jesuit missions
       A. Sault Ste. Marie
       B. St. Ignace
 VII. After the French

## The Origin of Certain French Place Names
## in Northern Michigan

### Introduction

The history of the French place names in Northern
Michigan is a part of the history of the United States. I
hope to explain briefly the origin of certain of these
names. It is a fascinating venture.

### The First Europeans

Probably the first Europeans who reached the shorelines of Lake Michigan at the beginning of the seventeenth
century were French adventurers. (Occasionally it is claimed
that Vikings and even Phoenicians reached Michigan much
earlier, but this is not certain and rather unlikely in the
case of the Phoenicians.)[1] The Frenchmen came from New
France. They left Quebec and Montreal, the most important
trading posts, with the hope of finding a water route through
the continent to Cathay (China) on the coast of Asia. There
is also no doubt that they remembered the vast stores of gold
and silver the Spaniards had discovered in Mexico and Peru
and thought there could be a chance to come to a land of
immense riches. Champlain, the founder of Quebec, had been
in Mexico before he came to New France.[2] Other forces that

---

[1] Frederick Willis Dunbar, _Michigan: A History of the Wolverine State_, Grand Rapids, Eerdmaus Publishing Co., 1965,
p. 47.

[2] _New Catholic Encyclopedia_, New York, McGraw-Hill, 1967,
vol. 3, p. 442. In the capacity of the King's geographer,
Champlain had visited the West Indies and Mexico before
coming to New France in 1603.

drove the French into the interior of this unknown continent
were the fur trade and the zeal of the French missionaries
to save the souls of the "savages."

## How Discoveries Were Made

The land of lakes and rivers was discovered by canoe.
The famous boat of the native Indian tribes was made of
birch bark. The bark canoe was a light vessel. This was very
important because a canoe often had to be carried. The word
"portage," which is well known to all canoeists and often
found on maps of the northern part of Michigan, was originally
a French word.[1] It is natural that the first discovered
regions were the shorelines of the lakes and river basins.
It is also natural that we find most of the French place
names at Michigan's shorelines.

## Certain French Place Names

Names like presqu'ile ("peninsula with narrow isthmus"),
L'Anse-au-Loup ("bright wolf"), Au Sable ("sand"), and Sault[2]
("rapids") are numerous. The name Les Chenaux Islands near
Cedarville, a small town in Mackinac County in the Upper
Peninsula, is also a reminder of the early French explorers.
Les Chenaux (the channels) is the plural of the French word
le chenal (the chanel).

---

[1] portage: the distance from one stream or body of water
to another, where a canoe has to be carried.

[2] La Nouvelle-France, d'après Champlain en 1632. The
word "Sault" appears on this map. The word also appears on
a map La Louisiane en 1674 "copie anonyme de-me carte de
Louis Jolenet."

## The Discoveries of Brule and Nicolet

It is regarded as probable that Etienne Brule[1] reached the vicinity of Sault Ste. Marie in the winter of 1618-19. He was the first white man to see what is now the state of Michigan.

Encouraged by Champlain, Jean Nicolet,[2] another Frenchman, had journeyed westward and passed the Straits of Mackinac in 1634. The discoveries of Brule and Nicolet gave the French some knowledge of the St. Mary's River and the Straits of Mackinac. The famous map of Champlain of 1632[3] shows the position of the strait, and the rapids (Sault) at the place where Sault Ste. Marie is now. The Mer douce (Lake Huron) and the Grand lac ("the big lake"--Lake Superior) are also shown. The name "Sault de Gaston" was the first name for the strait at Sault Ste. Marie. It indicates that Champlain evidently had his information from white men because the name was given in honor of a brother of the King of France.

## The Founding of the Jesuit[4] Missions

The next visitors to Michigan were two Jesuit priests, Father Isaac Jogues and Charles Raymbault.[5] They traveled to

---

[1] Dictionary of American History, 6 vol., James Truslow Adams, editor-in-chief, New York, Charles Scribner's Sons, 1940, vol. 1, p. 34.

[2] Ibid. (Note: ibid (Latin, "the same") is sufficient when no other reference comes in between.)

[3] Ibid.

[4] Jesuit: a member of a Roman Catholic religious order (Society of Jesus).

[5] Encyclopaedia Britannica, Chicago, London . . . Manila, William Benton (publisher), 1967, vol. 15, p. 370.

the rapids of the St. Mary's River in 1647.  They named the
place Sault Ste. Marie.  Sainte Marie was the name of the
chief mission in Huronia[1] from which the two Jesuits had come.

Because of its location, Sault Ste. Marie was a very
important mission and trading place on the Canadian side of
the strait.  In 1668 Father Jacques Marquette opened on the
south (Michigan) side of the rapids a mission post around which
grew up the earliest settlement of whites in Michigan.[2]  The
French took official possession of the interior of North America
in a ceremony at the Sault in 1671.[3]  Sault Ste. Marie
is still a significant town in Michigan.

St. Ignace, another important mission, was founded in
1670-71.  Father Charles Dablon, superior of the Jesuit
mission of the Upper Lakes, named the place for St. Ignatius.

He began the mission first on Mackinac Island.  In the
spring of 1671, Father Marquette came with members of the
Huron tribe from the upper end of Lake Superior.  Whether they
settled at once on the island or on the mainland north of the
straits, is not known.  Dablon's mission of St. Ignace was
soon, probably in 1672, being conducted at the latter location
with Father Marquette in charge.  It was moved, probably in 1741,
to the site on the mainland south of the island, where Jesuits
were in charge until 1765.

---

[1] Huronia: named for the Hurons, an Indian tribe living near
Lake Huron.

[2] Encyclopedia Americana, New York, Americana Corporation, 1967,
vol. 24, p. 318.

[3] ibid. "The French held a great council of the Indians at the
Sault in 1671, and proclaimed France as owner and ruler of all
lands south to the Gulf of Mexico and west to the Pacific Ocean."

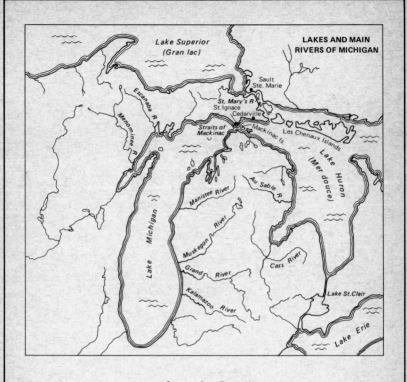

Lake Superior
(Gran lac)

**LAKES AND MAIN
RIVERS OF MICHIGAN**

Sault
Ste. Marie

St. Mary's R.
St. Ignace
Cedarville

Straits of
Mackinac

Mackinac Is.

Les Chenaux Islands

Escanaba R.

Menominee R.

Lake Huron
(Mer douce)

Manistee River

Au Sable R.

Lake Michigan

Muskegon River

Grand River

Cass River

Kalamazoo River

Lake St. Clair

Lake Erie

## After the French

The documented history of Michigan began at about the same time the English and Dutch people founded the first settlements on the east coast of this continent. For about 150 years the history of Michigan was a history of French-speaking people. The French were pushed out of Michigan by the English in the eighteenth century.[1] However, the French place names still exist as monuments to the early French explorers of this country.

---

[1] The Pilgrims arrived from England in December, 1620. The Dutch founded New Amsterdam in 1625.

# BIBLIOGRAPHY[1]

Bald, Frederick Clever, <u>Michigan in Four Centuries</u>, revised and enlarged edition, New York, Harper, 1961.

Besson, Lerois, <u>Upper Great Lakes Places of Significance in the Life of Father Jacques Marquette</u> City of St. Ignace (publisher), Michigan, 1966.

<u>Dictionary of American History</u>, 6 vols., James Truslow Adams, editor-in-chief, New York, Charles Scribner's Sons, 1940.

Dunbar, Willis Frederick, <u>Michigan: A History of the Wolverine State</u>, Grand Rapids, Michigan, Eerdmaus Publishing Co., 1965.

<u>Encyclopaedia Britannica</u>, Chicago, London . . . Manila, William Benton (publisher), 1967.

<u>Encyclopedia Americana</u>, New York, Americana Corporation, 1967.

Johnson, Ida Amanda, <u>The Michigan Fur Trade</u>, Lansing, Michigan Historical Committee, 1919.

Kelton, Dwight H., <u>Indian Names of Places Near the Great Lakes</u>, Detroit, <u>Detroit Free Press</u>, 1888.

<u>La Nouvelle-France</u>, d'après Champlain en <u>1632</u>. (map)

Moore, Charles, <u>History of Michigan</u>, Chicago, Lerois Publishing Co., 1915.

<u>New Catholic Encyclopedia</u>, New York, McGraw-Hill, 1967.

Sheldon, Electa M., <u>The Early History of Michigan</u>, Detroit, Kerr, Morley, 1856.

Trudel, Marcel, <u>Atlas Historique du Canada Francoes des Origines à 1867</u>, Québec, Presses de l'Université Laval, 1867.

[1] To review the form for a bibliography, see p. 297.

# For Reference

*Directions for the Term*

1. Use a pen or a typewriter, not a pencil.
2. Use large sheets of white, lined paper, with a red line defining the left-hand margin.
3. Write the title, properly capitalized, in the middle of the first line. Write the exercise number on the same line, but to the left near the red margin.
4. Write nothing on the line between the title and the body of the exercise. Leave the line blank.
5. Write the exercise on alternate lines only (every other line), leaving the instructor space for corrections.
6. **Indent** every paragraph, including the first one—that is, start to write about an inch to the right of the red line.

*A Checklist for Written Work*

This list presents "Directions for the Term" from another angle. It should contain whatever modifications the instructor and the class have made in the first list.

1. Did you read the directions before beginning to write?
2. Did you put down the exercise number as well as the title?

3. Did you leave the first line below the title blank?
4. Did you write on alternate lines, leaving every second line blank?
5. Did you indent the **first** paragraph as well as all others? (In writing an exercise, have the same number of paragraphs that the text has.)
6. Did you make your statements without writing **yes** or **no**?
7. Did you write statements only? (The questions are not to be copied.)
8. Did you put a period (point) after every statement, including the last one?
9. After you finished, did you read your work over, looking for the little errors which you knew better than to make?

## Directions for Rewriting

1. When your corrected work comes back to you, unless your instructor has other directions, rewrite only the sentences containing an error.
2. Give the number of the exercise and the title on this paper, as well as the original one.
3. Write the sentences containing an error as a numbered list (not as a paragraph).
4. Even though the error lay in a single word, rewrite the complete sentence.
5. If several sentences in succession contain an error, rewrite them by a single number as a section of a paragraph.
6. Hand in your original work with your corrected work.
7. If the work you have corrected comes back with any errors marked, turn back immediately to your original work and see what happened. Had you somehow overlooked a correction? Did you, with bad luck, make the same error again?
8. Keep all your papers. Every six weeks or so analyze your corrections and note the ways in which you have become more accurate.

## RULES OF PUNCTUATION

English uses less punctuation than a number of other languages. When you are in doubt about whether a comma is needed or not, your best course is to omit it. It is better to underpunctuate than to overpunctuate.

  I. Adverbial clauses
    1. An introductory adverbial clause is regularly followed by a comma (Section D, p. 135)

       When you hear anything further, be sure to let me know.

2. Normally, no comma is required when the adverbial clause follows the main clause (Section F, p. 176).[1]

> We pulled over to the side of the road since the car was now completely out of gas.

II. Compound sentences with a comma.

The usual compound sentence has two equal parts (two main clauses, each with its subject and predicate), although it can have more:

> The leader flourished his baton, and the band began to play. (2 main clauses)

> The leader smiled at the crowd, the soloist gripped the microphone, and the band played on. (3 main clauses)

When a comma joins the two main clauses of a compound sentence, it is followed by one of these conjunctions: *and, but, for, yet, or, nor, so:*

> Jorge and Hing were new in the country last semester, *but* they did good class work. They had heard lectures in English in their own countries, *so* they understood their American professors. They worked extremely hard, *yet* they managed to have some good times.

III. Compound sentences with a semicolon

A semicolon is used in a compound sentence when a conjunction is not used:

> Jorge is from Peru; Hing is from Taiwan.

> Jorge intends to major in civil engineering;

> Hing intends to major in physics.

IV. Sentence connectors

Sentence connectors, such as *therefore, nevertheless, however, moreover, in fact, consequently,* may be used after a semicolon, at the end of a sentence, or at the beginning of a sentence (Section E, p. 164):

> The situation was affecting everyone; *therefore* a solution was imperative.

> The situation was affecting everyone; a solution was imperative, *therefore.*

> *Therefore* everyone listened to the Mayor's announcement anxiously.

---

[1] However, see footnote, p. 176.

V. Two simple sentences
Any idea which can be expressed as a compound sentence can be expressed as two simple sentences:

> Jorge is from Peru. Hing is from Taiwan. They worked extremely hard. *Yet* they managed to have some good times.

> They were eager to see a lot of the country. *Therefore* they spent their vacation in inexpensive travel.

VI. No comma between pairs
No comma is used when a conjunction merely joins a pair of words:

> cold *and* rainy

> small *but* mighty

> functional *yet* pleasing in design

No comma is used when a conjunction joins a compound **verb,** not a compound sentence:

> Juan *reached* for the dictionary and *looked* up the word. (compound verb)

> Juan reached for the dictionary, and *he looked* up the word. (compound sentence)

When there are **two complete sentence patterns** between a capital and a period, each with its own subject and predicate, the sentence is compound, and a comma is used along with the conjunction.

VII. Relative clauses
1. When a relative clause points out the specimen meant, no commas are used:

> The river **which divides the United States from north to south** is the Mississippi.

Relatives clauses which do not require commas are called **restrictive** or sometimes **defining.**
2. When a relative clause merely gives an additional fact concerning a specimen already identified, often by a proper noun, the clause is called "descriptive" and set off by commas:

> Mozart, **who lived from 1756-1791,** wrote music enjoyed at concerts today.

Relative clauses which require commas are called **nonrestrictive** or sometimes **commenting**. Such clauses appear very commonly when the noun modified is a proper noun. Relative **who** and **which** appear in nonrestrictive clauses; relative **that** does not.

VIII. Possession indicated
  1. Use an apostrophe to indicate possession in persons and animals:

    singular:   the boy's sweater
                a dog's teeth

    plural:     five boys' sweaters
                two dogs' dinner

  2. Generally, *of* is used to indicate "possession" by objects without life:

    the leg *of* the table

    the third floor *of* the apartment

    **However:**   the university's budget
                   the budget *of the university*.

IX. The colon
  1. Use the colon after the salutation in a formal letter:

    Gentlemen:

  2. Use a colon after a formal introductory statement. (Such a statement will usually contain the word **following**):

    The following fact is clear: Civilization must develop new forms of energy and conserve the forms it has.

X. Items in a series
  Equal ideas in a series are separated by commas:

    The passengers read books, newspapers, and statistical reports. (nouns in a series)

    The sailboat moved down the river, across the bay, and out toward the open sea. (phrases in a series)

    The batter hit the ball, flung his bat aside, and raced for first base. (verbs in a series)

XI. Parenthetical elements
  1. Use commas to set off a nonrestrictive appositive element:

    Roberto, **my cousin,** is going to take some courses next semester.

> Peter the Great, **a talented tyrant,** tried to Westernize his kingdom.

2. Use commas to set off elements which interrupt the main thought:

> I understand, **of course,** that the problem is complex.
>
> I feel, **on the other hand,** that it is not insoluble.

3. Use commas to set off items after the first one in dates:

> America's Declaration of Independence was made public on July 4, 1776, in Philadelphia.

4. Use commas to set off items after the first one in addresses:

> My uncle, who lives at 230 West Congress Street, Tucson, Arizona, has invited me to come and try the sunshine.
>
> Street and avenue may properly be abbreviated on an envelope, but not in a composition.

## XII. Parallel structure

Elements performing the same function in a sentence should have parallel structure, that is, should be of similar structure type:

> I like swimming and fishing. (not "swimming and to fish")
>
> She read slowly and thoughtfully. (not "slowly and with thought")
>
> He is a sportsman, a writer, and a musician. (not "a sportsman, a writer, and plays the trombone")

## XIII. Hyphenation

The simplest way to take care of the problem of hyphenation is to decide **not** to divide a word at the end of a line but simply to put the whole word on the next line. This practice is acceptable.

If hyphenating, the sure way to divide a word correctly is to refer to the dictionary. Every word in the dictionary is divided into syllables by points (.) or a hyphen (-) and points:

> a.lone        self-con.fi.dent

Never write merely one or two letters at the end of a line, even if they are syllables:

> wrong: a-        brave-
>          lone        ly

Divide a word between two consonants:

> plan.ning        stop.ped

However, when you need to be really sure, consult the dictionary. Americans do.

# THE WRITING OF CAPITALS AND NUMBERS

I. Capitals

1. Capitalize the names of particular organizations:
Trinity Church, the Monarch Machine Tool Company, Civil Engineering II, Clare College

   **But:** a church, a company, a college, civil engineering

2. Capitalize the days of the week, months, and holidays:
Wednesday, February, New Year's Eve

   **But:** spring, summer, fall, winter

3. Capitalize the names of streets, avenues, parks, and rivers:
Fourteenth Street, 101 Street, Eighth Avenue, Golden Gate Park, the Missouri River

   The abbreviations acceptable on envelopes may not be used in a composition.

4. Capitalize adjectives derived from the names of countries and races:
Spanish, English, Indian, Jewish

5. Use capitals when a locality, however vaguely defined, is meant, not a direction:
the Midlands, the Great Plains, the Midwest

   However, capitals are not used to indicate simple directions of the compass: **north** of Boston, **east** of Suez.

6. Capitalize the names of historical events and documents:
the War of the Roses, the Battle of the Bulge, the Magna Carta

7. Use capitals when the name of a relationship takes the place of a proper name:
Won't you sing for us, **Father?**

   **But:** My **father** has a fine voice.

II. Numbers

1. Use a hyphen when a figure is written as two words:
thirty-nine, forty-two, ninety-one

2. In a formal composition, write out numbers to one hundred:
seventy-five, ninety-nine. (Informally, use figures beginning with 10.)

3. Use figures thereafter except when writing round numbers such as a hundred or a thousand:
a hundred    101    199    two hundred

## The Principal Parts of Irregular Verbs

The principal parts of irregular verbs are to be found in every dictionary; nevertheless, a list of such verbs is offered here as a convenience in the quick checking of spelling.

The *ing*-form of an irregular verb is not, strictly speaking, irregular, for it is formed from the simple form of the verb according to spelling rules 1, 2, or 3.

Regular verbs form the past tense and the past participle by adding *ed* to the simple form—or merely *d* if the simple form ends in *e*: ask—asked, erase—erased.

| Simple Form Infinitive | Past Tense | Past Participle | Present Participle |
|---|---|---|---|
| be | was, were | been | being |
| beat | beat | beaten, beat | beating |
| become | became | become | becoming |
| begin | began | begun | beginning |
| bend | bent | bent | bending |
| bet | bet | bet | betting |
| bite | bit | bitten | biting |
| bleed | bled | bled | bleeding |
| blow | blew | blown | blowing |
| break | broke | broken | breaking |
| bring | brought | brought | bringing |
| build | built | built | building |
| burst | burst | burst | bursting |
| buy | bought | bought | buying |
| catch | caught | caught | catching |
| choose | chose | chosen | choosing |
| cling | clung | clung | clinging |
| come | came | come | coming |
| cost | cost | cost | costing |
| creep | crept | crept | creeping |
| cut | cut | cut | cutting |
| deal | dealt | dealt | dealing |
| dig | dug | dug | digging |
| dive | dived, dove | dived | diving |
| do | did | done | doing |
| draw | drew | drawn | drawing |

| Simple Form Infinitive | Past Tense | Past Participle | Present Participle |
|---|---|---|---|
| drink | drank | drunk | drinking |
| drive | drove | driven | driving |
| eat | ate | eaten | eating |
| fall | fell | fallen | falling |
| feed | fed | fed | feeding |
| feel | felt | felt | feeling |
| fight | fought | fought | fighting |
| find | found | found | finding |
| flee | fled | fled | fleeing |
| fly | flew | flown | flying |
| forget | forgot | forgotten | forgetting |
| forgive | forgave | forgiven | forgiving |
| freeze | froze | frozen | freezing |
| get | got | got, gotten | getting |
| give | gave | given | giving |
| go | went | gone | going |
| grow | grew | grown | growing |
| hang | hung | hung | hanging |
| have | had | had | having |
| hear | heard | heard | hearing |
| hide | hid | hidden | hiding |
| hit | hit | hit | hitting |
| hold | held | held | holding |
| hurt | hurt | hurt | hurting |
| keep | kept | kept | keeping |
| kneel | knelt | knelt | kneeling |
| know | knew | known | knowing |
| lay (to put down) | laid | laid | laying |
| lead | led | led | leading |
| leave | left | left | leaving |
| lend | lent | lent | lending |
| let | let | let | letting |
| lie (recline) | lay | lain | lying |
| lie (tell an untruth) | lied | lied | lying |

| Simple Form Infinitive | Past Tense | Past Participle | Present Participle |
|---|---|---|---|
| light | lighted, lit | lighted, lit | lighting |
| lose | lost | lost | losing |
| make | made | made | making |
| mean | meant | meant | meaning |
| meet | met | met | meeting |
| pay | paid | paid | paying |
| put | put | put | putting |
| quit | quit | quit | quitting |
| read | read | read | reading |
| ride | rode | ridden | riding |
| ring | rang | rung | ringing |
| rise | rose | risen | rising |
| run | ran | run | running |
| say | said | said | saying |
| see | saw | seen | seeing |
| seek | sought | sought | seeking |
| sell | sold | sold | selling |
| send | sent | sent | sending |
| set (to put down) | set | set | setting |
| shake | shook | shaken | shaking |
| shine (shoes) | shined | shined | shining |
| shine (sun) | shone | shone | shining |
| shoot | shot | shot | shooting |
| shrink | shrank, shrunk | shrunk, shrunken | shrinking |
| shut | shut | shut | shutting |
| sing | sang | sung | singing |
| sink | sank | sunk | sinking |
| sit | sat | sat | sitting |
| sleep | slept | slept | sleeping |
| slide | slid | slid | sliding |
| speak | spoke | spoken | speaking |
| spend | spent | spent | spending |
| spin | spun | spun | spinning |
| split | split | split | splitting |
| spread | spread | spread | spreading |
| spring | sprang | sprung | springing |
| stand | stood | stood | standing |

| Simple Form Infinitive | Past Tense | Past Participle | Present Participle |
|---|---|---|---|
| steal | stole | stolen | stealing |
| stick | stuck | stuck | sticking |
| sting | stung | stung | stinging |
| stride | strode | stridden | striding |
| string | strung | strung | stringing |
| strive | strove | striven | striving |
| swear | swore | sworn | swearing |
| sweep | swept | swept | sweeping |
| swim | swam | swum | swimming |
| swing | swung | swung | swinging |
| take | took | taken | taking |
| teach | taught | taught | teaching |
| tear | tore | torn | tearing |
| tell | told | told | telling |
| think | thought | thought | thinking |
| throw | threw | thrown | throwing |
| thrust | thrust | thrust | thrusting |
| understand | understood | understood | understanding |
| upset | upset | upset | upsetting |
| wake | waked, woke | waked | waking |
| wear | wore | worn | wearing |
| weave | wove | woven | weaving |
| weep | wept | wept | weeping |
| win | won | won | winning |
| wind | wound | wound | winding |
| wring | wrung | wrung | wringing |
| write | wrote | written | writing |

Printer and Binder: The Murray Printing Company

78 79 80 81 82 83 84 85    10 9 8 7 6